D0394953

Happy Rural Seat

Happy Rural Seat

THE ENGLISH COUNTRY HOUSE
AND THE LITERARY IMAGINATION

by Richard Gill

NEW HAVEN AND LONDON
YALE UNIVERSITY PRESS, 1972

Published with assistance from the
Kingsley Trust Association Publication Fund
established by the Scroll and Key Society
of Yale College.

Copyright © 1972 by Yale University.
All rights reserved. This book may not be
reproduced, in whole or in part, in any form
(except by reviewers for the public press),
without written permission from the publishers.

Library of Congress catalog card number: 72-75192
International standard book number: 0-300-01524-0

Designed by Sally Sullivan
and set in Baskerville type.
Printed in the United States of America by
Vail-Ballou Press, Inc., Binghamton, N.Y.

Published in Great Britain, Europe, and Africa by
Yale University Press, Ltd., London.
Distributed in Canada by McGill-Queen's University
Press, Montreal; in Latin America by Kaiman & Polon,
Inc., New York City; in Australasia and Southeast
Asia by John Wiley & Sons Australasia Pty. Ltd.,
Sydney; in India by UBS Publishers' Distributors Pvt.,
Ltd., Delhi; in Japan by John Weatherhill, Inc., Tokyo.

Grateful acknowledgment is made to the following for permission to quote
from publications in copyright:
Chappell & Co., Inc. for "The Stately Homes of England" from *Operette* by
Noel Coward. Copyright © 1938 by Chappell & Co., Ltd. Copyright renewed.
The Viking Press, Inc., William Heinemann, Ltd., Laurence Pollinger, Ltd.,
and the Estate of the late Frieda Lawrence for *The Letters of D. H. Lawrence*,
edited by Aldous Huxley. Copyright 1932 by the Estate of D. H. Lawrence,
copyright © renewed 1960 by Angelo Ravagli and C. Montague Weekley, Ex-
ecutors of the Estate of Frieda Lawrence Ravagli.
Curtis Brown, Ltd., for *The Memorial* by Christopher Isherwood. Copyright
1946 by New Directions.
The Macmillan Company, A. P. Watt & Son, and Mr. Michael Yeats for *The
Collected Plays of W. B. Yeats* (copyright 1934, 1952 by The Macmillan Company) and for *The Collected Poems of W. B. Yeats* (copyright 1903, 1906, 1907,
1912, 1916, 1918, 1919, 1924, 1928, 1931, 1933, 1935, 1940, 1944, 1945, 1946, 1950,
1956 by The Macmillan Company. Copyright 1940 by Georgie Yeats).

823.09
G475h

180806

To the memory of my Mother and Father

MILLS COLLEGE   WITHDRAWN
LIBRARY

Beneath him, with new wonder, now he views,
To all delight of human sense exposed,
In narrow room Nature's whole wealth; yea more,
A Heaven on Earth: for blissful Paradise

....

                              Thus was this place,
A happy rural seat of various view.

                              Milton, *Paradise lost*

❧ Contents ❧

✣ Illustrations ✣

ꙮ Preface ꙮ

"Roofs," says a character of Ivy Compton-Burnett, "seem to give rise to situations." In its fictional context, the remark is ingeniously ironic, being the insouciant reply of a house guest accused of cuckolding the host in his own home. Taken generally, it happily admits of a less restricted range of reference. Certainly, the roofs of the English country house have given rise to situations of great and interesting variety. Books on the country house have, accordingly, been prompted by a corresponding variety of motives—scholarship, snobbery, sentimentality, or malice. While pseudoresearchers have managed to amuse or infuriate, serious students of English history, sociology, and architecture have broadened our knowledge of the country house as work of art, social institution, exemplar of traditional custom, and index of social change. Indeed, during the last few decades, particularly since World War II, when the fate of the country house became more dubious than ever, there has been a renewal of interest in its whole milieu as a subject for scholarly investigation. In the area of the fine arts, Christopher Hussey, Nicholas Pevsner, Sacheverell Sitwell, and John Summerson have provided thorough and attractive accounts of country-house architecture and decor. Social historians like G. M. Trevelyan and G. M. Young have enriched our sense of its daily life and conventions. Recently, economists such as H. J. Habakkuk, G. E. Mingay, and F. M. L. Thompson have brought to light the more prosaic and neglected details of the finances and material bases of the manorial establishment.

The context of my own study is literary rather than sociological. I am not concerned with the historic house as such; instead,

I have attempted to examine the function of the traditional country house as a recurring motif in English literature, at least in one area—modern fiction. In the process, it is true, I have tried to satisfy the incidental interest many readers have in the actual places that may have served as models for novelists. More important, I hope some justice has been done to the complicated and often devious ways of the artistic imagination with the world of social fact. But, while the historian has often turned to literature to document or illustrate his observations about the country house, I have assumed that an investigation of the relationship of the novelist to the country house and his representation of its life may assist our understanding of his fiction.

I have attempted to define my purpose and method more fully in the introductory chapter. Here a few words might be added about the literary scholarship and criticism already available on the topic. In view of the possibilities for studying the role of the country house in English literature, much less has been undertaken than one might expect. The best studies have nearly all been recent and have usually been confined to discussion of the country house in individual works or authors. Lionel Trilling, for example, who has been attracted to the subject on more than one occasion, has presented illuminating observations about E. M. Forster's Howards End, Jane Austen's Mansfield Park, and Henry James's Medley in *The Princess Casamassima*. Both Richard Chase and Robert Wooster Stallman have analyzed extensively the symbolic function of Gardencourt in *The Portrait of a Lady*. Going beyond individual works, T. R. Henn has written suggestively about the place of the great house in the poetry of W. B. Yeats; while John Holloway in *The Victorian Sage* has considered at some length the role played by the old ancestral halls in the fiction of Disraeli. Finally, in *The Garden and the City: Retirement and Politics in the Later Poetry of Pope, 1731–1743* (published in 1969), Maynard Mack has imaginatively speculated on the mythopoeic value that the villa at Twickenham in particular and the country-house ethos in general came to have for Pope during the production of his last great satires. Indeed, I very much regret that Professor Mack's eloquent and beautifully illustrated book appeared too late for me to take advantage of it in preparing my main text, though I have profited from its allusive erudition in the revision of parts of my first appendix.

Despite such studies, however, little has been done by way of survey or synthesis; and the fiction of the late nineteenth and twentieth centuries, where the country house seems ubiquitous, has been particularly neglected. In fact, to my knowledge, the only other book-length study that has some affinity with my own is Warren Hunting Smith's *Architecture in English Fiction,* published in 1934. Although Smith is not concerned with the country house per se, he does present an impressively detailed and suggestive review of the use of architectural setting in English fiction from its beginnings through the nineteenth century. For the student of modern literature, however, this otherwise valuable treatise has, regrettably, two serious limitations: it makes only a few minor references to the novels of the twentieth century; and its treatment of the actual literary function of architecture in fiction is too thin and undeveloped to satisfy present-day concern with complex symbolism and close explication of texts.

To the the works just mentioned and others cited where relevant below I am indebted for instruction and stimulus. There are also other debts more immediate and personal. I am especially grateful to Professor William York Tindall of Columbia University, who guided me through early stages of this study; his encouragement, advice, and good-humored patience shall be warmly remembered. I also wish to thank Professor Lionel Trilling of Columbia University for reading a late version of the manuscript; the interest he showed in the work and his valuable suggestions eased the way toward its completion. And I owe considerable thanks to Professor Alistair M. Duckworth of the University of Virginia, whose scholarly advice saved me from error and misjudgment.

To Sir John Wheeler-Bennett, K.C.V.O., C.M.G., O.B.E., is due a special word of gratitude, not only for providing information about Garsington Manor, his home in Oxfordshire, but for his invitation to visit there as well. The hospitality that Sir John and Lady Wheeler-Bennett graciously extended during one lovely afternoon at Garsington seemed to epitomize the sociability of the English country house at its best.

I am further indebted to Professor T. R. Henn of Saint Catharine's College, Cambridge, and the Yeats International Summer School, Sligo, Ireland, for a useful bibliography on the Big House in Anglo-Irish literature; to the administration and faculty of the Yeats International Summer School and to Dr. Oliver Edwards in particular for information about the houses associated with Yeats; and to Charles Lines of Pendrell Hall College, Staffordshire, England, for his instructive tours through a number of historic English houses.

I also owe thanks to a number of correspondents who kindly answered my inquiries: to the late Evelyn Waugh; to L. P. Hartley; to G. H. Marwood; to Miles Shepherd, F.L.A., Borough Librarian and Curator, Middlesbrough, Yorkshire; and to J. P. Wells, City Librarian, at the Central Library, Saint Aldates, Oxfordshire.

For further suggestions and interest, I am grateful to many of my colleagues at Pace College, but particularly to Dr. Bernard P. Brennan, Dr. Raymond S. Burns, Professor Gerard Cannon, Dr. Robert M. Dell, Dr. Edward R. Easton, Professor Walter Levy, Professor Jane Philips, Dr. Gilbert M. Rubenstein, Dr. John V. Saly, Dr. Muriel G. Shine, Professor William H. Sievert, Professor William X. Taylor, Dr. Bryce Thomas, and Dr. John Waldman.

For special assistance, I wish to thank Alice Lewis, Dr. Clarence W. Richey, and Ethel Waugh.

Finally, it is a pleasure to thank Merle Spiegel and Cynthia Brodhead of Yale University Press for editorial aid and advice that contributed invaluably to the final form of the book.

R. G.

🌿 Abbreviations 🌿

For the convenience of the reader, the following abbreviations have been used to cite references from various works quoted frequently in the text. The abbreviations occur parenthetically, with page or volume and page numbers, following the quoted passage. Works included in *The Novels and Tales of Henry James*, New York Edition, 26 vols. (New York: Charles Scribner's Sons, 1907–09), are indicated below by specific title and volume number within this edition. Parenthetical references in the text to James's multivolume novels are to volume number within the individual novel.

AA   Henry James, *The Awkward Age,* New York Ed., vol. 9.

AB   Henry James, "The Author of Beltraffio," New York Ed., vol. 16.

BA   Virginia Woolf, *Between the Acts* (New York: Harcourt, Brace & Co., 1941).

BC   Elizabeth Bowen, *Bowen's Court* (New York: Alfred A. Knopf, 1942).

BR   Evelyn Waugh, *Brideshead Revisited,* rev. ed. (London: Chapman and Hall, 1960).

CE   Henry James, "Covering End," *The Two Magics* (London, 1898).

CH   John Galsworthy, *The Country House* (London: J. M. Dent & Sons, 1957).

CY   Aldous Huxley, *Crome Yellow* (New York: Harper & Row, 1922).

EA	H. G. Wells, *Experiment in Autobiography* (New York: Macmillan Co., 1934).
EH	Henry James, *English Hours,* ed. Alma Louis Lowe (New York: Orion Press, 1960).
GB	Henry James, *The Golden Bowl,* 2 vols., New York Ed., vols. 23–24.
GS	Ford Madox Ford, *The Good Soldier* (New York: Random House, 1957).
HD	Evelyn Waugh, *A Handful of Dust* (New York: New Directions, 1945).
HE	E. M. Forster, *Howard's End* (New York: Alfred A. Knopf, 1945).
HH	George Bernard Shaw, *Heartbreak House* (London: Constable and Company, 1931).
IC	John Galsworthy, "In Chancery,'" Book 2, *The Forsyte Saga* (London: William Heinemann, 1950).
L	Henry Green, *Loving* (New York: Viking Press, 1949).
LCL	D. H. Lawrence, *Lady Chatterley's Lover* (New York: Grove Press, 1959).
LL	Henry James, "A London Life," New York Ed., vol. 10.
LS	Elizabeth Bowen, *The Last September* (London: Jonathan Cape, 1960).
MP	John Galsworthy, "The Man of Property," Book 1, *The Forsyte Saga* (London: William Heinemann, 1950).
MT	E. M. Forster, *Marianne Thornton: A Domestic Biography, 1797–1887* (New York: Harcourt, Brace, & World, 1956).
PC	Henry James, *The Princess Casamassima,* 2 vols., New York Ed., vols. 5–6.
PE	Ford Madox Ford, *Parade's End* (New York: Alfred A. Knopf, 1961).
PL	Henry James, *The Portrait of a Lady,* 2 vols., New York Ed., vols. 3–4.
PP	Henry James, "A Passionate Pilgrim," New York Ed., vol. 13.
SH	Evelyn Waugh, *Sword of Honour* (Boston: Little, Brown & Co., 1966).

SP   Henry James, *The Spoils of Poynton*, New York Ed., vol. 10.

TB   H. G. Wells, *Tono-Bungay* (New York: Dodd, Mead & Co., 1935).

TBP   Joyce Cary, *To Be a Pilgrim* (New York: Harper & Row, 1942).

TE   V. Sackville-West, *The Edwardians* (New York: Viking Press, 1961).

THD   Elizabeth Bowen, *The Heat of the Day* (London: Jonathan Cape, 1949).

TL   John Galsworthy, "To Let,'" Book 3, *The Forsyte Saga* (London: William Heinemann, 1950).

TM   Christopher Isherwood, *The Memorial* (Norfolk, Conn.: New Directions, 1946).

TP   John Galsworthy, *The Patricians* (New York: Charles Scribner's Sons, 1926).

WD   Henry James, *The Wings of the Dove*, 2 vols., New York Ed., vols. 19–20.

WL   Elizabeth Bowen, *A World of Love* (London: Jonathan Cape, 1955).

The Quest for Community

It was the old houses that fetched me. . . . These delicious old houses, in the long August days, in the south of England air, on the soil over which so much has passed and out of which so much has come, rose before me like a series of visions.
Henry James, *The Notebooks of Henry James*

The Stately Homes of England
How beautiful they stand!
Amidst their tall ancestral trees,
O'er all the pleasant land.
Felicia Hemans, *"The Homes of England"*

The Stately Homes of England
Altho' a trifle bleak,
Historically speaking,
Are more or less unique.
Noel Coward, *Operette* in *Second Play Parade*

For centuries the social structure of England has been embodied in the very landscape. In shire after shire the manorial pattern took hold, so that even today—despite suburban sprawl and shrinking green belts—the eye never really loses sight of the age-old feudal contours. Ultimately, as the historian G. M. Young observes, "the Domesday landscape, *terra pratum, pastura, silva* will be found underlying it all. . . . And its midpoint everywhere is the country house." [1]

Moreover, despite counterparts in the baronial system of the Continent, what has generically come to be called the "country house"—whether specifically designated as hall, abbey, park, or manor—is peculiarly English. Even the French chateau, while analogous, is not really identical: indeed, with the social genius of the Gallic *haut monde* gravitating toward the metropolitan rather than the provincial, the fashionable town house of the Faubourg Saint-Germain might be considered more nearly equivalent; but this domicile too, impressive as it may appear in the pages of Balzac and Proust, still lacks the dimension and quite special connotation of the Englishman's. The novelist V. Sackville-West, who was born in the great Jacobean mansion of Knole and who wrote its history, once made a point of the unique and almost indefinable essence of the British country house:

> France has her chateaux, Italy her historic villas . . . Germany her robber castles, but the exact equivalent of what we mean by the English country house is not to be found elsewhere.
>
> It may be large, it may be small; it may be palatial, it may be manorial; it may be of stone, brick, stucco, or even beams and plaster; it may be the seat of the aristocracy or the home of the gentry—whatever it is, it possesses one outstanding characteristic: it is the English country house. [2]

The reason for its uniqueness is, of course, that it is much more than a house in the country. As a nineteenth-century American ambassador once remarked, with a charmingly fresh sense of having made a sociological discovery, a basic difference between the English upper classes and those of many other modern cultures is their profound attachment to the land itself:

"They have *houses* in London, in which they stay while Parliament sits, and occasionally visit at other seasons; but their *homes* are in the country. Their turreted mansions are there, with all that denotes perpetuity—heirlooms, family memorials, pictures, tombs. . . . The permanent interests and affections of the most opulent classes center almost universally in the country." [3] Indeed, as the ambassador might have added, the country house is even more than an ancestral home and family seat: it is —or at least has been—a social, economic, and cultural institution, inextricably linked with the surrounding landscape and profoundly affecting not only those living under its roof but those within its purview as well.

Visiting the English country house, therefore, has long been one of the compulsory pleasures of the American abroad, whether he is received as an invited guest or simply as an anonymous tourist who pays his shillings at the gate. It might even be said that the American interest in this representative English institution has, from a cultural point of view, become a national pastime: from Washington Irving and Nathaniel Hawthorne and Henry James down to a host of roving journalists, Americans have recorded their impressions of one stately home after another, and works like *Bracebridge Hall, Our Old Home,* and *English Hours* remain among the most readable of our minor classics. The great country house, the American has often assumed, is the true habitat of the trueborn Englishman; nowhere else is the English style of life more enviably displayed. And nowhere else does the American himself display so revealingly his own long-simmering ambivalence toward the Old World, toward England and the ancient ways. For behind his anthropological mask, the visiting American who surveys the country house, with its historic landscape, spacious lawns, and perhaps a straying peacock, is often torn by the kind of dilemma young Henry James lightly touched upon when he found Warwick Castle the model of a great dwelling "which amply satisfies the imagination without irritating the democratic conscience." [4] If the great house in one moment speaks to him of human possibilities and opportunities, in another it brings back to mind the darker actualities of a hereditary and hierarchical order. To blot out these darker actualities, the American knows, is to indulge in genteel fantasy and even to risk the charge of outright snobbery; yet to be obsessed by them alone, he also realizes, is to miss seeing that the country house often functioned as an arbiter of taste, manners, and sociability—indeed, as the embodiment of that spirit of *noblesse oblige* that made the old order, at its best, a truly organic community.

Very illuminatingly, this sort of ambivalence comes out where it might be least expected. To cite twentieth-century examples, Sinclair Lewis in *Dodsworth* and Vincent Sheean in *Personal History,* respectively, allow us to see the country house from the clearly contrasting vantage points of a conservative midwestern businessman and a radical young journalist, both of whom, ironically enough, give expression to much the same attitudes toward what it represents. Lewis describes Sam Dodsworth's first visit to a typical English estate as an encounter eliciting highly mixed feelings on the part of the American:

> Most insecure of all was Sam that afternoon when they motored for tea to Woughton Hall, the country place of Sir Francis Ouston. . . . Here—so overwhelmingly that Sam gasped—was one of the great houses of which he had been apprehensive. Up a mile-long driveway of elms they came to a lofty Palladian façade, as stern as a court-house, with a rough stone wing at one end. "That's the old part, that stone—built about 1480," said Herndon.[5]

As Lewis continues the description of the house and its atmosphere, it is evident that Dodsworth regards the place with mingled apprehension, envy, and awe as a kind of epiphany revealing what repels and yet charms him in the old order. Vincent Sheean, speaking for himself in *Personal History,* recalls how he was invited to Knole soon after his youthful conversion to revolutionary Marxism and consequently found himself of two minds about the obviously privileged status of the place and its remarkable poetic beauty. However, remembering Knole and the hospitality of V. Sackville-West and her husband, Harold Nicolson, Sheean is not in the least doctrinaire; on the contrary, he is almost Jamesian:

One house in the country came to represent, almost to sum up, the imaginative and romantic appeal of England to me. . . . I grew to know the house, to feel something of its extraordinary persuasive power as a living thing, and to experience, however indirectly, the emotion it peculiarly evoked: the emotion of visible history. . . . Perhaps to be born in it would be to be overshadowed by it, obsessed by it, particularly in days when so much of its significance has become historical. But to a stranger, a foreigner, a barbarian, it was that rare wonder, a journey of the imagination in time. I should have understood little indeed about England if I had never known it.[6]

This rich and complex sense of the country house is sharpened by much of what may be found in English literature. Many a historic house has associations with some poet or novelist to whom it may have given birth or patronage. One thinks of Sidney at Penshurst or Pope in the gardens at Cirencester, of Byron savoring the gloomy charm of Newstead Abbey or Thackeray enjoying the hospitality of Clevedon, the model for Castlewood in *Henry Esmond*. One can imagine, too, the command performance of *As You Like It* at Wilton or of *Comus* in the now roofless great hall of Ludlow Castle. Moreover, as a social reality, the country house—whether an imposing noble pile of the sort Disraeli fancied or simply a comfortable manor house—has been an inevitable subject for any writer portraying the life of the English landed classes. The country house has given inspiration to the poet, stage settings to the dramatist, properties of horror to the Gothic romancer, and countless victims to both the satirist and the purveyor of murder mysteries. Many a novelist from Richardson and Fielding to Huxley and Waugh has attended to its rituals or chronicled its fortunes. And if some have castigated the follies of the country house, others have found there an image of the good life itself.[7] Indeed, basing the title of a novel on a country-house setting has become a characteristic convention of English fiction, as may be seen in such notable examples as *Mansfield Park, Bleak House, The Spoils of Poynton, Howards End, Crome Yellow,* and *Brideshead Revisited.*

In turning more closely to literature, we soon recognize that, while the country house may simply be used as an inevitable element of the English background, in a significant number of works—in, for instance, Ben Jonson's "To Penshurst" or in *Mansfield Park*—it is obviously much more than a literal setting: it is the chosen emblem of what the author considers humane order and enduring values. This is particularly so in the fiction of the late nineteenth and twentieth centuries—for reasons that should be at least briefly considered if the literary function of the country house is to be truly grasped and appreciated.[8]

Let us approach the matter by way of a literary illustration. In the last sequence of *Descent into Hell,* a religious fantasy by Charles Williams, Lawrence Wentworth, a character incapable of love or fellow-feeling, finds himself clinging to a rope that appears to hang from nowhere into a great abyss. Having no other choice, he lowers himself into the unknown depth. Despite his motion descent is slow and the destination obscure. Eventually he does reach the bottom of the rope and then discovers a dark, endless space. There he is momentarily besieged by menacing faces and meaningless voices, but they soon give way to silence and nothingness. He knows, then, where he is: he is in hell, and his punishment is not its darkness nor its depth, but its isolation. In hell he is alone, as he wished to be in life.[9]

To the reader of modern literature this final scene does not come as a complete surprise. It is really a recognition scene, for Williams has merely given a rather obvious allegorical form, an unashamedly simple apotheosis, to one of the dominant themes of modern literature: the hell of modern man is isolation. Whether presented as cosmic alienation, social estrangement, or simply human loneliness, isolation in some form is made to seem man's ultimate condition or enigmatic choice. A roster of modern protagonists would include mostly outsiders, solitaries, "isolatoes" [10] of some kind, whose predicament is crystallized in the memorable image from Eliot's *Waste Land:*

> We think of the key, each in his prison
> Thinking of the key. . . .[11]

Characters like J. Alfred Prufrock, Stephen Dedalus, and Leopold Bloom would occupy a special place in the list precisely because they are prototypes of others similarly alienated. Even social rank makes little difference: from Graham Greene's seedy Londoners up to the fashionable Mrs. Dalloway and down again to Beckett's tramps, the number is legion. For some authors— particularly Conrad, Joyce, Lawrence, and Auden—isolation is an obsessive concern.[12] Conrad's novels, needless to say, present variations on this theme by tracing the tortured destinies of Axel Heyst, Razumov, Decoud, and Lord Jim. Yet even novelists for whom isolation is not the primary theme often portray characters familiar with its agonies. Aldous Huxley, for example, describes Philip Quarles, the cerebral protagonist of *Point Counter Point*, in words hauntingly like Conrad's: "All his life he had walked in solitude, in a private void, in which nobody, not his mother, not his friends, not his lovers had been permitted to enter." [13] Even Somerset Maugham, for all his seeming ease in Zion, writes his most serious novels about outsiders like the diffident Philip Carey in *Of Human Bondage* and the footloose painter, Charles Strickland, in *The Moon and Sixpence*.

It may seem, of course, that the theme of isolation is best illustrated by works from the earlier decades of the century, particularly those in the symbolist or "modernist" tradition. Recent antimodernist mutations in English fiction might appear, at first glance, to indicate a turning away from the problems of the self and to imply a renewed confidence in the possibility of restoring the broken circuits of vital communal feeling. On closer examination, however, this is not the case: despite a return to traditional novelistic modes and materials, the poignancy of isolation still remains. The fiction of C. P. Snow—for some, the best instance of a new direction—often confirms the theme of isolation in unexpected ways. In precept and practice, Snow has rejected the modernist tradition and its preoccupation with the lonely psyche and has exploited obviously "public" themes. His most typical novels show men engaged in some group endeavor, operating in a large complex of institutional relationships; but these, he recognizes, often conceal rather than relieve the individual's loneliness. *The Masters*, perhaps his finest novel, illustrates this very movingly. Here the surface is decidedly public: the scene is a Cambridge college, and the characters are nearly all dons shown largely in their professional roles. The plot turns on the election of a new master, precipitated by the fatal illness of the one in office, and presents what is to be taken as a microcosm of political life: candidates step forward, sides form, supporters maneuver, stay, or depart with a choreographic nuance that is accentuated by the low-keyed, almost documentary style. But the power struggle is not the only source of drama: at least some of the tension is due to the fact that the jockeying and bargaining take place while the incumbent master, old and dying, lies alone in his room above it all. And if Snow's impersonal manner is mistaken by the reader, one of the characters is there to correct him. A perceptive don, knowing that not even the dying master's wife can give him comfort, exclaims: "We're all alone, aren't we? Each one of us. Quite alone." [14]

Furthermore, modern literature abounds with symbolic images of isolation. For example, physical setting, whether a natural landscape or a man-made structure, is very often a symbol for the alienation of its occupants. To be specific, consider how often the setting is an island. Once a favorite image for poets like Byron and Shelley, to whom it epitomized natural loveliness and idyllic freedom from the oppressions of the mainland, the island has increasingly come to suggest the poignancy of human loneliness or the dangers of self-absorption. "Yes! in the sea of life enisled, / . . . We mortal millions live *alone*," Matthew Arnold cried to Marguerite—only making explicit what fellow poets from Baudelaire and Tennyson to Yeats and Auden more subtly imply. Such poems as "The Lady of Shallot," The Lotus-Eaters," "Un Voyage à Cythère"—even "The Lake Isle of Innisfree"—evoke places of retreat rather than fulfillment, so that Auden's call that "we rebuild our cities, not dream of islands" [15] seems a reprimand considerably overdue. And the island image, so long the property of poets, has in recent times been appropriated by writers of fiction because it evidently resounds for them with identical overtones. Joseph Conrad, perhaps the novelist most obsessed with the theme of isolation, makes the island a primary symbol in several novels. In *Victory*, for example, the island of Samburan, the abandoned coaling station where Heyst lives apart from the world, becomes an embodiment of his own

psychic withdrawal and the dangers of his detachment. Elsewhere, D. H. Lawrence strikes an unmistakable symbolic note
in the very title of "The Man Who Loved Islands"; and the plot
itself presents, as we might expect, a frigid escapist who, less
attractive than the humane Heyst, also tries to widen the distance between himself and his fellows by going from island to
island, each more isolated than the last, until he perishes by
himself on one blanketed by the snows of a northern sea.[16]

More recently, Durrell's *Alexandria Quartet,* as seems fitting
in a work with a symbolist, even Laurentian, awareness of landscape, brings back the island in its familiar role. The first novel,
Justine, opens with the self-exile of Darley, the novelist-narrator,
to an island outside the city; the final one closes with his recognition that this haven cannot last. As if in response to the nostalgic
lament of another artist-exile, Rimbaud—*"Je regrette l'Europe
aux anciens parapets"* ("Bateau Ivre")—Darley considers turning
westward toward "the old inheritance" of Italy and France.
"Surely there is still some worthwhile work to be done among
their ruins," he speculates, "something which we can cherish,
perhaps even revive." Thus novelist Durrell almost echoes poet
Auden's imperative to rebuild cities, not dream of islands.[17]

Like islands, enclosures of one kind or another—particularly
buildings—also become emblems of isolation. For artists and
decadents, structures like Tennyson's Palace of Art, Axel's castle,
Des Esseintes's bizarre villa, or the towers of Joyce and Yeats
suggest the temptations and hazards of aesthetic renunciation of
the communal world. In fiction, ever since Balzac described the
commonplace boardinghouse of Madame Vauquer in the ominous terms of a prison, other dwellings—from the tenements of
Zola to the *palazzi* of Henry James—have been insinuating a
claustral atmosphere. Whether described in the Gothic manner
of Hawthorne and Dickens or in the more sophisticated modes of
Elizabeth Bowen and Henry Green, the house has suggested
introversion and separateness as well as intimacy and relationship. In particular, it is revealing to note how often individual
rooms, like so many secreted shells, figuratively confirm the
isolation of their occupants. The death cell of Stendhal's Julien
Sorel and that of his shabbier descendant Camus's Meursault are

both actual jails, but they may be taken emblematically as well; between them stands a century-long line of other cell-like quarters—among them, the darkened chamber of Dickens's Miss Havisham, Mr. Osborne's forbidding study in *Vanity Fair,* the cramped garret of Raskolnikov, Eliot's sordid furnished rooms, the sterile bedroom of Joyce's Mr. Duffy. Indeed, with these in evidence, is it surprising that Samuel Beckett should house his lonely characters in dingy cellars and even ash cans?

Yet if isolation is generally recognized as a dominant theme of modern literature, there is another significant theme, a genuine countertheme, which also requires emphasis. This may be identified as the theme of "community" or "communion"—the reaffirmation of those values, symbols, and patterns of behavior that, in Erich Fromm's words, relieve the "moral aloneness" of the individual and give him the feeling of "belonging." [18] This is what Conrad spoke of as "solidarity" and D. H. Lawrence called "togetherness," before the word was debased by modern pedagogues and the women's magazines. Indeed, despite the attention contemporary literary criticism has given to the theme of isolation as a singular and separate obsession of the modern imagination, modern novelists and poets have really been concerned with isolation *and* community as a polarity, so that the significance of one cannot be properly understood without an awareness of its dialectical relationship to the other. The writers themselves have been quite explicit about this, even to the point of using the same language. "It is being cut off that is our ailment," Lawrence wrote in a letter. He added his diagnosis elsewhere: "We have frustrated that instinct of community that would make us unite in pride and dignity." [19] Almost echoing Lawrence, the chorus of Eliot's *Murder in the Cathedral* strikes the same note:

> What have you if you have not life together?
> There is no life that is not in community.[20]

As artists living in a time when the values and patterns begetting a feeling of belonging have undergone constant diminution, modern writers have also had to cope with the problem of discovering or inventing the dramatic and symbolic means for projecting their sense of true community and the possibility of its restoration. In other words, the haunting images of isolation —such as the islands and enclosures mentioned above—have to be convincingly balanced by equally compelling images of human relatedness and vital association. In face of the blankness of the social landscape, the difficulties of this task are obvious. They also help to account for the experimentation and tentativeness of the artist's portrayal of community, which, even when carried through, may be only dimly perceived by his readers or seem less resonant than the more familiar motifs of loss and estrangement. Conrad, whose works are often read as monodies on isolation, was perhaps more fortunate than most modern novelists in that he had a personal store of communal symbolism upon which to draw: namely, his own experience of ships and the traditional code of the sea. Just as he employed the islands of *Nostromo* and *Victory* as symbols of isolation, he also found countersymbols of community in the ship and the whole regimen of the sailor's world. "Our ship, the ship we serve, is the moral symbol of our life," he once explicitly declared,[21] as if to sum up what is evocatively rendered in *The Nigger of the Narcissus, The Shadow-Line,* and even *The Heart of Darkness.*

Other modern writers, not so fortunate as Conrad but with the same intent, have often transformed ordinary social affairs such as parties into ritual enactments of community. Indeed, there is a variety of works in which "parties" of some sort—tea parties, cocktail parties, dinner parties, weekend parties, traveling parties —are so essential to plot and theme that the title of Henry Green's *Partygoing* could be fittingly used over and over again. Evidently such parties recur not simply to bring people together as plot demands but to suggest some kind of attempted community, whether frustrated or attained. Sometimes, in fact, the writers reveal this purpose by alluding to religious and sacramental rites in otherwise mundane contexts. The simple party for two in Joyce's *Ulysses,* where Leopold Bloom plays host to Stephen Dedalus, provides a good instance, since their moment of communion is confirmed by the emphasis upon the eucharistic character of the shared cocoa, "Epp's massproduct." So also the "parties" in the works of other writers often take place under religious auspices: Christian, of course, in Eliot's *Cocktail Party* and Auden's *Age of Anxiety;* Moslem and Hindu in Forster's *Passage to India;* and primitive in Lawrence's *Plumed Serpent.* Even purely secular affairs unsupported by any churchly allusion are often portrayed as attempts to achieve a sense of unity and harmony. The novels of Virginia Woolf in particular repeatedly employ the party as a symbolic action: an evening party provides the climax of the long, trying day in *Mrs. Dalloway;* the dinner over which Mrs. Ramsay presides in *To the Lighthouse* establishes among the guests a feeling of relatedness that lingers long after her death. Even the more sober fiction of C. P. Snow usually takes advantage of a background like Cambridge to punctuate routine proceedings with a note of ritual by studied reference to the custom of high table and common room.[22]

Another recurring symbol used to convey the idea of community is a certain kind of woman: the intuitive, elemental, or—to use Shaw's word—"vital" woman who keeps reappearing in modern fiction in various guises—Forster's Mrs. Wilcox and Mrs. Moore, Conrad's Mrs. Gould, Joyce's Molly Bloom, Virginia Woolf's Mrs. Ramsay, Joyce Cary's Sara Monday.[23] Vibrant, loving, maternal, possessing not knowledge but some deep wisdom, often strangely passive, sometimes mysterious, this woman seems to create for those around her, by her very existence, by her special quality of being, the occasion for community—not simply with her alone but among themselves as well. She may be young, though often she is not; she may be wife, mother, mistress; but none of these functions really suggests her almost uncanny power to reach others, to relieve, subdue, transform, and reconcile them. An excellent manifestation of such a woman is Mrs. Gould, who, as Conrad observes, is "highly gifted in the art of human intercourse which consists of delicate shades of self-forgetfulness and in the suggestion of universal comprehension." For such a woman, moreover, community extends beyond the present, back into the past and onward into the future in an unbroken, connecting arch. Mrs. Wilcox, we are told, "worshiped the past" and revealed the "instinctive wisdom the past alone can bestow" (*HE*, p. 28). Mrs. Gould reflects that "our daily work must be done to the glory of the dead and for the good of those who come after." [24] And for these women, nothing illustrates the sense of the past and of the future so clearly as the feeling for the finer things that have survived and should survive—above all, houses. When Mrs. Wilcox learns that the Schlegel sisters must give up their London home because the landlord has decided to replace it with flats, she grieves at their loss. Even Sara Monday, a servant, shows genuine fondness for the homes of her master, Tom Wilcher. "How well Sara looked after both my houses," Wilcher remembers, "how she cleaned and polished them and how she cherished and loved them" (*TBP,* p. 28). And in both *Howards End* and *To the Lighthouse,* those who return to the homes of the dead Mrs. Wilcox and Mrs. Ramsay find themselves under a kind of spell that joins all together once again, as though each woman lingered as a benevolent spirit of place.

Which brings us to the significance of the country house in modern fiction. Of all the available symbols of community, the outstanding one for the English novelist is obviously the country house. As an institution representing the structure and traditions of English society, it is a microcosm which has the advantage of being public and familiar, yet malleable enough to serve the protean interests of individual novelists. Not only identifiable symbolists like James, Forster, and Virginia Woolf, but documentary realists like Wells and Galsworthy, as well as satirists like Huxley and Waugh, have all found in the country house a means of embodying the qualities and values of community, whether in a state of decay, transformation, or renewal—as may be readily seen by considering its role in such varied works as *The Princess Casamassima, Tono-Bungay, Parade's End, The Edwardians, Between the Acts,* or *To Be a Pilgrim.* Indeed, the number of modern novels featuring the country house is great enough to suggest that the problem of community, too broad and diffuse for any single comprehensive treatment, might be studied within this area. My purpose in what follows, therefore, is to group together for consideration the outstanding works of modern fiction—often unassociated—that employ the country house as a symbolic setting, to examine the communal values their authors wish to represent, and to show, through analysis of literary techniques and conventions, precisely what the house contributes to the formal structure and total meaning of individual novels. In doing this, I have not atempted to mention, let alone discuss, all the fictional houses that might be found. My intention is not to make a mere inventory, but to study the literary function of an important community symbol, the greater understanding of which may help to illuminate the work of individual novelists as well as the literature of the period as a whole.[25]

Once the country house is recognized as a symbol of community, its specific advantages for both the novelist and his readers soon become evident. A good symbol, as Susanne Langer has noted, possesses definite physical attributes—a point that is often ignored when the meaning of symbols and not their adequacy is emphasized. Speaking of the Cross of Christianity, one of the most powerful symbols known, she observes that much of its value is due to its physical form: it is "easily made—drawn on paper, set up in wood or stone . . . even traced recognizably with a finger in a ritual gesture." [26] And though admittedly a literary symbol does not always possess such an elemental simplicity, it too must be readily grasped by the imagination to form a memorable pattern in the mind and to offer a magnetic focus for a rich complex of feeling. The country house definitely reveals these attributes: it is unmistakably *there*. Like a great stage, it quite literally gathers people together and shows them meeting, separating, colliding, uniting. Depending upon the novelist's intention and tone, all the concrete elements of the house and its setting—rooms and furnishings, gardens and landscape—may combine in a subtle network of supporting images. The appearance, scale, and style of the house may bespeak the taste and sensibility of the occupants or expose their surrender to vanity and ostentation. The reach of park and spread of acre may imply a wish for apartness and distance from others or an expansive openness of spirit; the owners may isolate themselves behind their gates or reach out to the surrounding countryside and their neighbors in an affable way. Within the house, individuals may withdraw themselves to lonely rooms or join one another in hall or on terrace. The long gallery, with its row of

family portraits running like a passageway into the past, makes it
seem one with the present. And the whole regimen of country-
house life, like that aboard Conrad's ships, may manifest a stable
order based on unchanging custom and comfortable habit.

Physically, the house provides a definite unity of place, which
in any attempt to portray community is important for thematic
as well as aesthetic reasons. And this unity of place augments the
sense of other unities: the unity of past, present, and future;
unity with nature; indeed, the unity of human experience. Vi-
brating to the life rhythms of departures and arrivals, separations and reunions, deaths and births, the house itself—lived in,
left, and remembered—becomes the hub of the narrative and the
axis of meaning. In an era of travelers, wanderers, seekers, the
house remains a "still point" in an overturning world. Today,
moreover, a symbol that so impressively embodies what Walter
Pater called the "sense of home" has a special resonance. We live
in a world where, as Susanne Langer observes, "the displacement
of the permanent homestead by the modern rented tenement—
now here, now there—has cut another anchor-line of the human
mind," a world where, as she goes on, most people have "no
home that is a symbol of their childhood, not even the definite
memory of one place to serve that purpose." [27] The fictional
house may then become for both writers and readers alike a sur-
rogate for something missed; and an imaginative act may recover,
at least temporarily, the feeling of community that has been lost.

This does not necessarily mean that the inhabitants of the
country house and their way of life are purposely idealized, any
more than the seamen and shipboard life are idealized by Conrad. As a matter of fact, sharply contrasting attitudes toward the
historic country house may be found, varying with the authors
and their times. As we shall see, some admire, others are openly
critical and satirical, and a good many remain ambivalent. Of
these last, the essayist C. E. Montague is a good example; he
makes his point of view explicit enough to be unmistakable. In
some places, Montague acknowledges, the actual squire may have
been a "petty tyrant or a dull boozer," and "the whole bucolic
concern when brought into the thin dry clarity of utilitarian
lamplight" was perhaps "an affront to reason and conscience";

nonetheless, he is also ready to surmise that at its best the system "worked out the relation of rural landlord and tenant into a form almost easy, often almost affectionate." And finding the house itself "the most agreeable of all human mansions," Montague concludes that it somehow seems to transcend its original social context: "Like Louis's Versailles and Wolsey's Hampton Court, the country houses of the English 'ruling class,' now almost dispossessed, may be finer than their makers." [28]

In any case, during the twentieth century and especially in recent decades, harsh criticism has lost much of its point. The country house in the traditional sense has largely ceased to exist: it is no longer a going concern but an economic disability. Paradoxically, in fact, the decline of the country house seems to have strengthened its possibilities as a symbol. With its former power having shifted to other centers of authority far more impersonal and even ominous, animosity has given way to nostalgia, and elegy has vied with satire to have the last word. As David Daiches points out, it cannot be an accident that since World War II visiting old country houses has become such a popular British pastime.[29] Nor is it coincidental that a number of leading authors—Osbert Sitwell, V. Sackville-West, Percy Lubbock, Elizabeth Bowen, Joyce Cary—have affectionately composed autobiographical accounts of the life they knew in actual country seats like Renishaw, Knole, Earlham, Bowens Court, or Castle Cary. What the house has lost in reality, it seems to have recovered as a symbol whose import satisfies our modern needs. "The 'household of continuance' has gone now," wrote Oliver St. John Gogarty in his warm recollection of Lady Gregory and Coole Park. "Two years is the average length of rental. Mansions are no more. The very apartments in which we live are hardly stationary. All are caught in the eddy of ever widening circles and of ever lessening intensity." [30] Today, both writers and readers may be less concerned with what the house was or is and more with what it suggests: an image of community antithetical to the dislocation and isolation they actually know.

Indeed, the more perceptive of those who witnessed the first stages of the decline of the country house in the late nineteenth century obviously recognized this and eloquently expressed their appreciation of the representative value of what was passing away. John Ruskin, for example, was evidently thinking of the fate of the ancient places when he made memory the sixth lamp of architecture and argued that domestic buildings took on perfection as they became immemorial, "animated by a metaphorical or historical meaning." Declaring it "an evil sign of a people when their houses are built to last for one generation only," Ruskin extolled the house of continuity:

> There is a sanctity in a good man's house which cannot be renewed in every tenement that rises on its ruins; and I believe that good men would generally feel this; and that having spent their lives happily and honourably, they would be grieved, at the close of them, to think that the place of their early abode . . . was to be swept away. . . . I say that a good man would fear this; and that, far more, a good son, a noble descendant, would fear doing it to his father's house. I say that if men lived like men indeed, their houses would be temples—temples which we should hardly dare to injure, and in which it would make us holy to be permitted to live.[31]

And there was another who could also call the house a "temple" without Ruskin's impulse to preach, who also was devoted to dwellings "animated by metaphorical and historical meaning," though he managed to edge his sentiment with irony. He was what the occasion perhaps required—an outsider, an American.

❧ 1 ❧

The Great Good Place

HENRY JAMES AND THE COUNTRY HOUSE

*Of all the great things that the English have
invented and made part of the credit of the
national character, the most perfect, the most
characteristic, the only one they have mastered
completely in all its details, so that it becomes a
compendious illustration of their social genius and
their manners, is the well-appointed, well-
administered, well-filled country house.*
                              Henry James, *English Hours*

Among the early images of himself that Henry James presents to the reader of his autobiography is one of a small boy lying comfortably on the carpet of a Fourteenth Street parlor, entranced with Joseph Nash's *Mansions of England in the Olden Time*.[1] The image is charming in itself, but its essential significance derives from our being able to see the link between the small boy's momentary enchantment and the mature James's abiding preoccupation with the English country house. Indeed, James displayed in the pages of his works—themselves architecturally conceived as windows in the "house of fiction"—such a remarkable number of his own mansions and manorial estates that they might almost seem intended as rivals to those historic houses of brick and stone represented in Nash's lithographs. Gardencourt, Medley, Poynton, Mellows, Fawns, Summersoft, and many others all bring to mind imaginary landscapes of great beauty and splendor, haunting in their glorious ripeness, sometimes themselves haunted by insinuations of decay and evil. Obviously their number, carefully chosen names, and evocative power suggest that they are meant to be taken as something more than fictional background in the conventional sense, and to the reader who understands this, they come to have an unmistakable symbolic resonance.

To be sure, since James drew upon the life of the English upper classes for the substance of much of his fiction, the typical country house with its familiar regimen was an inevitable part of his *mise en scène;* the more literal requirements of his subjects, however, did not demand the subtle lavishness and dedication he brought to its portrayal. Observation of its recurrence and function in work after work soon makes evident that James looked upon the country house not simply as an actuality of English society but also as a symbol, one of the most attractive variants of the "great good place."

His preoccupation with the country house should, therefore, associate him with other novelists who approached it out of much the same motive and need as his own. In fact, to place the houses of James in the company of those depicted by, say, Jane Austen, Disraeli, Forster, Bowen, or Ford—without necessarily implying strong lines of influence in any direction—provides an illuminating perspective on James himself and helps to rescue him from the ill-considered attacks to which his seemingly solitary and exposed position has often made him vulnerable. Misunderstanding of this aspect of James has been exhibited on both sides of the Atlantic. Parrington dismissed his concerns as a genteel "nostalgia for culture." Van Wyck Brooks, taking a volume to say much the same thing, maintained that James idealized English society uncritically. In England, Rebecca West, at least in her early study of James, belittled his "twittering over the teacups." Even Ezra Pound, an admirer and descendant of sorts, regretted the master's "passion for high life." [2] Although their phrases may stick in the mind and block the sympathetic understanding of some, they are wide of the mark. But the error involved is not simply the identification of James with commonplace snobbery and social trivia; it is the obtuse unawareness of the validity of his concern with a community symbol.

James, such critics seem to forget, was as much concerned with the problem of human isolation as with "society." Some of his most notable works, as L. C. Knights has noted, present "the trapped, the caged, the excluded consciousness" with an apprehension that shows him to be the first of the moderns.[3] And, though Knights is thinking largely of such characters as Basil Stransom in "The Altar of the Dead" and John Marcher in "The Beast in the Jungle" (a character whose psychology, incidentally, gives him a remarkable affinity with Joyce's Gabriel Conroy and James Duffy), it is also true that even James's great heroines—Isabel Archer, Fleda Vetch, Milly Theale, Maggie Verver—are also isolated figures, forced to make their terrible choices alone and without spiritual support. Again, the betrayal theme—what Graham Greene calls the "Judas complex" [4]—that runs through James's work is, like the theme of cuckoldry in other modern writers, an indication of concern with the problematic nature of human ties and the unreliability of the most intimate relationships. Even his technical development of the restricted point of view, the filtering of impressions through the sensibility of a single character, bespeaks—like Joyce's use of the "stream of consciousness"—the recognition of the privacy of the self in world where a public, communicable relation to others appears undependable.

Ignoring this side of James, hostile critics inevitably brand his concern with society as superficial. What should be emphasized, instead, is that, for James as for other modern writers, the theme of isolation is intimately and dialectically related to the theme of community. He is not concerned with the self alone, nor with society in the fashionable sense only—nor even, save in some general respect, with the relation of the individual self to society in the realistic tradition of the great nineteenth-century novels.[5] Ultimately, James is most concerned with the relation of the self to others in a state of community that transcends the familiar institutions and social forms he describes, though these undoubtedly remained for him the best and most natural means for embodying its fulfillment or its diminution. T. S. Eliot, perhaps because of his own analogous situation, recognized James's intention quite clearly. Replying to the usual charges against the novelist, Eliot remarked that the fact that "his view of England—a view which gradually dissolves in his development—was a romantic one is a small matter. His romanticism implied no defect of observation of the things he wanted to observe . . . it issues, rather, from the imperative insistence of an ideal which tormented him. He was possessed by the vision of an ideal society." [6]

Like other modern writers preoccupied with the theme of ideal human relationships, James needed and sought and affirmed those "values, symbols, patterns" that Erich Fromm considers the means for creating the feeling of communion and belonging. Certainly, James's celebrated sense of the past, his almost chivalric commitment to a code of personal honor and loyalty, his awareness of suffering as an inevitable strand in "the continuity of the human lot" (*PL*, 2 : 327), and his dedication to the discipline of art are all values pointing away from the ego toward self-transcendence. Again, a story like "The Altar of the Dead," which presents Basil Stransom burning candles before a Catholic shrine for his dead friends and relations, illustrates James's understanding of the importance of "practised communion" [7] or ritual (even apart from religious beliefs) for assuaging the sense of loss and isolation. But the most favored emblem of all, the most repeated

figure in the Jamesian carpet, appears to be the English country
house. Perhaps it is not even too daring a speculation to say that
the houses in Nash's folios that James found entrancing as a
small boy furnished what eventually became the dominant symbol of the novelist's social imagination. In any case, it is evident
that he turned again and again to the English country house,
from the early *Passionate Pilgrim* to the most subtle novels of
his last period, because it meant more than a conventional setting: it was a "local habitation" for many of his own values; a
unifying focus to which his multitudinous impressions of the
good life might gravitate and from which, in turn, they might
be abundantly released; even, at times, a measure of his own disenchantment and a vehicle for expressing his disillusion.

Critics friendly to James have at least dimly realized that the
country house had some such significance for him. Returning to
the novelist once again in 1933, T. S. Eliot observed: "The elaborate complications in which many of James's problems involve
themselves, now seem remote; what is not remote is his curious
search, often in the oddest places, like country houses, for spiritual life." Joseph Warren Beach, commenting on the "rarified
and transcendental atmosphere in which James lifts us," also goes
on to note that he has given this atmosphere "a semi-physical
counter-part in the air of the English country house . . . in
which every provision is made for the convenience of people bent
on a liberal freedom of intercourse." And F. R. Leavis finds that
in one novel at least, *The Portrait of a Lady,* James considers a
"possible world in which the country house, with its external
civilization, shall also be a centre for the life of the spirit; in
which manners shall be the index of an inner fineness." Even
Ezra Pound, though he frowns upon James's "passion for high
life," recognizes nonetheless that in a novel like *The Awkward
Age* James "does give us the most subtly graded atmospheres of
his houses most excellently"—adding significantly but with im-
perspicuous brevity, "and indeed, this may be regarded as *his*
subject." [8] However, although Eliot, Leavis, Beach, and Pound
are among the most perceptive of James's critics in their understanding of the role of the country house, they present their insights in passing, so to speak, and leave them unexplored, thus

allowing them to be taken more superficially than they must intend. They do not examine James's actual houses in depth, nor consider their remarkable number and range or their function from one work to another. On the other hand, the critic who produces a thorough and discerning analysis of a typically Jamesian house usually confines himself to the context of a single work; he gives little or no emphasis to its possible relation to other houses in James, and very rarely suggests any comparison between its function and the traditional place of the country house in English fiction before and after James. Hence, there are good reasons for concentrating upon the country house as one of the most significant motifs in James's work and for undertaking the comprehensive examination it so obviously invites but has not yet actually received.[9]

The symbolic function of the English country house should first of all be recognized as the culmination of the Jamesian way with setting. In selecting his fictional backgrounds, James hardly ever turns to nature: he obviously prefers familiar architectural sights and representative monuments allowing the imaginative fusion of the historical and the personal, the traditional and the visionary. Indeed, Madame Merle in *The Portrait of a Lady* appears to sum up the novelist's own awareness of the human implications of such a setting quite explicitly. When Isabel Archer declares that she does not care what kind of physical home her suitors may offer and expresses equal indifference to a "castle in the Apennines" and a "brick house on Fortieth Street," Madame Merle rebukes her:

> That's very crude of you. When you've lived as long as I you'll see that every human being has his shell and that you must take the shell into account. By the shell I mean the whole envelope of circumstances. There's no such thing as an isolated man or woman; we're each of us made up of some cluster of appurtenances. What shall we call our "self"? Where does it end? It overflows into everything that belongs to us— and then it flows back again. . . . I've a great respect for *things!* One's self—for other people—is one's expression of

one's self; and one's house, one's furniture, one's garments, the
books one reads, the company one keeps—these things are all
expressive. [*PL*, 1 : 287–88]

To be sure, Madame Merle is a fictional character, even an unsympathetic one, but we must not infer from this that she cannot
speak for her creator, particularly when the total action of this
novel expresses the inadequacy of Isabel Archer's almost Mani-
chaean disregard for the complexities of the social, material world
in her pursuit of unconditioned freedom. Moreover, in speaking
for himself, James invariably associates his own experiences with
the places where they occurred. How often in the famous prefaces, for example, does he weave into the history of the work
under consideration the very atmosphere of the place that fostered its genesis or execution, so that, between the lines allowing
us intimacy with the novelist's art, we are also made aware—
through some evocative detail of night walks in the West End,
of sounds from the Rue de Luxembourg, of the view from an
ancient palazzo—of the large human world of London or Paris
or Venice beyond the desk and the study window. How often,
in fact, does he reveal that many of his great life-transforming
experiences were simply those moments of intense, almost mystical response to the historic buildings and storied monuments of
Europe.

Thus, rather like a modern film director, James takes his characters "on location" not for the sake of scenic background and
gratuitous charm but to provide symbolic settings relevant to his
theme. Familiar tourist spots recur because they offer the possibility of a public kind of symbolism through association with
social and cultural actualities. Indeed, when James's Americans
enter a palazzo or a château, a cathedral or a museum, the building itself becomes an element in their plight before Europe's challenges and contradictions. *The American* opens in the Louvre
but closes in the cathedral of Nôtre Dame, thus posing in two
Parisian landmarks the contrast between Christopher Newman's
early aesthetic aspirations and his final moral renunciation of
possible revenge. When Daisy Miller visits the castle of Chillon,
she reveals herself to be a true daughter of democracy by remain-

ing unimpressed by its "feudal antiquities" and "dusky traditions," but the pleasing naïveté displayed at this historic haunt only leads the way to another one that destroys her—for she dies, as Harry Levin dryly comments, like an early Christian martyr, of overexposure in the Roman Colosseum.[10] James's continental dwellings, in fact, often appear to be forbidding, menacing, even prisonlike. Newman's first sight of the Bellegardes' château is intimidating: all the Gothic elements of the setting—iron gates, bars, towers, the clang of a rusty bell—work upon the American to elicit the perhaps too obvious conclusion: "It looks like a Chinese penitentiary." [11] And in "The Aspern Papers," the gloomy Venetian palazzo produces a similar effect, with the aging mistress of the dead poet and her unfortunate niece living there shut off from the world and the present.

Compared with such residences as these, the English country house appears all the more inviting and hospitable. Indeed, young James was on one occasion quite explicit about the contrast. During his apprentice years in Italy, when a lady suggested that the Roman villa would be a subject for him, he demurred. "A Roman villa," he replied, "seems to have less of a human and social suggestiveness, a shorter, lighter vibration, than an old English country house, round which experience seems piled so thick." [12]

There is more than one reason for this, particularly since the demands of James's social imagination were so varied. First of all, with his remarkable pictorial sense, James was aware of the psychological implications of physical space. In the works mentioned above and others, images of constricted spaces and enclosures—of "cages," in particular—create a claustrophobic sense of isolation. The nightmarish predicament of being pursued or trapped in some narrow, bounded place frequently recurs as a symbolic action. Many of the somber, introverted houses that James found in Italy and France became just such symbols of isolation. The English country house, on the other hand, because of its very physical appearance—its great space, hospitable openness, and gracious beauty—inevitably became their countersymbol; begetting a genuine expansion of spirit, it suggested not isolation but sociability. Moreover, even when James does pre-

sent the country house as a kind of enclosure, he still emphasizes
its positive qualities; it becomes a protective shelter, a refuge:
from one point of view, a kind of mother symbol, from another,
a sanctuary or temple.[13]

James needed ceremony and ritual to give texture to the drama
of social intercourse; and like Conrad, who made his patterns of
moral community out of the rugged but traditional ways of ships
and sailors, James found his in the more elegant but no less traditional and familiar regimen of country-house life. Indeed, even
Rebecca West—who, as we noted above, once caustically described
the stories of James as so much "twittering over the teacups"—
has recently come to see more profound significance in his preoccupations. James would have preferred, she now maintains,
"the Shakespearean days when the formality of a palace had a
visible connection with salvation and damnation. But he could
not write his books about the contemporary English court for it
hardly existed . . . he took the English aristocratic life as the
next best thing." [14] Her remark would be even more to the point
if she had specified that this life was really the life of the country
house. There, surely, was his court.

This is not to say, however, that James necessarily idealized
English life and the English upper classes. James, being an American and Henry James, an outsider on two counts, never really
lost his ambivalence toward Europe or England itself. At once
enamoured and detached, he found in the great houses not only
nourishment for his imagination but also irritants to his democratic conscience. Indeed, the difficulty the reader may sometimes
have with interpreting James's treatment of the house is really
due to the fact that he is often given a double view of it: at once
artist and historian, James celebrates the house as a social symbol
and observes it as a social fact. In consequence, his awareness of
the disparity between the symbolic ideal and the social actuality
is often naggingly present. This uneasiness is evident in his early
stories and essays and becomes more aggravated in his later works.
Significantly, in a number of them, the house itself—the chosen
symbol of community and order—becomes the victim of an uncertain fate. It is left to decay, it changes from hand to hand, it
is bought and sold and rented out—and, in the case of Poynton,

haggled over, ransacked, even destroyed. In fact, without this ambiguity, the Jamesian drama of the country house might remain conventional and dilute.

Although James chose the country house as both symbol and setting, it might be said from another point of view that the country house had chosen him, that it was, in his own idiom, one of the *données* that came inevitably to hand. Before discussing the outstanding places in his fiction, we must consider some of the influences, historical and literary, that helped to shape his vision of the English country house.

To begin with, his family had in a sense made the choice for him. As he wrote of his early years,

> I saw my parents homesick, as I conceived, for the ancient order and distressed and inconvenienced by many of the more immediate features of the modern, as the modern pressed upon us, and since their theory of our better living was from an early time that we should renew the quest of the ancient on the very first possibility I simply grew greater in the faith that somehow to manage that would constitute success in life." [15]

Their "quest of the ancient" became his own and eventually led him to many corners of the Old World, but to none more frequently than to the manor homes of England. From his first independent trip to England in 1869 until his last years, James made countless visits, both as tourist and as guest, to a variety of country houses. There his quest seemed fulfilled, the true paradigm of the ancient order luminously revealed.

Indeed, even his casual writings about these visits—in travel sketches, notebook jottings, and letters—are usually suggestive, for James often records in them direct responses and explicit attitudes toward country-house life that later become dramatically and symbolically transmuted into fiction. Particularly illuminating in this respect are his early travel essays, which readers of his fiction tend to neglect. Not only the essay "Abbeys and Castles" but others on Haddon Hall, Compton Wynyates, Warwick, and Stokesay allow us to follow James's pursuit of his symbol. Most of them, in fact, fall into a pattern that soon becomes familiar;

there is even a pleasing monotony about the features of the house selected for emphasis. "The house was most agreeable," he writes of one that might very well be the model for Gardencourt: "It stood on a kind of terrace, in the middle of a lawn and garden, and the terrace overhung one of the most copious rivers in England." Moreover, despite the visual beauty of park and terrace and house, James's interest is never purely aesthetic; like most nineteenth-century travelers, like Irving, Hawthorne, or Ruskin, he invariably complements his remarks on architecture and style with reflections on their human context, their associations with time past. "Every step you take in such a house," he writes of an old Norman residence that was once an abbey, "confronts you in one way or another with the remote past. You devour the documentary, you inhale history." And it is this easy communication of the present with the past that constantly delights him:

> It is not too much to say that after spending twenty-four hours in a house that is six hundred years old you seem yourself to have lived in it six hundred years. You seem yourself to have hollowed the flags and to have polished the oak with your touch. . . . You look up and down the miniature cloister before you pass in; it seems wonderfully old and queer. Then you turn into the drawing room, where you find modern conversation and late publications and the prospect of dinner. The new life and the old have melted together; there is no dividing line.[16]

Of course, since James's notion of England was already formed in childhood by what he found in Nash's lithographs, the pages of *Punch,* and the Victorian novelists appearing in *Cornhill* magazine, many of the places he visited for the travel sketches are those "whose every aspect is a story or a song"; and one or another of them recalls a favorite author whom James associates with the scene. As we might expect, allusions to writers who depicted the life of the castle and the country house constantly recur. At Haddon Hall, for example, James is put in mind of Shakespeare—not the Shakespeare of the tragedies, but the mellow creator of the social comedies. Its court, stately flight of steps, terrace, and balustrade offer, he suggests, the "ideal *mise*

en scène" for *Twelfth Night* or *Much Ado About Nothing.*
Again, at Lynton, he is led to think of Tennyson and the *Idylls
of the King* because its ruined castle suggests wild Tintagel.[17]
And so, throughout the sketches, the literary names multiply,
from Addison and Scott and Jane Austen to James's near contemporary George Eliot.

It would be misleading, however, to imply that James's travels
reflect only the interest of an antiquarian or a conventional literary pilgrim. The English landscape and ancient houses offered
something more than echoes from the past and intimacy with
literary settings: they also gave to James a sense of human possibilities, a measure for human aspirations. At Stokesay, for example, he does not relish the romantic medieval atmosphere for its
own sake, but happily finds there evidence for a new turning in
history, a new beginning. "The place is a capital example of a
small *gentilhommière* of the thirteenth century," he notes. It is
no longer a fortress, but a house; and for him, "this is part of
the charm of the place; human life there must have lost an earlier grimness; it was lived by people who were beginning to believe in good intentions. They must have lived very much together; that is one of the obvious reflections in the court of a
medieval dwelling." And throughout the sketches, as James savors
the same details of landscape and house, it soon becomes apparent that he is really viewing them with an almost Baudelairean
sense of the power of images drawn from the familiar physical
world to evoke a larger spiritual realm of meaning and value.
At Wroxton Abbey, for example, he dwells on the "expressive
rooms," the "observing portrait of a handsome ancestral face,"
and the "great soft billows of the lawn"—images that will run
through his stories and novels; and he goes on to expound meanings that his later fiction will only imply: "Everything that in
the material line can render life noble and charming has been
gathered into it with a profusion which makes the whole place
a monument to past opportunity." [18]

For the young James, almost everything about the country
house seems to suggest symbolic possibilities. Even the surrounding landscape, the garden and the park, is not without emblematic qualities: indeed, it puts him in mind of man's Edenic

state. William Troy, one of the first to recognize the symbolic use of setting by James, in observing the number of climactic scenes that occur in gardens wondered if the choice was conscious or accidental. If an accident, it was, Troy concluded, a fortunate one, for the garden symbol provides a wonderful point of concentration for the widest possible associations.[19] That it was not an accident, however, seems obvious from "Abbeys and Castles," which shows James to be quite aware of the Biblical overtones of the setting. Walking about the park with his host, James hears him describe it as the "paradise of a small English country gentleman"; and he gives his own point to what is only a cliché by adding: "It was indeed a modern Eden, and the trees might have been trees of knowledge." Given this remark from the apprentice years, it is difficult to conclude that the creator of *The Princess Casamassima* and *The Turn of the Screw* remained oblivious to the associations which the gardens of Medley and Bly would have for the perceptive reader. Moreover, in most of these sketches, the simplest routines of country-house life—strolling about the terraces and grounds, churchgoing of a summer afternoon, visiting, and the inevitable taking of "fine strong tea and bread and butter" [20]—are singled out in a way that reveals his appreciation of their ritual character. After reading these sketches we realize that it is not by chance that *The Portrait of a Lady* so readily establishes a sense of community by opening with the tea on the lawn at Gardencourt, or that the country house parties in the later, satirical works create an atmosphere of pseudocommunity in the manner of the symbolic parties of Joyce and Eliot by showing a less gracious age parodying the amenities of another time.

To be sure, James also realized, even as a young man, that many of the things about this life that enchanted him were "in some degree or other characteristic of a rich, powerful, old-fashioned society." The owners of these things were conservative, he admits, while sorting out his mellow impressions of Warwickshire. "Of course they were stubbornly unwilling to see the harmonious edifice of their constituted, convenient world the least bit shaken. I had a feeling, as I went about, that I would find some very ancient and curious opinions still comfortably domiciled in the fine old houses whose clustered gables and chimneys appeared here and there, at a distance, above their ornamental woods." [21] And decades later, he still displayed the same detachment. Indeed, in an essay on Old Suffolk published in 1897, James in one passage considers the place of the country house in relation to the English social hierarchy and manages to give the writing an almost visionary quality without any lapse of realistic awareness. It deserves quotation in full:

> The very essence of England has a way of presenting itself with completeness in almost any fortuitous combination of rural objects at all, so that, wherever you may be, you get reduced and simplified, the whole of the scale. The big house and the woods are always at hand; with a "party" always, in the interval of shooting, to bring down to the rustic sports that keep up the tradition of the village green. The russett, low-browed inn, the "ale-house" of Shakespeare, the immemorial fountain of beer, overlooking that expanse, swings with an old-time story-telling creak, the sign of the Marquis of Carabas. The pretty girls, within sight of it, alight from the Marquis' wagonetter; the young men with one eye-glass and the new hat sit beside them on the benches supplied for their sole accommodation, and thanks to which the mediator on manners has, a little, the image gathered from faded fictions by female hands, of the company brought over, for the triumph of the heroine, to the hunt or the county ball. And it is always Hodge and Gaffer that, at bottom, *font les frais*—always the mild children of the glebe on whom, in the last resort, the complex super-structure rests.[22]

The passage might seem, on first glance, no more than a conventionally charming set piece, nourished more by reading than by observation. But consider it closely: surely, the pointed references to the "mild children of the glebe," to their place and function in the "complex superstructure"—*font les frais*, bearing the cost of it—reveal that James's response to the English scene, no matter how fond, is much more than one of dreamy reverence and uncomplicated nostalgia. Unlike the Duchess in *The Awk-*

ward Age who prefers the historian who "leaves the horrors out," James did not remain uncritical of those aspects of English life that irritated his "democratic conscience."

Furthermore, if James was realistic about the past, whose barbarism or provincialism might be softened by the passage of time, he could be more than shrewd about the present. The hard edges of contemporary actuality, even economic actuality, did not go unobserved. In "An English New Year," for instance, he gives a moving account of a gloomy Christmas season during the depression of the late 1870s. And in other essays, he recognizes that the economic blight also touched his beloved country houses. The great mansions were beginning to stand empty, and their vacancy gave him still another insight into their actual social meaning. Passing a deserted one in Monmouthshire and noting, as always, the long grey facade, the towers, the "usual supply of ivy," and the "rook-haunted elms," he pauses thoughtfully: "But the windows were all closed and the avenue was untrodden; the house was the property of a lady who could not afford to live in it in a becoming state and who let it, furnished, 'for the shooting.' The rich young man occupied it but for three weeks in the year and for the rest of the time left it prey to the hungry gaze of the passing stranger." James does not indulge in melancholy, however, but concludes with a remark that might stand as an epigraph to such novels as *The Princess Casamassima, The Spoils of Poynton,* and *The Awkward Age:* "It seemed a great aesthetic wrong that so charming a place should not be a conscious, sentient home. In England all this is very common. It takes a great many plain people to keep a 'perfect' gentleman going; it takes a great deal of wasted sweetness to make up a saved property." 23

Even the "saved property" itself, James understood, gave no warrant that its owners would also possess an authentic style of life and truly superior manners. It is true, he admits elsewhere, that in England conservatism has "all the charm and leaves dissent and democracy . . . nothing but their bald logic." All that pleases the aesthetic sense appears to be conservative—"the cathedrals, the colleges, the castles, the gardens, the traditions, the associations, the fine names, the better manners, the poetry." But does conservativism always live up to the charm and nobility of its setting? It apparently does not—and, like Yeats, who recognized in "Ancestral Houses" that even the offspring of a mansion of bronze and marble may be "but a mouse," James plays ironically with the discrepancies he encounters. "There is an odd link," he wryly observes, "between large forms and small emanations." And, when he adds that an American is "not incapable of taking a secret satisfaction in an incongruity of this kind," [24] his remark assists our reading of such works as "A London Life" and *The Awkward Age*.

Moreover, James did not always find country-house life itself the be-all of existence, as his personal letters frankly testify. "The gilded bondage of the country house," he wrote to Charles Eliot Norton in 1886, "becomes onerous as one grows older, and the waste of time in vain sitting and strolling about is a gruesome thought in the face of what one wants to do with the remnant of existence." [25] Indeed, it is difficult not to conclude that in his description of Prince Amerigo's life in England, James is being autobiographical. "He had paid . . . many an English country visit," James says of the Prince. "He had learned, even from of old, to do the English things, and to do them, all sufficiently, in the English way . . . yet with it all, he had never so much as during such sojourns the trick of a certain detached, the amusement of a certain inward critical, life . . . 'English society,' as he would have said, cut him, accordingly in two" (*GB*, 1 : 328).

Reservations such as these are easy enough to find in James. While citing them, however, we must also maintain perspective: to identify his more qualified responses to certain aspects of English life with anything like rejection would involve as mistaken a sense of James's manner of valuation as to find in his attachments to English forms only evidence of an uncritical, snobbish acceptance. For James, the relation between the moral life and the life of manners, between the ethical way and the aesthetic way, is always more complicated than either the moralist or the aesthete are willing to allow. Responsive to the positive and frequently conflicting claims of both, James is also aware that, when viewed together, the puritanical, reforming social conscience of one and the restricted, morally uncommitted, "plastic" consciousness of the other often display a complementary weak-

MILLS COLLEGE
LIBRARY

ness in their mutual simplifications. His own sensibility, being essentially dialectic, does not express itself in a simple moral ledger of virtues and faults which demands or yields a final balance. Rarely, therefore, does James appear to be reaching for the "last word" about English society.[26]

This may be characterized as ambivalence; yet it might also be remembered that ambivalence, while possibly a sign of weakness, may also be a manifestation of strength—a full, alert responsiveness to all the complexities of a given moral and social situation. In any case, James shows a much more questioning and even critical attitude toward English life than his hostile critics have been just enough to admit; on the other hand, he announces his preferences and appreciations with candor.

It is undeniable, therefore, that whatever reservations James may express about England, he found in the country house a public embodiment of his own personal vision—so much so, in fact, that it seems to have played an important part in his final decision to settle in England rather than remain in America. In 1881 James returned home after an absence of six years; he visited his family in New England and went on to New York. During that winter, he took his notebook into his confidence, as he put it: he recorded his impressions and sorted out his thoughts. The famed set of entries begun in the Brunswick Hotel, Boston, continued in New York, and finally completed back in Cambridge, are now documentary; for in them James announces his choice and contemplates the influential years immediately preceding. "My choice is the old world," he confides to his notebook, "my choice, my need, my life. There is no need for me today to argue about this; it is an inestimable blessing to me and a rare good fortune, that the problem was settled long ago, and that I have now nothing to do but act on the settlement." [27] And, while trying to recover the impressions of the years just past, the years spent in Italy and France and England, he recalls most fondly of all his visits to the English countryside during the preceding summer. He stayed in a number of different houses during July and August and it is apparent that they came to epitomize for him, if anything could, the forces determining his choice; for he closes one of the last entries of this crucial winter with what amounts to a paean celebrating the archetypal, transcendental quality of the English country house, its meaning for him and for his future work:

> I went down into Somerset and spent a week at Midelney Place, the Lady Trevilian's. It is the impression of this visit that I wish not wholly to fade away. Very exquisite it was (not the visit, but the impression of the country); it kept me a-dreaming all the while I was there. It seemed to me very old England; there was a peculiarly mellow and ancient feeling in it all. . . . I think I have never been more *penetrated*—I have never more loved the land. It was the old houses that fetched me—Montacute, the admirable; Barrington, that superb Ford Abbey, and several smaller ones. Trevilian showed me them all; he has a great care for such things. These delicious old houses, in the long August days, in the south of England air, on the soil over which so much has passed and out of which so much has come, rose before me like a series of visions. I thought of a thousand things; what becomes of the things one thinks of at these times? They are not lost, we must hope; they drop back into the mind again, and they enrich and embellish it. I thought of stories, of dramas, of all the life of the past— of things one can hardly speak of; speak of, I mean, at the time. It is art that speaks of those things; and the idea makes me adore her more and more. Such a house as Montacute, so perfect, with its grey personality, its old-world gardens, its accumulation of expressions, of tone—such a house is really, *au fond*, an ineffaceable image; it can be trusted to rise before the eyes in the future.[28]

At the start of his career, in fact, James had already presented in one of his first long stories a situation to which he would return in later years—the problem of the American who goes to England with the claim to ancestral property. Indeed, "A Passionate Pilgrim" (1878) and *The Sense of the Past* (1917) respectively introduce and conclude James's treatment of this symbolic situation of the American encounter with an English house; and by their very position in the sequence of his works—very much like that of Evelyn Waugh's *A Handful of Dust* and *Brideshead Revisited* or Elizabeth Bowen's *The Last September* and *A World of Love*—they not only show how compelling the motif of the house was for James but also provide convenient poles by which to gauge his development of it.

"A Passionate Pilgrim" is simple enough in itself and might not engage our attention for long except for the theme that it introduces and the disagreement it has aroused among several critics. The pilgrim-hero Clement Searle is, as his first name implies, a "claimant," who believes he has the rights to an old English mansion through his relation to an ancestor who left it generations before. Arriving in England an impoverished, sick, middle-aged man, he is further worn down by fruitless litigation and disappointment. In despair, he is prompted by a fellow American to visit the family seat of Lackley Park and see it for himself.[29] The estate is typical of those James visited and described in his early travel essays—one with numerous pastoral acres, a landscaped park, and a long winding avenue leading toward the great Tudor house rising above terraces and gardens. Searle glories in the beauties of the place and regretfully speculates upon what his life might have been surrounded by such perfection. During his visit he also meets his distant cousins— another Searle, the present holder of the estate, a dilettantish but brusque English squire; and his sister Margaret, a sweetly timid middle-aged spinster. The squire displays the house and its treasures. Margaret and Searle fall in love with each other, but his claim to the property is naturally dismissed as idiotic by her brother. Almost expelled from the house, Searle dies soon after in Oxford; and he is buried, as he sentimentally requested, under the yews of an English churchyard.

Critics hostile to James—particularly Rebecca West and Van Wyck Brooks—have gone to "A Passionate Pilgrim" for evidence to discredit him. Identifying James with Searle, they see in the story merely a dramatization of what they take to be James's own personal plight as a self-exiled American with an unrealistic attachment to the past.[30] Actually, though "A Passionate Pilgrim" is one of James's earliest and least subtle stories, it hardly prompts such an oversimplified interpretation. First of all, the story has

not one American but two—Searle himself and the narrator who
befriends him; neither one can be completely identified with
James himself, and each one presents contrasting attitudes toward England. Searle, it is true, is obsessed with things English
and waxes lyrical before them; but he is, as the narrator perceives, a mixture, "full of glimpses and responses, of deserts and
desolations"; even on first meeting, the other American immediately predicts that Searle's "perceptions would be fine and his
opinions pathetic" (*PP*, p. 350). The narrator, in contrast, comes
to England with an "educated eye," as Searle himself admits;
and, speaking from a commonsensical, even ironic detachment,
he is quick to notice the extravagances of his compatriot as well
as the anomalies in the English scene around him. It seems a
mistake, therefore, to identify James exclusively with either one;
in fact, for the reader familiar with James, it is the interplay of
their contrasting attitudes—and even their irresolution—that
now provides the genuine interest of the tale.[31]

To be sure, there is something of James's own feeling for
England in Searle's nostalgic longing, and it springs from much
the same need as his character's. Searle, significantly, admits that
he is homesick; but when the narrator takes this as a reference
to America, he becomes more precise: "I meant I was sick for a
home" (*PP*, p. 345). Declaring himself "a conservative by nature"
(*PP*, p. 352), Searle describes his American dilemma: "I had the
love of old forms and pleasant rites, and I found them nowhere
—found a world all hard lines and harsh lights, without shade,
without composition, as they say of pictures, without the lovely
mystery of colour" (*PP*, p. 357). An English estate such as Lackley Park, therefore, seems to give body to all he has craved. "To
think of 'others' having hugged this all these years," he exclaims
on first view of it. "I know what I am, but what might I have
been? What do such places make of a man?" (*PP*, p. 367). And
the narrator himself testifies to the charms of Lackley. "The scene
had a beautiful old-time air," he tells us:

> The peacock flaunting in the foreground like the genius of
> stately places; the broad terrace, which flattered an innate taste
> of mine for all deserted walks where people may have sat after

heavy dinners to drink coffee in old Sèvres and where the stiff brocade of women's dresses may have rustled over grass or gravel; and far around us, with one leafy circle melting into another, the timbered acres of the park. [*PP*, pp. 378–79]

Moreover, while the narrator seems to admire Lackley largely from an aesthetic point of view as a kind of "palace of art," Searle goes further in his admiration: to him, it is also a "house of life." "You've some history among you all," he explains to his English cousin:

You've some poetry, you've some accumulation of legend. I've been famished all my days for these things. . . . When I think of what must have happened here; of the lovers who must have strolled on this terrace and wandered under the beeches, of all the figures and passions and purposes that must have haunted these walls! When I think of the births and deaths, the joys and sufferings, the young hopes and the old regrets, the rich experience of life—! [*PP*, p. 380]

There can be doubt of the high valuation, but James even in this early work prevented it from becoming a "superstitious" one. Through the narrative itself and the narrator, we are reminded of what was to become a recurring theme in James's later work: the house itself embodies a sense of ideal community, but the inhabitants themselves very often may not. Indeed, "A Passionate Pilgrim" is one of the first fictional treatments of the incongruity that he dwells upon in the travel essays discussed above, "the odd link between large forms and small emanations." [32] There is the ironic contrast between what Searle expects and what he actually discovers. Famished for experience, he believes he will find in England and particularly in Lackley all that he has envisioned and missed. Actually, his visit to Lackley proves this to be illusory. His cousin Margaret Searle is also middle-aged and as starved for life as Clement himself. A Sleeping Beauty, as the narrator calls her, she confesses: "I think I've hardly lived" (*PP*, p. 396). And her brother, in turn, hardly shines as an example of human possibility: a blunt man, "breathing the fumes of hereditary privilege and security" (*PP*, p. 387), he condescends to be hospitable to Searle, proudly shows off his house and possessions, and brags unashamedly about the family ghost—the ghost of a poor curate's daughter maltreated by his ancestors. That episode in the family history, moreover, turns out to be one of cowardice, betrayal, and callousness. And, melodramatic as this may be, the ghost suggests the dimension of evil, guilt, and human suffering present in the house and its history; and thus it introduces a symbol that James employs with greater subtlety in the works to follow.

The reader is tempted to ask: Is the supposed celebration of the country house and England really an exposure after all? What is he to make out? Very little that is definite, it seems. At this stage James obviously had no clear resolution for the contrasting, even conflicting perspectives of Searle and the narrator. "A Passionate Pilgrim" remains an exploration of attitudes—attitudes that sometimes seem to cancel each other out. Moreover, the deaths of both Searle and his cousin, the master of Lackley, add to the reader's sense of stalemate. Searle simply dies, unable to settle down in England or to return to America. The squire is thrown from his horse; but his death remains a surface irony. It is merely fortuitous, and even if Searle had survived his cousin, there is no indication of what his coming into Lackley Hall might thematically imply.

Undeniably, "A Passionate Pilgrim" leaves much to be desired as a work of fiction. To say, however, as one critic does, that its plot is "little more than a convenient device upon which to arrange long passages of travel notes" is to miss the significance of this early story for James's development.[33] Many of the passages about Hampton Court, Oxford, and Lackley itself do at times smack of reportage, particularly when compared with the composed fictional narrative of the later James; nevertheless, it must be remembered that by transforming the country house which James had already described in his youthful sketches into a central image of a work of fiction, "A Passionate Pilgrim" introduced a motif that, like a fresh musical figure rich in overtones, offered generous opportunities for expansion and orchestration. Indeed, Ford Madox Ford—who was to make the country house a pivotal image in his own *Parade's End* tetralogy—found this first presentation of James "the apotheosis of the turf, the deer, the oak trees, the terraces of manor houses," claiming that the

milieu had never been "done" so before and never again would
be so done.[34] And we may agree. In his more finished novels
James became more sparing in his description of background,
more deliberately symbolic in his choice of concrete detail, allowing delicate brush strokes to suggest what is here heavily out-
lined and thickly painted. In "A Passionate Pilgrim," Lackley
Park is as lavishly and unashamedly described as a mansion in
Disraeli—and there is, in this instance, a certain satisfaction to
be found in this early, more primitive treatment. It seems appropriate that James in his first presentation should give the
house unmistakable body, mass, presence. Lackley becomes solidly
established in the imagination, and our recollection of it provides
a reliable touchstone for expanding the brief, more elliptical
treatments of the country house in James's later works.

Moreover, "A Passionate Pilgrim" also makes us more directly
aware of themes and images that usually attend the country
house whenever it recurs in James: the same emphasis on ceremony, on "pleasant rites and old forms"; the ghost as symbol of
insight; the problematic distinction between the house as "palace
of art" and "house of life"; the incongruities between the house
and its occupants. To be sure, these are more richly and more
subtly elaborated in the works to come, as we shall see; but to
identify them in their more elementary state helps to clarify from
the outset James's intentions and our own pursuit of them.

Before arriving at Lackley, Clement Searle assumed, so to
speak, that a "palace of art" would also be a "house of life";
but his actual experience there proved that the two cannot be
so readily identified. Through his great middle period, James remained preoccupied with this problematic relationship between
art and life, beauty and suffering, aesthetics and morality; and
in three outstanding novels—*The Portrait of a Lady* (1881), *The
Princess Casamassima* (1886); and *The Spoils of Poynton* (1897)
—he executed a number of variations on this theme.[35] Each
novel, it is true, has its own special subject; but it is important
to recognize that, when read in sequence, they comment on each
other and disclose an unfolding dialectic of great subtlety and
power. From one point of view, all three seem to repeat the basic

situation and motifs of "A Passionate Pilgrim." In each, a young person—who is in one way or another a homeless outsider, a "passionate pilgrim" of sorts, aspiring to a higher plane of being —finds himself on the threshold of a new life; and this life quite literally presents itself in the form of a great house: Gardencourt in *The Portrait of a Lady,* Medley in *The Princess Casamassima,* and Poynton itself. The protagonist's recognition of the worth of the great house is a measure of his own, but his encounter with it eventually poses ultimate and painful choices, so that in the end his decisions concerning them involve his whole life and destiny. The story of Isabel Archer, Hyacinth Robinson, or Fleda Vetch—whatever else each may be—is also the story of a country house.

Like Clement Searle, Isabel Archer leaves behind her a culturally and emotionally impoverished American scene to begin a new life abroad. Her pilgrimage, at the start more auspicious than his, is to be in the end longer and even more tortuous. Yet for a time it follows similar contours. It begins in England with her visit to Gardencourt, a country house which in its graceful leisure and inviting hospitality is all that Clement Searle hoped to find in Lackley and pathetically missed. The very opening scene presents one of the "pleasant rites" for which he longed— a small, congenial group enjoying tea on the lawn during a perfect summer afternoon. James obviously conceived the occasion as a true "ceremony of innocence" in the manner of Yeats, even referring to the tea as a "ceremony," an "innocent pastime" (*PL,* 1 : 1). These mellow, golden-hued passages are among the loveliest that James ever wrote, but he does more than create an atmosphere: he composes a symbolic setting. At Gardencourt, Isabel is awakened to human possibilities undreamed of before. Indeed, as several critics have noted, the very name of Gardencourt suggests the archetype of all human beginnings, Eden itself, the paradisiacal state of innocence.[36]

Gardencourt, however, is the commencement of Isabel Archer's pilgrimage, not the conclusion. If her story opens in a kind of Eden, the rest of it, as one critic perceives, may be taken as a nineteenth-century *Paradise Lost.*[37] Isabel in her proud self-reliance and illusion of total freedom aspires toward the highest in

human experience; blindly and mistakenly, she chooses the worst
within her reach by marrying Gilbert Osmond. Nevertheless her
fall, rather than destroying her in the usual tragic sense, becomes
a "fortunate fall" that gives her insight through suffering. From
her lonely isolation she travels the hard path toward human
community and the acceptance of the common human lot.

The psychology of Isabel Archer and the meaning of her destiny have, of course, been discussed at length; what is relevant to
our present purpose is that James describes her moral pilgrimage
so consistently in terms of Gardencourt and the other houses
Isabel knows. As Richard Chase observes, "the idea of leaving
and entering a house, the contrast of different kinds of houses,
the question of whether a house is a prison or the scene of liberation and fulfillment—these are the substance of the metaphors
in *The Portrait of a Lady*." Gardencourt is, of course, the pivotal
house of the novel.[38] It is the stage upon which Isabel begins her
new life, and it is the stage to which she returns after her disillusionment with Gilbert Osmond for what may be called, not a
second chance, but rather a second choice. Her two visits to Gardencourt measure not only her misfortune but also her moral
progress. The first one gives her a vision of beauty, leisure, ritual,
a vision to some extent tainted by her own self-seeking; the second visit, prompted by concern and love for her dying cousin
Ralph, enables her to accept the burden of her own moral destiny.

Of all the country houses in James, Gardencourt is perhaps
the closest to the ideal. It is an appropriate image of "the great
good place," the true community. Along with its Biblical associations, its name also implies, as Stallman observes, that here nature and civilization are combined in a harmonious relationship.[39] Indeed, the description of Gardencourt in the opening of
the novel emphasizes the easy continuities between the natural
and the civilized:

> It stood upon a low hill, above the river—the river being the
> Thames some forty miles from London. A long gabled front of
> red brick, with the complexion of which time and the weather
> had played all sorts of pictorial tricks, only, however, to im-
> prove and refine it, presented to the lawn with its patches of

ivy, its clustered chimneys, its windows smothered with creep-
ers. . . . Privacy here reigned supreme, and the wide carpet
of turf that covered the level hill-top seemed but the extension of a luxurious interior. The great still oaks and beeches
flung down a shade as dense as that of velvet curtains; and the
place was furnished, like a room, with cushioned seats, with
rich-coloured rugs, with the books and papers that lay upon
the grass.[40] [*PL*, 1 : 2–4]

But Gardencourt is more than a pleasure dome above the sacred
river Thames, more than a palace of art. Lackley itself was that.
Gardencourt is also a house of life: its aesthetic attributes correspond to the moral and spiritual attributes of its occupants; its
luxury and spaciousness express the magnanimity, generosity,
and kindness of old Mr. Touchett and his son Ralph. It is significant, furthermore, that although Gardencourt offers a "peculiarly
English picture" (*PL*, 1 : 1), it is not a typical English estate. Mr.
Touchett, the owner, is an American; he has not inherited the
house, he has purchased it. By this James apparently means to
have Gardencourt represent a synthesis of what he thought best
in American and English culture. The beautiful old house with
its historical ties to the past has certainly brought out the best
of Mr. Touchett, who has become "conscious of a real aesthetic
passion for it" (*PL*, 1 : 3) and has adapted himself to its pleasing
amenities and social rituals. At the same time, Mr. Touchett displays no conceited sense of place or privilege; he has been suc-
cessful in life, yet, as James wittily remarks, "his success had not
been exclusive and invidious, but had much of the inoffensive-
ness of failure" (*PL*, 1 : 2). In fact, the serenity of Gardencourt is
probably due in part to the moral equipoise that James found in
this synthesis: here, he did not have to cope with the arrogance
and injustice of the aristocratic system depicted in "A Passionate Pilgrim," and he was not yet haunted by his later awareness
of "the black and merciless things that are behind great possessions." [41]

As a house of life, however, Gardencourt is not spared the
inevitable suffering of life. The house has a history, James tells
us, which in his chronicle means that in one period or another
it has been "bruised," "defaced," "repaired," and "disfigured"

(*PL*, 1 : 3). Nor is Mr. Touchett presented as untouched by the limitations of the human lot. Rather, as we see him in the late afternoon light, drinking tea from an "unusually large cup" (*PL*, 1 : 2),[42] we realize that he is draining the cup of life itself, taking the "rest that precedes the great rest" (*PL*, 1 : 4). To this aspect of Gardencourt, Isabel remains oblivious on her first visit. Enjoying the house, she playfully asks her cousin Ralph if there is a ghost. Evidently there is, but Ralph's reply makes clear that this ghost is not a haunting reminder of past evil, like the one at Lackley Hall, but the sign of some profound spiritual insight. "I might show it to you," Ralph tells Isabel, "but you'd never see it. . . . You must have suffered first, have suffered greatly, have gained some miserable knowledge" (*PL*, 1 : 64). Ralph, initiated by his own illness, has obviously seen the ghost; before the end of the novel Isabel herself shall see it; but at this point she rather presumptuously responds: "It's not absolutely necessary to suffer; we were not made for that" (*PL*, 1 : 65).

Nevertheless, Isabel responds to the beauty of Gardencourt. "I've never seen anything so lovely as this place," she admits to her uncle. "I've been all over the house; it's too enchanting" (*PL*, 1 : 18). And James dwells on her sense of revelation:

> Her uncle's house seemed a picture made real; no refinement of the agreeable was lost upon Isabel; the rich perfection of Gardencourt at once revealed a world and gratified a need. The large low rooms, with brown ceilings and dusky corners, the deep embrasures and curious casements, the quiet light on dark, polished panels, the deep greenness outside, that seemed always peeping in, the sense of well-ordered privacy in the centre of "property"—a place where sounds were felicitously accidental, where the tread was muffled by the earth itself and in the thick mild air all friction dropped out of contact and all shrillness out of talk—these things were much to the taste of our young lady, whose taste played a considerable part in her emotions. [*PL*, 1 : 73]

Other characters, in contrast, reveal their moral inadequacy by their failure to appreciate Gardencourt and to understand the sense of community it implies. Mrs. Touchett refuses to reside there; she is "not fond of the English style of life" (*PL*, 1 : 26), as James expressly puts it, and maintains a separate house in Italy. Henrietta Stackpole, the breezy American journalist, would like it better if it were a boarding house. Madame Merle—who, as one critic notes, always seems to be going in and out of other people's houses without having any fixed place [43]—makes a revealing distinction between the house and its inhabitants. "I don't venture to send a message to the people," she admits to the departing Isabel later in the novel, "but I should like to give my love to the place" (*PL*, 2 : 380).

Gardencourt is the major moral-aesthetic symbol of *The Portrait of a Lady*. Throughout the novel Isabel leaves and enters other houses; in fact, though the novel opens at Gardencourt, Isabel's story begins chronologically, as Stallman and Chase have emphasized, with the flashback to her old family home in Albany and reaches its climax in Gilbert Osmond's Palazzo Roccanera. These houses suggest other ways of living, however; their meaning and value must be gauged by returning to Gardencourt as a symbolic reference point. Robert W. Stallman, who was in fact one of the first to perceive the function of the houses in *The Portrait of a Lady*, has traced the symbolic pattern of their relationships very carefully. There might be no need to explore this much further, except that he appears to overlook some of the subtleties involved in James's dialectical arrangement. Writing of the juxtaposition of Gardencourt with the Albany house in the first half of the novel and with Osmond's palazzo in the second, Stallman observes that "in the first set of counterpointed houses Isabel is rescued from prison; in the final set she returns to imprisonment." This observation on imprisonment is suggestive as far as it goes; nevertheless—aside from the fact that it is based on Stallman's totally unsympathetic and therefore questionable view of Isabel as a "pretentious and shallow creature," who is trapped into "ending ironically where she began"—it can be misleading. It does not emphatically define the special function of Gardencourt; and by claiming that Osmond's Roman palace "is the Albany house all over again," it confusingly equates them.[44] The qualities of Gardencourt have been considered; here we should stress that the Albany house and the Palazzo Roccanera are not to be taken as exact duplicates: along with the resemblances go significant contrasts.

In regard to this point, Isabel's first conversation with her aunt is very revealing. When Mrs. Touchett visits Albany, the house there has already become too silent, solitary, and melancholy for young Isabel; obviously, she must leave it if her life is to begin at all. Yet despite her eagerness to go off to Europe with her aunt, Isabel cannot share the older woman's rejection of the American house. "In Florence we should call it a very bad house," Mrs. Touchett informs her niece, condescendingly dismissing the place as "very bourgeois" (*PL*, pp. 34, 35). Ironically, Mrs. Touchett at the same time makes a very bourgeois proposition for its disposal: she suggests that it can be sold for a high price. "The position's of value," she explains, "and they'll probably pull it down and make a row of shops." Never having considered such an idea, Isabel is fond enough of the house to hope that it will at least remain standing. When Mrs. Touchett questions this attachment by reminding Isabel that her father had died there, the girl's reply expresses James's own sense of a human habitation and, in fact, echoes Clement Searle's response to Lackley Park:

> "Yes, but I don't dislike it for that," the girl rather strangely returned. "I like places in which things have happened—even if they're sad things. A great many people have died here; the place has been full of life."
>
> "Is that what you call full of life?"
>
> "I mean full of experience—of people's feelings and sorrows. And not their sorrows only, for I've been happy here as a child." [*PL*, pp. 34–35]

It is, indeed, this sense of the "house of life," her capacity for happiness *and* suffering, that keeps Isabel from being unsympathetic as a heroine and eventually leads to her most profound insights. On the other hand, Mrs. Touchett's idea of a house turns out ironically to be a house of death. "You should go to Florence if you like houses in which things have happened—especially deaths," she counsels Isabel. "I live in an old palace in which three people have been murdered" (*PL*, p. 35). And the remark not only exposes Mrs. Touchett, but foreshadows some-thing of Isabel's own fate in the palazzo of Gilbert Osmond.

Of course, all that is missing from the Albany house prepares Isabel to appreciate her uncle's English mansion, whose "rich perfection . . . at once revealed a world and gratified a need." Nevertheless, even while responding to the loveliness of Garden-court, Isabel checks herself with the thought of the thousands of people less happy than herself and asks what one should do with "the misery of the world in a scheme of the agreeable to one's self." And though "it must be confessed that this question never held her for long" (*PL*, p. 62), it is one that reveals Isabel's essential humanity and sensitivity to the world beyond herself— virtues which the moral climate of the Albany house has evidently helped to nourish and which, as she eventually discovers, are not at all out of place in the mellow atmosphere of Gardencourt itself.

The intended parallels between the Italian residence of Gilbert Osmond and the Albany house are coupled with subtle antitheses. In fact Stallman, who overemphasizes the prison parallelism of the American and Italian dwellings, does at one point note the more complex set of relationships established by color imagery. The Albany house and Gardencourt are linked, he observes, through their association with the color green; on the other hand, Isabel's yellow bedroom in the Palazzo Roccanera recalls the yellowish-white walls of her family home; it is red, however, that is the distinctive color of Osmond's palace. Isabel, as Stallman sums up, begins in the greenness of Albany and Gardencourt but ends imprisoned behind walls covered with red damask.[45]

Ironically, of course, Isabel herself cannot discern the reveal-ing similarities and differences to be found in the houses she so casually leaves and enters; and her imperceptiveness in this re-gard is but another manifestation of the romantic, even tragic naïveté that ultimately brings about her fall. James, however, in his symbolic presentation of Osmond's houses establishes mean-ingful contrasts with Gardencourt that the reader cannot mistake. In fact, before Isabel ever meets Osmond, James's description of his Florentine villa prepares us for a world disturbingly different from the gracious world of the Touchetts and their English coun-

try house. Superficially, the interior of Osmond's villa suggests
another palace of art, like Gardencourt itself; we are shown "a
seat of ease, indeed of luxury, telling of arrangements subtly
studied and refinements frankly proclaimed" (*PL,* 1 : 326). Books
in profusion, magazines, and watercolors reflect a life not necessarily creative nor strenuously intellectual but at least agreeably
and harmlessly dilettante. The first view of the exterior, however, evokes instead the ambiguous character of the place and its
resident. A long, rather blank-looking structure, with a solid
"incommunicative" facade and cross-barred windows, the villa is
obviously a symbolic prison, rather like Balzac's Maison Vauquer.
And later in the novel, when Isabel pays her first visit there, the
prison imagery, again accented by James, forecasts her unfortunate destiny well before its unfolding. "There was something
grave and strong in the place," James comments; "it looked somehow as if, once you were in, you would need an act of energy
to get out. For Isabel, however, there was of course as yet no
thought of getting out, but only of advancing" (*PL,* 1 : 364). Like
the heroine of a Gothic romance, she enters a haunted house but
ironically takes it for a palace of enchantment not unlike Gardencourt itself.[46]

Like the Florentine villa, the more elaborate Palazzo Roccanera in Rome, to which Isabel and Osmond retire after their
marriage, is also a prison. Indeed, Isabel belatedly discovers this
for herself, but once again the reader is prepared for what comes
by the reactions of other characters to the palazzo. Mr. Rosier,
for one, having fallen in love with little Pansy, Osmond's daughter, sees the "dark and massive structure" of her father's house
as a dungeon, a kind of domestic fortress, which smells to him
of "crime and craft and violence" (*PL,* 2 : 100).[47] With greater
penetration, Ralph Touchett discerns that Osmond, despite his
air of moral superiority, really lives for the world and wishes
only to impress it—"to surround his interior with a sort of invidious sanctity, to tantalize society with a sense of exclusion, to
make people believe his house was different from every other"
(*PL,* 2 : 144). It is neither accidental nor unexpected, therefore,
that Isabel should conceive her own disillusionment with her
husband metaphorically in terms of his house. As James presents

it, she has obviously mistaken Osmond's values for those of an English house like Gardencourt; she has taken his expressed love of the "conventional" to be a "noble declaration," supposing it to mean "the love of harmony and order and decency and of all the stately offices of life." She discovers that in reality Osmond has made her a prisoner:

> She could live it over again, the incredulous terror with which she had taken the measure of her dwelling. Between those four walls she had lived ever since; they were to surround her for the rest of her life. It was the house of darkness, the house of dumbness, the house of suffocation. Osmond's beautiful mind gave it neither light nor air; Osmond's beautiful mind indeed seemed to peep down from a small high window and mock her. [*PL*, 2 : 196]

Isabel's recognition of her imprisoned state and isolation is undoubtedly one of the great moments in the novel; yet it is not the final moment. To emphasize her discovery of her predicament without giving equal consideration to what follows upon it encourages the superficially ironic notion that Isabel merely ends where she began, exchanging one prison for another. It is true, of course, that the novel ends with the acceptance of her life with Osmond, a life behind the dark walls of his palazzo; but the intervening chapters between her disillusionment and her acceptance depict more than her isolation: indeed, they dramatize the beginning of Isabel's self-transcendence and her growing awareness of community with others. And the scene in which James portrays her sense of community at its most intense is as finely rendered as her moment of tragic recognition. As Joyce in "The Dead" depicted the release of Gabriel Conroy from his isolation by describing his contemplation of the snow falling over Dublin and all Ireland, over the living and the dead, so James—keeping to his own architectural symbols—places Isabel before Roman ruins where she may view her own private sorrow in the perspective of history and the sorrows of generations. Having just discovered the deceptive role Madame Merle has played in her life and in her marriage, Isabel goes for a drive alone:

She had long before taken this old Rome into her confidence,
for in a world of ruins the ruin of her happiness seemed a less
unnatural catastrophe. She rested her weariness upon things
that had crumbled for centuries and yet still were upright. . . .
Small it was, in the large Roman record, and her haunting
sense of the continuity of the human lot easily carried her from
the less to the greater. She had become deeply, tenderly ac-
quainted with Rome; it interfused and moderated her passion.
But she had grown to think of it chiefly as the place where people had suffered. This was what came to her in the starved
churches, where the marble columns, transferred from pagan
ruins, seemed to offer her a companionship in endurance and
the musty incense to be a compound of long-unanswered
prayers. [*PL*, 2 : 327–28]

Her sense of what might be called a community of suffering—
her awareness of "the continuity of the human lot" and the
"companionship of endurance"—does not imply, however, a
state of passivity. As James comments elsewhere in the novel,
"suffering, with Isabel, was an active condition; it was not a chill;
a stupor, a despair; it was a passion of thought, of speculation, of
response to every pressure" (*PL*, 2 : 189). It eventually brings
about her return to Gardencourt and leads to positive participa-
tions and commitments. Moreover, before returning, Isabel senses
that there is "something sacred in Gardencourt" (*PL*, 2 : 296).
And when in defiance of Osmond she goes back to England to
attend her dying cousin Ralph, she seems motivated not only by
her love for him but by her deep need for the place itself: "Gardencourt," she reflects, "had been her starting point, and to those
muffled chambers it was at least a temporary solution to return
. . . if it had been a rest to her before, it would be a sanctuary
now" (*PL*, 2 : 391).

Structurally, of course, the second visit of Isabel to Gardencourt parallels her first and thus dramatizes the contrast between
the free, open world of her early expectations and her present
state of unhappiness. "She left the drawingroom and wandered
about—strolled into the library and along the gallery of pictures,
where, in the deep silence, her footstep made an echo. Nothing

was changed; she recognized everything she had seen years before; it might have been only yesterday that she stood there."
Like Keats before the Grecian urn or Yeats before those religious
images keeping a marble or bronze repose, Isabel grows aware
of the difference between the serene permanence of art and the
tragic instability of the human lot. "She envied the security of
valuable 'pieces' which change by no hair's breadth, only grow
in value, while their owners lose inch by inch youth, happiness,
beauty" (*PL,* 2 : 403).

But this visit to Gardencourt does more than measure her
losses; it is also the occasion for new stages of transformation in
Isabel. Attending the dying Ralph, she discovers a sense of human
relationship that places her beyond the suffering she has experienced. "Here on my knees," she confesses to Ralph, "with you
dying in my arms, I'm happier than I have been for a long time.
. . . In such hours as this what have we to do with pain? That's
not the deepest thing; there's something deeper." And Ralph, in
turn, reminds Isabel that she has never been completely isolated:
"And remember this . . . that if you've been hated you've also
been loved. Ah but, Isabel—*adored!*" (*PL,* 2 : 416, 417).

Ralph dies during her visit, but the manner in which Isabel
learns of his death also marks a stage in her moral progression.
On her first visit to Gardencourt, when she asked Ralph if there
was a ghost in the house, he affirmed that there was and told her
that if she lived to suffer enough she might one day see it. This
time she does see a ghost—and it seems the spirit of Ralph himself. "It seemed to her for an instant that he was standing there—
a vague, hovering figure in the vagueness of the room. She stared
a moment; she saw his white face—his kind eyes; then she saw
there was nothing. She was not afraid; she was only sure." Isabel
has obviously fulfilled the "necessary condition" (*PL,* 2 : 418),
James reminds us; she has been initiated by her own suffering,
and this too unites her with Ralph, who once told her that he
had long ago seen the ghost himself (*PL,* 1 : 64).

After Ralph's death Isabel lingers for a time at Gardencourt
because she shudders when she thinks of Rome. "There was a
penetrating chill in the image, and she drew back into "the deepest shade of Gardencourt" (*PL,* 2 : 421). In what follows, however,

Gardencourt becomes more than a retreat or a refuge; it gives her the moral strength to make her great decision. In the final pages of the novel, Isabel is seated quietly at dusk on the great lawn outside the house, only to find herself confronted by Caspar Goodwood and hearing his proposal once again. His reappearance and his energetic suit bring to an end her period of vacillation: she decisively rejects Goodwood and returns to Osmond. Isabel's action at this point has been much debated, but we should note that what evidently gives it meaning is the setting itself. The scene in which Goodwood proposes to Isabel is really a temptation scene. The place itself, with all its connotations of Eden, suggests that she is being tested once again.

Goodwood comes as a tempter who offers Isabel not only the most plausible arguments for leaving Osmond and coming with him but the first breath of white-hot passion she has ever really experienced. "You don't know what to do—you don't know where to turn," he cruelly insists. "You're afraid to go back. You're perfectly alone; you don't know where to turn" (*PL*, 432–33). He justifies his proposal by reminding her of the misery she faces with Osmond and the happiness he can give her. Ironically, in offering her an argument seemingly based on prudence, he echoes the words of the basic Christian dictum that he who would save his life must first lose it: "You must save what you can of your life," he disarmingly explains; "you mustn't lose it all simply because you've lost part" (*PL*, 2 : 434). As Goodwood continues, it becomes obvious that his whole premise runs counter to the sense of relationship presented by Ralph and Gardencourt itself: "We can do absolutely as we please; to whom under the sun do we owe anything?" Finally, a Miltonic allusion makes the implications of the scene even more evident. "The world's all before us," he proclaims to the besieged Isabel (*PL*, 2 : 435). Since this is precisely the same allusion made much earlier in the novel with respect to Isabel herself ("The world lay before her—she could do whatever she chose," *PL*, 2 : 36), it is clear that her acceptance of Caspar Goodwood would only be another presumptuous act of folly which would make her appear untouched by all she has suffered.

For Isabel the temptation is a powerful one nonetheless. "She had wanted help, and here was help; it had come in a rushing torrent." Almost willing to sink in the "fathomless waters" of Goodwood's ardor, she has sense of drowning that gives her a momentary rapture. Isabel justly fears this death by water, however, and beseeches Goodwood to leave her. Gaining some control over herself, she discovers a place to which she can turn—significantly, the house itself:

> She never looked about her; she only darted from the spot. There were lights in the windows of the house; they shown far across the lawn. In an extraordinarily short time—for the distance was considerable—she had moved through the darkness (for she saw nothing) and reached the door. Here she only paused. She looked all about her; she listened a little; then she put her hand on the latch. She had not known where to turn; but she knew now. There was a very straight path. [*PL*, 2 : 436]

The symbolic function of Gardencourt here at the very close of the novel is therefore unmistakable; and unless it is recognized, the implications of Isabel's action are easily lost. The return of Isabel to the house—literally and symbolically indicated by the lights from the window of the house—dramatizes the strength of her commitment to the sense of community there embodied. The straight path leads, it is true, back to Osmond and loneliness; by taking it, however, Isabel reveals that she is no longer the passive victim of Osmond's deception and her own delusion, for she returns to Italy by her own conscious, deliberate choice. As Edwin T. Bowden observes in his excellent analysis of Isabel's decision, the moral choice is here a heroic choice—"the choice of life over death, of participation over isolation." Recognizing a moral obligation to Pansy and even to Osmond himself, Isabel must reject Goodwood and return to Italy, but she does not go back to the same state of isolation. "By forgetting self in the dedication to larger life the self is no longer isolated." [48]

Finally, there seems no reason to conclude that Isabel may not yet know a measure of happiness; she will at least know the contentment of relieving the unhappiness of others. Perhaps she will come to resemble those archetypal women in twentieth-century

fiction—Mrs. Gould, Mrs. Wilcox, Mrs. Ramsay—who by their
sensibility and insight manage to impart community to those
about them. At least, suffering has taught Isabel something of
their self-forgetfulness and comprehension of the universal lot.

After *The Portrait of a Lady*, the next novel with an English
setting is *The Princess Casamassima,* and here another country
house—Medley Hall—plays a role analogous to that of Gardencourt. In fact, while passing from one novel to the other with
this resemblance in mind, we are struck by further similarities
that underly their contrasting surfaces. It is true that Hyacinth
Robinson, the poor little bookbinder involved in a revolutionary
conspiracy fomenting in a London slum, may seem to have little
in common with the proud, high-spirited American heroine. Yet
nevertheless both characters were for James perceptive outsiders
whose confrontations with the great society of England and
Europe offered the most compelling occasions for exploring the
aesthetic, social, and moral themes that pressed him hardest.
From one point of view, Hyacinth and Isabel may be viewed as
complementary characters, with their novels in several significant
ways dialectically counterpointing each other.

The Princess Casamassima considers a question already raised
by the earlier work. During her first stay at Gardencourt, Isabel
was haunted in the midst of her own newfound happiness by the
suffering of others. "What should one do," she pondered, "with
the misery of the world in a scheme of the agreeable for one's
self?" Cultivating the garden of her own soul, she reminded herself that there were a great many places which "were not gardens
at all—only dusky, pestiferous tracts, thick with ugliness and
misery" (*PL,* 1 : 71). The guilty question might apply to the
whole country-house world, to beautiful old England itself, which
provides the most charming phase of her initiation. James at this
point does not force the issue, nor does he need to within the
framework of the novel. Gardencourt itself is primarily a moral
symbol rather than a historical representation. And Isabel herself
is finally exonerated when through her own suffering she comes
to recognize and accept what is involved in the human lot.

Isabel's question, nevertheless, evidently lingered and darkened
for James himself, for what is *The Princess Casamassima* but the

dramatization of an answer? What is Hyacinth Robinson but one of the inhabitants of the "dusky, pestiferous tracts" of a London "planted thick with ugliness and misery"? Even James's later account of the genesis of the novel suggests that his sympathetic identification with Hyacinth was not unalloyed with a measure of guilt. Writing of the way Hyacinth seemed to spring up at him out of the London pavement, James remembered giving him much of his own capacity for wonder and curiosity: "To find his possible adventure interesting I had only to conceive his watching some public show . . . I had watched myself, and of his watching very much as I had watched." But at the same time, James found the germ of the novel in the pathetic difference between himself and his underprivileged character: he recognized that the world which spoke of "freedom and ease, knowledge and power, money, opportunity and society"—and which for him had conveniently opened—must be a world which his character must see "only from the outside—in mere quickened consideration, mere wistfulness and envy and despair." [49] The story which James conceived for Hyacinth Robinson, therefore, inevitably involves once again the problem of the relationship between what we have called, in James's own idiom, the "palace of art" and the "house of life." Despite many differences, *The Princess Casamassima* explores a basic theme of *The Portrait of a Lady* from the vantage point of a protagonist whose social circumstances are intentionally the very opposite of those in which we discover Isabel Archer. The world from which Hyacinth Robinson emerges is, James wishes to remind us, the underside, the shadow side, of the high, bright world opened to Isabel by old Mr. Touchett and his son Ralph.

Isabel's story commences on the sunny, hospitable lawns of Gardencourt; Hyacinth's, in a sordid London slum. This world of Lomax Place with its poverty and misery seems a prison from which there is no escape. As James describes it, the hideous conditions of the place and its working class inhabitants contradict and challenge all the splendid, humane values that the other world espouses. Indeed, Hyacinth himself embodies the contradiction of the society around him and above him: raised as an orphan by an impoverished seamstress, he is in reality the bastard son of an English lord and a plebeian French girl. As a book-binder, he also plays an ambiguous role; he is a young man of some sensibility, yet he is also a workman caught, like the rest of his fellows, in a narrow, cheerless existence. Moreover in presenting this James blinks at none of the social ugliness and inequalities his chosen theme compels him to consider. The problems represented by Lomax Place and Hyacinth are described as intolerable: they cry out for some solution, some relief. Interestingly enough, and perhaps unexpectedly, James realizes that the most direct, decisive, and cogent answer may seem to be the revolutionary one, and he is willing to look it full in the face. Taking a cue from the extreme ideologies of the age, he portrays Hyacinth as inevitably attracted to the anarchist movement and, out of his longing for justice and change, committing himself to the most violent commands of its international apparatus.

James is just to the social criticism voiced by his revolutionists, and much of the power of the novel derives from this. But though he is willing to explore and dramatize the revolutionary position, he does not embrace it. Indeed, through the career of Hyacinth, he depicts the limitations and inadequacies of a revolutionary absolutism.[50] At this stage, no world might seem more distant from Hyacinth's than Isabel Archer's. Nonetheless, the careers of the two characters do follow similar contours: both are in the process of moral discovery; both, in fact, experience an enlargement of vision. Whereas Isabel is forced to learn that freedom must involve relationship and that even a palace of art must participate in the suffering of the human lot, Hyacinth eventually discovers the converse: that there is much more to life than suffering, that beyond the small, oppressive world of Lomax Place there is also the large world of beauty, art, and culture, without the vision of which even the most sensitive and deeply engaged moral consciousness remains constricted and joyless. And in our present context the most important resemblance of all is that Hyacinth's transformation begins, like Isabel's, with a visit to a great country house.

Ironically, as soon as Hyacinth commits himself to total revolutionary action, he is invited by the Princess Casamassima herself to stay for a time at Medley Hall, a beautiful old English estate.

Here he finds his social convictions and allegiances tempered, if not actually tested, by the new experience. Like Isabel at Gardencourt, Hyacinth finds that Medley reveals a world and gratifies a need. All the civilized and noble things from which he has been shut off are at least momentarily accessible to him, and Medley becomes the distillation of the good life itself. From his first moments there, he has an almost visionary sense of the possibilities and promises life offers after all: "He had never in his life been in the country—the real country, as he called it, the country which was not the mere ravelled fringe of London, and there entered through his open casement the breath of the world enchantingly new and after his recent feverish hours unspeakably refreshing" (*PC*, 2 : 3–4). Almost like a child in a fairy tale, Hyacinth roams in amazement through the great high rooms of Medley, through its gardens and parkland: "Round the admirable house he revolved repeatedly, catching every aspect and feeling every value." Wherever he rambles, he finds "his whole walk peopled with recognitions; he had been dreaming all his life of just such a place and such objects, such a morning and such a chance" (*PC*, 2 : 7).

At Medley, Hyacinth in truth undergoes a kind of conversion; and although some would say that he is merely converted to snobbery, it must be emphasized that what moves Hyacinth is not the social status of Medley, but the quality of life—the realm of being, so to speak—that it suggests to his imagination. As Lionel Trilling has argued, if Hyacinth is a snob, he is in great company—the "company of Rabelais, Shakespeare, Scott, Dickens, Balzac, and Lawrence, men who saw the lordliness and establishment of the aristocrat and gentleman as the proper condition for the spirit of man." Hyacinth has, indeed, according to Trilling, "Yeats's awareness of the dream that a great house embodies, that here the fountain of life 'overflows without ambitious pains.' " [51]

But if Medley transports Hyacinth to a new level of perception, this does not imply that James idealizes the country house or the social system of which it is a part. Rather, here again, the novelist distinguishes between the house as a symbol of the opportunities of civilized existence and the house as historic actuality. Hyacinth is allowed to drink the "cup of an exquisite experience—a week in that enchanted palace" (*PC*, 2 : 41); but while for him Medley seems to belong to a timeless, transcendent realm of the imagination, the reader is repeatedly reminded of its entanglement with the evils of the historical past and the prosaic exigencies of the present. The Princess herself shows Hyacinth the "queer transmogrified corner that had once been a chapel" (*PC*, 2 : 16) before the persecution of the Old Faith; their visit to a haunted chamber recalls an ancestral crime, for here the ghost of a dispossessed and murdered eldest son is rumored to appear. Medley, the Princess also discloses, is not really her property: she has merely rented it for a few months from owners obviously needy enough to let it for a pittance.

Furthermore, the visit that Hyacinth pays to Broom, the nearby estate of the Marchands, satirically displays the limitations and insipidities of English country life in a way that becomes more prominent in the short fiction James was to write during the nineties. Conversing with the daughter of Lady Marchand, the poor bookbinder is mistaken for one of her own class and so has a glimpse of its preoccupations: "She asked Hyacinth with what pack he hunted, and whether he went in much for tennis, and she ate three muffins" (*PC*, 2 : 29). Elsewhere, a strong case against other features of the English upper class is presented in the portrait of Captain Sholto, the trifling but rather sinister "gentleman" who trails after the Princess. He is a "curious and not particularly edifying English type," as she describes him: "He was nothing whatever in himself and had no character or merit save by tradition . . ." (*PC*, 2 : 82). Indeed, in her summation of the state of things in England, the Princess echoes a biting observation of James himself. "It's the old regime again," she declares to Hyacinth, "the rottenness and extravagance, bristling with every iniquity and every abuse, over which the French Revolution passed like a whirlwind" (*PC*, 2 : 23).[52]

To be sure, this ardent and conspiring woman cannot be claimed to speak absolutely for the creator. On the contrary, James's point of view is expressed dialectically through several characters balanced one against the other; and if the Princess is allowed her fiery revolutionary stance, old Mr. Vetch seems to express James's suspicion of any program promising a total reno-

vation of things. Indeed, James describes the old republican as
having "outlived the democratic glow of his prime": "The idea
of great changes . . . took its place among the dreams of his
youth; for what was any possible change in the relations of men
and women but a new combination of elements? . . . The figures
on the chessboard were still the passions and jealousies and stupidities of man . . ." (*PC*, 2 : 103–04).

The complexity of James's own attitude is, in fact, dramatized
by the conclusion of the novel; and it is Hyacinth who perhaps
comes closest to representing the moral-aesthetic vision of James
himself. Divided in his sympathies, Hyacinth is loyal to those
who suffer society's injustice and also loyal to the new vision
imparted by Medley and his brief tour of France and Italy. "He
saw the immeasurable misery of the people, and yet he saw all
that had been, as it were rescued and redeemed from it: the
treasures, the felicities, the splendours, the successes of the world"
(*PC*, 2 : 217). Hyacinth commits suicide, it is true; however, as
Trilling observes, by the time his story draws to end, "his mind is
in a perfect equilibrium, not of irresolution but of awareness."
The two views of society that he comes to hold do not—like the
dying Clement Searle's in "A Passionate Pilgrim"—cancel each
other out: they interpenetrate. Hyacinth's "sense of the social
horror of the world," to quote Trilling once more, "is not diminished by his newer sense of the glory of the world. . . . Never,
indeed, is he so sensitive to the sordid life of the mass of mankind as after he has had the revelation of art." [53]

This is first shown with great vividness, it should be added, in
the middle of the novel, upon Hyacinth's return from Medley to
Lomax Place. Coming back to find that the little seamstress has
become ill during his absence, Hyacinth suddenly feels guilty at
"having lingered at Medley while there was distress in the
wretched little house to which he owed so much" (*PC*, 2 : 85–86).
Nevertheless, he now sees the place with greater detachment and,
paradoxically, with a greater sense of pathos. Throughout the
last half of the novel as well, Medley remains for Hyacinth—
much like Gardencourt for Isabel Archer—a symbolic touchstone
for higher values. Indeed, his week at Medley eventually becomes
for him "a far-off fable, the echo of a song; he could read it over

as a romance bound in vellum and gold, gaze at as he would have gazed at some exquisite picture. His visit there had been perfect to the end . . ." (*PC*, 2 : 126).

Medley becomes, in fact, such an embodiment of the ideal to Hyacinth that by its standard he passes judgment not only on the pitiful shabbiness of Lomax Place but on the philistine ugliness to which the Princess perversely submits herself in a spirit of revolutionary puritanism. Ironically, while his aesthetic responses have matured, she has succumbed to the notion that to serve the wretched even personal taste must be sacrificed and has moved into a dreary stucco house in Madeira Crescent, a quarter less squalid but somehow meaner than Lomax Place. If the Princess wished to mortify the flesh, she has chosen, Hyacinth perceives, to mortify the spirit as well.

The complex sense of things that Hyacinth acquires at Medley, we may conclude, enriches rather than demeans life and its relationships. Some have insisted otherwise. Irving Howe, though he is penetrating about the ambiguities of the novel, charges that in Hyacinth's vision the "alloy of snobbism is not always distinct from the gold of culture." [54] Actually, however, if we take "snobbism" as a concern with status, there is no evidence of this: Hyacinth never displays any admiration for social rank, position, or privilege as such, nor does he reveal any impulse toward exclusiveness. On the contrary, what Hyacinth admires in Medley are qualities intrinsically valuable apart from the social class with which they have been coupled historically.

The values embodied by Medley are, therefore, neither shallow nor superfluous, and from this point of view, *The Princess Casamassima* comments upon *The Portrait of a Lady:* for while the earlier novel demonstrates that aesthetic values uninvolved with moral relationships prove spiritually empty, the later one recognizes that a morality allowing no place for the aesthetic may fail to satisfy the spirit itself.

If these two novels tend to counterbalance each other, *The Spoils of Poynton* rounds still another dialectical turn and copes with the problem of art and life in a more fascinatingly complex way. While in *The Princess Casamassima* James recognizes that the palace of art may be raised—guiltily and perhaps unavoidably

—upon human suffering, in the novel written a decade later he goes beyond this sharp antithesis and dramatizes, instead, an evolution of attitudes. Very much like other nineteenth-century writers who discovered that the aesthetic values they cherished had ultimately to become part of a larger, more inclusive moral perspective, James in *The Spoils of Poynton* takes the reader from one level of awareness to another toward a more comprehensive vision. Like Tennyson in "The Palace of Art," Ruskin in *The Stones of Venice,* or Kierkegaard in *Stages on Life's Way,* he does justice to the beautiful but at the same time transcends it. He inevitably sees the cultivated aesthetic consciousness as a level well beyond that of the philistine and the materialist—and thus as a morally superior and valuable phase of human consciousness in itself; nevertheless in *The Spoils of Poynton* he obviously regards it as a limited phase and possibly a dangerous one by viewing it from a still higher level of ethical awareness.

Every aspect of *The Spoils of Poynton,* indeed, supports this theme, and even what some critics have deemed artistic anomalies in the narration are eminently fitting. Consider, for example, the seemingly awkward shift in the narrative point of view. R. P. Blackmur asks, "Who will say it is right or wrong that this novel which belongs to Fleda Vetch's fullness of action should have begun in the consciousness of Mrs. Gereth?" [55] Actually, we must say it is right—and more than right. If the story at first does seem to belong to Mrs. Gereth and, quite imperceptibly, becomes Fleda's, this shift in the point of view transports the reader from one level of awareness to another in a definitely unfolding sequence. Again, while the opening chapters make the reader sympathize with the mother who wishes to save her beautiful house from falling into the rapacious hands of her son's fiancée, the rest of the novel presents the more agonizing plight of the girl who is torn between love for the son and her recognition that she can have him only by sacrificing his honor and her own. And this realignment of plot is as it should be, since it dramatizes the profound moral sensitivity of the girl in contrast to the cultivated but constricted sensibility of the mother. Lastly, and what in our context must be considered in detail, the houses of the novel also provide a symbolic manifestation of the same theme.

The houses in *The Spoils of Poynton,* like those elsewhere in James, suggest contrasting realms of value; and they are presented in a sequence that conveys the progressive expansion of moral awareness with which the novel is concerned. Critical discussion has naturally settled on Poynton itself, the battleground of the novel; here, however, it must be emphasized that there are three houses to be considered: Waterbath, the grotesquely unattractive home of the self-seeking Brigstocks; magnificent Poynton, the charming country house which Mrs. Gereth must vacate for her son Owen; and Ricks, the simple dower house to which she is forced to move. The first contrast is a perfectly obvious one: Waterbath in all its ugliness and pretentiousness against the resplendent, authentic beauty of Poynton. And on this level, the theme is also obvious enough: tasteless materialism is found wanting by the genuinely superior standards of cultivation it threatens to destroy. But this almost elementary antithesis is complicated by the introduction of Ricks, for the dower house also plays a symbolic role in the moral scheme of the novel. Just as Poynton by its very existence stands as a rebuke to Waterbath, so also does humble Ricks comprise elements needful to the moral life but missing from both the other houses. Emphasis on Poynton alone or on the ironic contrast between Poynton and Waterbath, failing to give Ricks its due weight, thus ignores James's subtle development of the theme.

Significantly, Waterbath is not directly described by James; it is viewed through the exasperated sensibility of Mrs. Gereth. Confiding her reaction to the ugliness of the place to the sympathetic Fleda, she vents herself in delightfully comic invective. "Horrible—horrible!" she cries, with a laugh, "and it's really a comfort to be able to say it." Moreover, her own taste allows her to perceive that Waterbath reflects the stupidities and vulgarities of the Brigstocks. "The house was bad in all conscience," she admits, "but it might have passed if they had only let it alone. This saving mercy was beyond them; they had smothered it with trumpery ornament and scrapbook art. . . . They had gone wildly astray over carpets and curtains; they had an infallible instinct for disaster." The worst horror, in her eyes, is "the acres of varnish, something advertised and smelly, with which

everything is smeared" (*SP*, pp. 6–7). And from the whole aesthetic inventory of the outraged Mrs. Gereth, it is obvious that
Waterbath is the familiar result of money and bad taste, a kind
of parody of the ideal palace of art.

Poynton, in contrast, is a true palace of art. It is the product
not of money but of knowledge. There are "places much grander
and richer," Mrs. Gereth is willing to admit to Fleda, but there
is "no such complete work of art, nothing that would appeal so
to those who are truly informed" (*SP*, pp. 12–13). Fleda herself
responds to the perfect beauty of Poynton with tears of submission that do her great credit in Mrs. Gereth's eyes. In fact, the
girl experiences much the same sense of revelation that Hyacinth
knew at Medley: "Preoccupations and scruples fell away from
her; she had never known a greater happiness than the week she
passed in this initiation" (*SP*, p. 22). It is true that before the end
of the novel Fleda's vision transcends even Poynton; nevertheless,
James does justice to the aesthetic way it represents and conveys
through Fleda's reflections and Mrs. Gereth's complaints much
of his own sense of the high moral value of art. Fleda comes to
recognize that so perfect a beauty as that of Poynton embodies a
way of life morally higher than any possibly to be conceived by
the crass world of Waterbath:

> Pausing at open doors where vistas were long and bland, she
> would, even if she had not already known, have discovered
> for herself that Poynton was the record of a life. It was written
> in great syllables of color and form, the tongues of other coun-
> tries and the hands of rare artists. It was all France and Italy,
> with their ages composed to rest. For England you looked out
> of old windows—it was England that was the wide embrace.
> . . . What struck Fleda most in it was the high pride of her
> friend's taste, a fine arrogance, a sense of style which, however
> amused and amusing, never compromised nor stooped. She
> felt indeed, as this lady intimated to her that she would, both
> a respect and a compassion that she had not known before.
> [*SP*, p. 22]

Poynton, in Fleda's eyes, is just as much a moral record of a
life as an aesthetic one because it is based on standards, discipline,

even self-sacrifice. In Mrs. Gereth's cry that the "world is full of gimcracks in this awful age," there is social criticism of a kind. Though the woman's obsession with her beautiful things might seem like materialism, it is actually a kind of piety, for the "piety most real to her was to be on one's knees before one's high standards." Moreover, aesthetic devotion, like the religious, makes its demands, as Mrs. Gereth's rebuke to her son reveals: "The best things, as you know, are the things your father and I collected, things all that we worked for and waited for and suffered for. Yes . . . there are things in the house that we almost starved for! They were our religion, they were our life, they were us!" (*SP*, pp. 30–31). And even when the conflict between mother and son becomes so desperate that only stripping Poynton of its furnishings will satisfy Mrs. Gereth, Fleda perceives the loftiness of her motive:

> The girl's dread of scandal, of spectators, and critics, diminished the more she saw how little the vulgar avidity had to do with this rigor. It was not the crude love of possession; it was the need to be faithful to a trust and loyal to an idea. The idea was surely noble: it was that of the beauty Mrs. Gereth has so patiently and consummately wrought. [*SP*, p. 46]

Mrs. Gereth does ransack Poynton and appalls Fleda by removing every piece of furniture and every article to Ricks: but it is significant that the motive which spurred this action is the very same one that moves her to restore them. "It was absolutely unselfish," Fleda recognizes. "She cared nothing for mere possessions. She thought solely and incorruptibly of what was best for the things" (*SP*, p. 214). In these actions, there can be no doubt that James gives to Mrs. Gereth her own kind of sublimity. She is not evil, not the witch that Blackmur maintains that she is: [56] she does not serve herself, she really serves the high, demanding aesthetic standard beyond herself. In this, she undoubtedly represents a stage of being far above the level of the covetous Brigstocks and her dull-witted son Owen.

It must also be noted, however, that for James this stage is not the final stage. He naturally celebrates what is valuable in the aesthetic way, but he is also aware of its limitations. Through

Fleda, once again, we see these limitations, first in Mrs. Gereth and then actually in Poynton itself. For example, despite her exquisite sensibility, Mrs. Gereth, we are told, "had really no perception of anybody's nature—had only one question about persons: were they clever or stupid?" (*SP*, p. 138). Fleda obviously meets her demand for intelligence; but the young girl possesses what the older woman lacks: moral imagination, or what James describes as the "faculty that easily embraced all the heights and depths and extremities of things; that made a single mouthful, in particular, of any tragic or desperate necessity" (*SP*, p. 35). Fleda comes under the spell of Poynton and sympathizes with Mrs. Gereth's attachment to the place; nevertheless, she begins to perceive that the Poynton way of life, for all its fine discriminations—perhaps even because of them—has fostered peculiar weaknesses and obsessions: "The great drawback of Mrs. Gereth's situation was that, thanks to the rare perfection of Poynton, she was condemned to wince whenever she turned." Like the aesthetes of the nineties, she has lived for so long "in such warm closeness with the beautiful," that life has become for her a "kind of fool's paradise," sheltered from the appalling ugliness of the rest of the world (*SP*, p. 12).

Furthermore, this devotion to art, rather than extending Mrs. Gereth's sense of life, has tragically narrowed it: "The truth was simply that all Mrs. Gereth's scruples were on one side and that her ruling passion had in a manner despoiled her of her humanity" (*SP*, p. 37). Hypersensitive to aesthetic values, she exhibits an atrophied moral sense to her fellows. If she treats her things as if they were human ("They know me," she exclaims to Fleda, "they return the touch of my hand," *SP*, p. 31), she treats people as if they were things. Fleda, in fact, comes to realize that she herself is accepted "only as a priestess of the altar" (*SP*, p. 37)—a suspicion Mrs. Gereth confirms in her own comic way: "You'll at any rate be a bit of furniture," she confesses to Fleda. "For that, a little, you know, I've always taken you—quite one of my best finds" (*SP*, p. 245). Even the bitter family struggle itself is aggravated by this moral imperceptiveness. "What a strange relation between mother and son," Fleda again reflects to herself, "when there was no fundamental tenderness out of which a solu-

tion might irrepressibly spring" *(SP,* p. 44). Perhaps nowhere is
the contrast between the sensibilities of the two women more
vivid than in their attitudes toward the impending marriage of
Owen and Mona Brigstock. Loving Owen, Fleda conceals her
feelings in order not to force his hand to a dishonorable action.
Mrs. Gereth can only dismiss this attitude as one of "idiotic
perversity," rebuking the girl for her "sweet little scruples." On
the other hand, her own solution to the problem of Mona is almost grandly inhuman: "Our only chance is the chance that she
may die" *(SP,* p. 219).

It is revealing that Mrs. Gereth's moral inadequacies are reflected in her aesthetic limitations as well. Her relation to art, it
soon becomes clear, is at bottom the relation of the collector—
indeed, Mrs. Gereth herself claims that this is "her personal gift,
the genius, the passion, the patience of the collector" *(SP,* p.
242). Even Poynton itself—work of art that it is—remains the
ideal of the collector, as Fleda herself also comes to recognize.
On the other hand, Fleda does paint and is, therefore, an artist
of sorts: not an accomplished artist, to be sure, but enough of
one—and that may be James's point—to distinguish between the
collector's or dilettante's passive worship of the beautiful and
the true artist's deep commitment to creativity and all its entanglements with human emotion and human suffering. Poynton,
she perceives, "had stripped its mistress of all feeble accomplish-
ments . . . her hand had sooner been imbrued with blood than
with ink or with water color" *(SP,* p. 13). At Waterbath Fleda
had struggled to paint, but "the sight of the family splotches"
(SP, p. 148) defeated her. Poynton discourages her for another
reason: it is an "impossible place for producing; no active art
could flourish there but a Buddhistic contemplation" *(SP,* p.
141). Thus the reader finally comes to see that Mrs. Gereth exists
as a treasure hunter, and that Poynton is not so much a house as
a museum.

In this connection the third house, Ricks, takes on special
meaning. Recognizing the superiority of Poynton to Waterbath
and, then, the limitations of Poynton itself, Fleda finds that it is
the simple dower house that really satisfies the needs of her moral
imagination. From a strictly aesthetic point of view, of course,
there can be no comparison between elegant Poynton and humble

Ricks; inevitably, Mrs. Gereth despairs of the place, wondering
only how a house in the depths of Essex could look so "suburban"
(*SP,* p. 148). Fleda, however, looks beyond the appearance of
Ricks and, like Isabel Archer at her grandmother's house in
Albany, responds to its human associations and overtones. A
maiden aunt of Owen Gereth has lived at Ricks, and though she
is dead and gone, the very human stamp she has left upon it
touches Fleda:

> It was faded and melancholy, whereas there had been a danger
> it would be contradictious and positive, cheerful and loud. The
> place was crowded with objects of which the aggregation some-
> how made a thinness and the futility a grace; things that told
> her they had been gathered as slowly and as lovingly as the
> golden flowers of the other house. She too for a home could
> have lived with them: they made her fond of the old maiden-
> aunt; they made her even wonder if it didn't work more for
> happiness not to have tasted, as she herself had done, of
> knowledge. . . . The poor lady had passed shyly, yet with
> some bruises, through life; had been sensitive and ignorant
> and exquisite: that too was a sort of origin, a sort of atmosphere
> for relics and rarities, though different from the sorts most
> prized at Poynton. [*SP,* p. 53]

It is this involvement with human experience, with human suffering, that makes Ricks a house of life for Fleda. Characteristically, it is this quality of Ricks that Mrs. Gereth fails to compre-
hend. When Fleda confesses her "indulgent fantasy" about the
maiden aunt—that she was sure the woman had "deeply suffered," Mrs. Gereth caustically replies: "I'm sure I hope she did."
To be sure, we can enjoy the comic sophistication of Mrs. Gereth,
but the contrasting response of the two women to Ricks illustrates
nonetheless the limitations of a merely clever, aesthetic awareness
and the dimensions of the moral imagination that embraces "all
the heights and depths and extremities of things" (*SP,* pp. 54–55).

Fleda loves Ricks from the very first and, rather like Isabel
Archer at Gardencourt, looks upon it as a "blest refuge" (*SP,* p.
135). Eventually, moreover, she manages to convey something of
her own vision to Mrs. Gereth herself. Returning to Ricks late in
the novel, after Mrs. Gereth has restored to Poynton the plun-

dered furnishings, Fleda is amazed to find the place decorated
with beautiful things. Mrs. Gereth sees no beauty in them:
"They're the wretched things that were here," she exclaims, "that
stupid, starved old woman's" *(SP,* p. 246). But Fleda grows lyrical
about their human implications:

> Ah, the little melancholy, tender, tell-tale things: how can they
> *not* speak to you and find a way to your heart? It's not the
> great chorus of Poynton; but you're not, I'm sure, either so
> proud or so broken as to be reached by nothing but that. This
> is a voice so gentle, so human. . . . [*SP,* p. 248]

Ricks, Fleda tries to convince Mrs. Gereth, has a special beauty
of its own: it gives the "impression in which half the beauty
resides—the impression, somehow, of something dreamed and
missed, something reduced, relinquished, resigned: the poetry,
as it were, of something sensibly *gone.*" Ricks possesses an in-
tangible, spiritual element denied to magnificent Poynton:
"There's something here that never will be in the inventory,"
Fleda explains. And for once even Mrs. Gereth appears ready to
listen:

> "Does it happen to be in your power to give it a name?"
> Mrs. Gereth's face showed the dim dawn of an amusement at
> finding herself seated at the feet of her pupil.
> "I can give it a dozen. It's a kind of fourth dimension. It's a
> presence, a perfume, a touch. It's a soul, a story, a life. There's
> ever so much more here than you and I." [*SP,* pp. 248–49]

Fleda's reply reminds us of the almost visionary sense of the
continuity of the human lot that descends upon Isabel Archer
in the ruins of Rome, another place where people have suffered;
and it is significant, therefore, that here as in the other novel, an
allusion to ghosts is employed to embody a profound insight.
"Oh, if you count the ghosts!" replies Mrs. Gereth to Fleda's
suggestion that they are not alone.

> "Of course I count the ghosts, confound you! It seems to me
> ghosts count double—for what they were and for what they are.
> Somehow there were no ghosts at Poynton," Fleda went on.
> "That was the only fault."

Mrs. Gereth, considering, appeared to fall in with this fine humour. "Poynton was too splendidly happy."

"Poynton was too splendidly happy," Fleda promptly echoed.

"But it's cured of that now," her companion added.

"Yes, henceforth there'll be a ghost or two." [*SP*, pp. 249–50]

This exchange makes evident both that the limitations of an aesthetic sensibility like Mrs. Gereth's are due to the omission of human suffering from its perspective and that the beauty to which such a sensibility responds is in the last analysis a limited kind of beauty. The highest art does not ignore the depths and extremities of human experience, but rather partakes of them. In truth, for James, a moral limitation manifests itself as an aesthetic limitation; and, conversely, the aesthetic way is not denied but fulfilled by the ethical way.

Furthermore, the meaning that Fleda finds embodied in Ricks helps to explain the almost melodramatic finale of the novel—the burning down of beautiful Poynton itself. This ending has often puzzled readers: from one angle, the surprise and horror of it seems gratuitous in a master like James; yet, as Elizabeth Stevenson suggests, if the fire seems unnecessary, it is, nonetheless, gratifying; the destruction of the house and the spoils does satisfy our "sense of the way things *ought* to happen." [57] In our present context, we may go further and argue that, even if the fire is accidental, the destruction of Poynton is the necessary tragic coda to the central action of the moral-aesthetic theme. At the close of the novel, Poynton should be associated with Ricks, as certain verbal echoes, hitherto unnoticed, apparently imply. In the passage quoted above, Fleda speaks of the special beauty of Ricks as residing in the impression it conveys of "something dreamed and missed, something reduced, relinquished, resigned: the poetry, as it were, of something sensibly *gone*." Ironically, in the last pages this remark applies as much to Poynton as to Ricks, as the repetition of its key word *gone* helps to remind us. When Fleda goes down to Poynton and receives the horrible news about the fire, she uses the word again with the same force and meaning. "Poynton's on fire?" she inquires of the stationmaster. "Gone, miss—with this awful gale," he answers.

And she expresses her shock in the agonized utterance of a single word: *"Gone?" (SP,* p. 264).[58] May we not make the inference, therefore, that Poynton itself now shares something of the special quality of Ricks, because it too has become inextricably involved with life. Isabel Archer, we may remember, envied the beautiful objects of Gardencourt because they never changed but only grew in value, while their owners inevitably lost youth, happiness, beauty; Poynton, in contrast, takes on another kind of beauty by sharing in the fate of all mortal and material things.

Moreover, this transformation of Poynton seems reinforced by the ambiguity of the words *lost* and *saved* as they are used in the closing paragraphs of the novel. As I have indicated in the discussion of the last scene in *The Portrait of a Lady,* it is possible that James wishes the reader to respond to the Christian allusion involved in these words. In *The Spoils of Poynton,* this seems unmistakable. "Do you mean that great house is *lost?"* Fleda asks once again of the stationmaster, who admits that it must be. And when she mechanically inquires once more, "Poynton's *gone?"* the man can only reply: "What can you call it, miss, if it ain't actually saved?" *(SP,* pp. 264–66). On the literal level, Poynton is lost: the house is destroyed and all the spoils with it. On the level of Christian symbolism, there is a possible ambiguity: on one hand, Poynton is lost, as a damned soul is lost; on the other, James may have intended a paradox—Poynton is actually "saved" by being lost. It partakes of the beauty of Ricks itself: "something dreamed and missed, something reduced, relinquished, resigned." [59] Splendid, happy Poynton itself finally suffers, and the flames that consume it—like those in Dickens, Brontë, Meredith—destroy only to purify. Through the refining fire Poynton, the palace of art, becomes—in recollection, at least —another house of life.

In the novels just discussed, the country house is a major setting and a paramount symbol—indeed, in *The Spoils of Poynton,* it is the hub of the plot and theme. However, few of the novels and stories in which James dealt with the English scene are without some symbolic reference to the country house, even though it may not be central and seems casually introduced as background. This is true even in the works of the nineties which show James becoming more and more critical of English society and the country-house style of life.[60]

Indeed, it is noteworthy that in the works designed to give ironic glimpses of English *moeurs* in a changing time, James never forsakes the house itself. Quite the contrary: in its beauty and spaciousness, its soothing calm and privacy, its perpetuation of a gracious past into a vulgarized present, the country house continues to be a reminder of a higher order of being, a kind of mute censor of the tasteless and even decadent life he often finds within it. During his middle period, in fact, James returns to an early theme. In his youthful travel sketches, as noted above, James often remarked upon the incongruity between what appealed to him in the English setting and what appalled him in English life. Now, with a mixture of irony and regret, he again plays with the poignant contrast between the great house and the smallness of its occupants.

In several works, whatever the basic action and meaning, the country house carries this secondary theme. In "The Author of Beltraffio," for example, the contrast is particularly clear. The narrator, a young American author visiting the celebrated Mark Ambient, arrives at his country house naïvely prepared to see everything through the soft focus of literary and historical association. "That was the way many things struck me that time in England," he tells us, "as reproductions of something that existed primarily in art or literature. It was not the picture, the poem, the fictive page, that seemed to me a copy; these things were the originals, and the life of a happy and distinguished people was fashioned in their image." He not only admires his literary host, but finds "genius in his house too." It is a "palace of art," he declares rhapsodically, and might serve besides as "the dearest haunt of the old English *genius loci*" (*AB*, p. 8). To the reader, however, it is soon evident that the house of Mark Ambient is not at all a happy house but one tense with irresoluble conflicts. Mrs. Ambient is not only a philistine who lacks understanding of her husband and his art but a thin-lipped puritan who, by identifying his aestheticism with depravity, actually believes he is a moral threat to their young son.

Ironically, the American narrator himself is slow to perceive what is right in front of him; instead, he prattles on about "the literary allusions of the landscape" and "the decent English air" (*AB*, p. 40). When he finally discovers the truth of the situation, the beautiful house that formerly distracted him only accentuates the discord. After hearing Ambient disclose that his wife hates art, hates literature, and accepts only sham, the narrator reviews his surroundings: "I looked up at the charming house, with its genial colour . . . and I answered with a smile that those evil passions might exist, but that I should never expect to find them there" (*AB*, pp. 47–48). Finally, the dreadful climax takes place within the house itself: Mrs. Ambient allows her ailing son to die rather than have him grow up under what she considers the corrupting influence of his father. Thus another palace of art becomes a house of death.

In "A London Life," the heroine, another American, experiences an equally unsettling revelation; and here James employs the country house once again to create a kind of moral chiaroscuro. Young Laura Wing, paying a visit to Mellows, the country estate of her married sister and brother-in-law, Selina and Lionel Berrington, also arrives with high expectations of English domestic life. She dreams of English talk, "the rare sort of talk that was not the mere bandying of chaff." But in her year at Mellows, she is soon disillusioned: "There had never been an idea in the house . . . since she came at least; and there was wonderfully little reading." The men about her are concerned merely with horses and shooting, while the women in her sister's set delight in harrying each other with scandal in "a kind of horse-play of false criminal charges" (*LL*, p. 276). Most alarming of all, she discovers that both Selina and Lionel are involved in adulterous affairs which threaten to break out in scandalous court proceedings.

What makes the situation all the more poignant to her is the appealing setting in which she must learn these truths. "A year ago she knew nothing; and now she knew pretty well everything; and the worst of her knowledge . . . had come to her in that beautiful place, where everything spoke of peace and decency, of happy submission to immemorial law. The place was the same, but her eyes were other: they had seen such sad bad things in so short a time" (*LL*, p. 271). And this juxtaposition of the house as kind of arbiter ironically incriminating the sordid lapses of its occupants recurs as a refrain throughout the tale. Even while visiting Plash, the charming dower house of Lady Davenant, Laura muses on the contrast:

> The room had its bright durable social air, the air Laura liked in so many English things—that of being meant for daily life, for long periods, for uses of high decorum. But more than ever today was it discordant that such a habitation, with its chintzes and its British poets, its well-worn carpets and domestic art— the whole effect so naïve and sincere—should have to do with lives that weren't really right. [*LL*, pp. 271–72]

Again, in considering her brother-in-law, whom she pities rather than dislikes, Laura speculates on the differences between Lionel, the unadmirable adult, and the promising influences that must have surrounded his earliest years:

> She marveled at the waste involved in some human institu- tions—the English landed gentry for instance—when she noted how much it had taken to produce so little. The sweet old wainscoted parlour, the view of the garden that reminded her of scenes in Shakespeare's comedies, all that was exquisite in the home of his forefathers—what visible reference was there to these fine things in poor Lionel's stable-stamped composi- tion? [*LL*, p. 291]

The sight of Lionel's small sons in their nursery prompts the same question:

> She asked herself of what *they* would have to show twenty years later for the frame that made them just then a picture. Would they be wonderfully ripe and noble, the perfection of human culture?
>
> The contrast was before her again, the sense of the same curious duplicity (in the literal meaning of the word) that she took in at Plash—the way the genius of such an old house was all peace and decorum and yet the spirit that prevailed there,

outside the schoolroom, contentious and impure. She had often been struck with this—with that perfection of machinery that can still at certain times makes English life go on of itself with a stately rhythm long after corruption is within it. [*LL*, p. 292]

The house in this sense also enters into Laura's trying conversations with Selina and Lionel. Outraged by his vulgar behavior, Laura challenges him in the name of his own house: "I don't think you care any more for your home than Selina does," she rebukes him. "And it's so sacred and so beautiful, God forgive you" (*LL*, p. 309). And, in talking to Selina, she can hardly bring herself to utter the word divorce under the "somewhat austere ceilings of Mellows," whose eighteenth-century decorations—festoons, urns, and trophies—seem "so many symbols of domestic affection and irrevocable union" (*LL*, p. 324).

In the end, Laura is so appalled by the scandal of Mellows that she foolishly throws herself at a young man whom she hopes will save her from its impact. But what remains with the reader is not simply this particular climax but the spectacle of a great decent house in the hands of those unworthy to live within it.

This employment of the country house for purposes of irony rather than mere atmospheric support recurs so often in James that it is no wonder that even his most controversial "ghost" story, "The Turn of the Screw," which might seem to call for rather horrific effects, offers but another variation. Despite the superficial resemblance of this story to Gothic fiction, Bly is not the conventional haunted house of Mrs. Radcliffe. Instead of appearing sinister and forbidding, it has much the same charm as other country houses in James. On first seeing Bly, the governess enjoys "a thoroughly pleasant impression" of the house, of its "broad clear front, its open windows and fresh curtains and the pair of maids looking out," and during her early weeks there, she finds herself luxuriating in the "beauty and dignity of the place." [61] Later, when the governess encounters the evil ghosts —whatever interpretation is put upon them—the beauty of Bly reminds the reader of the dark realities that may lie behind the most engaging appearances and at the same time gives him the sense of a decent, daylight world by which to measure them. In this sense, Robert Heilman's interpretation of Bly as an emblem of paradise is suggestive; and, without endorsing his almost allegorical reading, we may consider "The Turn of the Screw" as a "story of the decay of Eden." [62]

Indeed, from a broad archetypal perspective, the works just considered are all so many stories of the country house as a kind of Eden—or, at least, pastorals of a golden world, lovely but lost.

It should by now be evident that no matter how often James employed the country house as a symbol of possible community he did not idealize the actual style of life he found within it. On the contrary, the longer James stayed in England, the more realistic he became about the whole subject of English manners; in fact, as the century drew to a close, he found English high society in a state of decline that alarmed the moralist within him as much as it stimulated the novelist. Even his notebook entries during the nineties are instructive on this point because for once James went beyond his usual preoccupation with "story" and technique as such to an explicit formulation of the social themes underlying his later fiction. Stimulated by his browsing through *Notes sur Londres,* a commentary on the decay of English society by Henriette Consuelo, James added his own testimony about the "demoralization of the aristocracy" and "their traffic in vulgar things, vulgar gains, vulgar pleasures." And as a novelist, he saw in "the *déchéance* of the aristocracy through its own want of imagination, of nobleness, of delicacy" and the "great modern collapse of all the forms and 'superstitions' and respects," a rich theme for a "large satirical novel." [63]

James never really produced this one large satirical novel; nevertheless, a host of his stories written during the nineties do fall into a sequence of satirical tableaux linked together by his concern with the follies and absurdities of the English upper classes. A number of these inevitably make certain aspects of country-house life the objects of satire. Indeed, stories like "The Real Thing" (1893), "The Death of the Lion" (1894), "Broken Wings" (1900), and "The Two Faces" (1901) do coruscate and bristle precisely because of James's ability to look upon the customs and rituals of the country house world with the detachment of an anthropologist gifted with a sense of irony. In some, James relishes the satirical possibilities of the country house as a spectacle almost operatic in its ostentation and staginess. Theater imagery, in fact, often recurs. In "Broken Wings," for example, the guests agree in the idiom of drama critics that, compared to any stage piece, "Mundham *was,* theatrically, the real thing; better for scenery, dresses, music, pretty women, bare shoulders, everything—even coherent dialogue." [64] Like any other stage, the country house provides the opportunity for dramatic entrance; and in James's fiction those outside English society but aspiring to enter are quite conscious of themselves as untried players before the most critical of audiences and, like Mrs. Headway descending the great staircase at Longlands in "The Siege of London" (1883), attempt to make the most of their initial bow.

Elsewhere in these stories the stages of the action are often linked, as D. W. Jefferson has pointed out, with "such routines as dressing or assembling for dinner, the question of who goes in with whom often being relevant." [65] In the opening of "Broken Wings," for instance, the painter Straith, finding himself unmatched with any other guest in the procession to the dining room and so obliged to enter alone at the end of the line, realizes that the artist may be invited to decorate the fashionable world but remains excluded from its inner circles. In "The Two Faces," the issue of proper dress provides the climax. Lady Grantham, the jilted mistress of Lord Gwyther, manages revenge by encouraging his attractive but artless young bride to overdress for her debut at a country house. "The poor creature's lost," one guest avows, because "overloaded like a monkey in a show." [66] Throughout his satirical fiction, moreover, James displays weekend parties as parodies of the very community he associated with the ideal of the country house. The gatherings he describes are often motivated by hostility, and the country house simply provides a zone of combat where the belligerents may join forces. Sometimes, in fact, James resorts to military metaphors.

The country-house world, James also perceived, worshiped Mammon along with Moloch, and in a number of his late stories he makes a point of displaying its "materializations," [67] its surrender to things and its indifference to intellectual and aesthetic values. An excellent example is "The Real Thing" (1893), the story of the Monarchs, the middle-aged couple who were once welcome visitors to great houses but who now hire themselves out as models to a painter. The Monarchs, the painter sees, are representative—they are, in their own words, "the *real* thing; a gentleman, you know, or a lady." Ironically, what they came to represent for the painter are the superficialities of the country-house style of life:

> It was in their faces, the blankness, the deep intellectual repose of the twenty years of country-house visiting. . . . I could see the sunny drawing-rooms, sprinkled with periodicals she didn't read, in which Mrs. Monarch continuously sat . . . I could see the rich covers the Major had helped to shoot and the wonderful garments in which, late at night, he repaired to the smoking-room to talk about them. I could imagine their leggings and waterproofs, their knowing tweeds and rugs, their rolls of sticks and cases of tackle and neat umbrellas; and I could evoke the exact appearance of their servants and the compact variety of their luggage on platforms of country stations.[68]

In his indictment of English high society, the painter in "The Real Thing" is not alone among James's artists. In fact, taken together, the many painters and writers in James's fiction form a kind of chorus, crying out against the very class that courts and pretends to laud them. The encounter of the artist with the country house is, therefore, an uneasy one. Inevitably enchanted with what the country house offers his senses and imagination, the typical Jamesian artist usually finds its life alien to his own needs and values. Indeed, the grotesque climax of "The Death of the Lion" (1894) seems to epitomize the fate of the artist in the world of the country house. Here, Mrs. Wimbush, the wife of a brewer and mistress of Prestidge, manages to catch the celebrated writer Neil Paraday for an extended visit to her "universal menagerie" and exhibits him as a "prime attraction, a creature of almost heraldic oddity." [69] But the round of performances proves too much for the exhausted novelist: catching a chill, he retires to his room and dies—much to the disappointment of his hostess. And what is perhaps more appalling, his last manuscript, to which he gave his dying thoughts, is lost forever in the bustling activity of Prestidge. Elsewhere, the artist finds that he must retreat from the worldliness of the country house in self-protection. At the close of "Broken Wings" (1900), for example, when the painter Stuart Straith and the widowed novelist Mrs. Harvey finally join together, they renounce the fashionable world which has long separated them: "We shall, thank heaven, never go again to Mundham. The Mundhams are over." [70]

The satirical élan possessing James in these stories also seasoned a few of the novels composed around the turn of the century, particularly *The Awkward Age* (1899) and *The Sacred Fount* (1901). Indeed Newmarch, the setting of *The Sacred Fount,* might be taken as the ironic apotheosis of places like Prestidge and Mundham. The story—the narrator's fantastic obsession with the possible adulteries of the guests—is, of course, mystifying enough in itself to preoccupy readers; but Newmarch bristles with enigmas of its own. In fact, for once in James, the symbolic setting is not truly consonant with the plot but almost seems to function autonomously. The descriptions of Newmarch, becoming more heavily weighted and more insinuating as the novel proceeds, beget a tension lacking in the finespun narrative itself. There is an indefinable air about Newmarch, a strangeness, an impersonality, unnervingly evoked by the curious tone of the narrator and his allusions to its ambiguous enchantments, to its half-lit gardens, motionless woods, and still ponds. Newmarch, one begins to see, is for James a deliberately stylized construct of the country house and its ritualistic formalities—almost expressionistic in effect, even Kafkaesque. The reader may be told of its noble freedom, its beauties and felicities, but Newmarch is a world of appearance and artifice. And the narrator himself, spellbound though he seems, confesses to claustrophobia as he turns from the interior and the assemblage to gaze through a window at the natural world beyond the house:

> The night was mild and rich. . . . I found the breath of outer air a sudden corrective to the grossness of our lustre and the thickness of our medium, our general heavy humanity. I felt its sweet taste, and while I leaned for the refreshment on the

sill I thought of many things. One of those that passed before me was the way that Newmarch and its hospitalities were sacrificed, after all, and much more than smaller circles, to material frustrations. We were all so fine and formal, and the ladies in particular at once so little and so much clothed, so beflounced and yet so denuded, that the summer stars called to us in vain. We had ignored them in our crystal cage, among our tinkling lamps; no more freely to alight than as if we had been dashing in a locked rail-way train across a lovely land.[71]

The antithesis between the social and the natural, the artificial and the spontaneous—here drawn with a sharpness unusual in James—appears to raise questions transcending the specific context of the novel. Newmarch, society, civilization, we are led to infer, may be a "crystal cage" stifling to the spirit. In such a passage, we seem to hear what T. S. Eliot has called the "first voice," [72] the personal voice of the author, of James himself, as he presses toward the boundary—should we not say the fateful region beyond the boundary?—of the social world which was his favorite stage and the source of his symbolism. To go beyond Newmarch and the "crystal cage" would be to move toward the cosmic, the metaphysical, even the religious. There are hints of such a tendency in James, in the "deeper psychology" of "The Jolly Corner" and the tentative Christian allusions of *The Wings of the Dove*. Even so, the problem of human fulfillment remained for James one that would be dramatized, if not actually solved, within the social world he knew. The "crystal cage" is not his final version of the country house.

In other late works of James, even those of the "major phase," the country house plays a more complex symbolic role. "Covering End" (1898) and "Flickerbridge" (1903), like *The Spoils of Poynton* (1897), make the house the pivot of the action. The unrelated characters of two important novels—*The Wings of the Dove* (1902) and *The Golden Bowl* (1904)—appear to visit the same country house of Matcham; and the American Mr. Verver and his daughter Maggie enjoy Fawns, their English home, in a manner that recalls the Touchetts at Gardencourt. Despite chro-

nology, however, there is no unambiguous last testament from
James about the country house. Instead, he continues to trace
a dialectical pattern by viewing the house from more than one
coign of vantage.

The old country places specified in the titles of "Covering
End" and "Flickerbridge" once again epitomize James's ideal—
perhaps too explicitly but at least attractively. "Covering End,"
in fact, seems a restatement of the issues of *The Princess Casamassima* with comic variations. Here, the house is visited by not
one but two outsiders: Mrs. Gracedew, an American widow on
tour; and Captain Yule, an English politician who has just inherited the estate but has never seen it. Paradoxically, the Captain is the one who fails to respond to the ancient pile, for he
is, in his own words, "a pure, passionate, pledged Radical" (*CE,*
p. 390). Nothing of its past speaks to him: "It was as if the two
hard spirits, the grim *genius loci* and the quick modern conscience, stood an instant confronted" (*CE,* p. 250). Mrs. Gracedew, on the other hand, representing James's ideal conservatism,
waxes lyrical.[73] "To look, in this place," she declares, "is to
love" (*CE,* p. 286). The pair, though attracted to each other,
naturally clash. The captain argues out of his troubled sense of
the large social questions involved. "I see something else in the
world than the beauty of old show-houses and the glory of show-
families," he explains. "There are thousands of people in England who can show no houses at all, and I don't feel it utterly
shameful to share their poor fate." Mrs. Gracedew is not indifferent to his concern. "We share the poor fate of humanity whatever we do," she replies, "and we do something to help and con-
sole when we've something precious to show" (*CE,* pp. 314–15).
But for her, the house transcends social and ideological conflict
and becomes a spiritual symbol, as her metaphors reveal: "This
is the temple," she exclaims:

> What do politics amount to, compared to religions? Parties
> and programmes come and go, but a duty like this abides.
> There's nothing you could break with . . . that would be like
> breaking *here*. . . . This *is* the temple—don't profane it! Keep
> up the old altar kindly—you can't set up a new one as good.
> [*CE,* p. 318]

Mrs. Gracedew and Captain Yule are eventually reconciled, however, and their marriage not only provides one of the most conventionally happy endings in James but obviously represents the union of what is best in the modern and the traditional.

Although "Covering End" might seem to return to the familiar eulogies of the early James, other late works have lost none of the astringency of his satirical vignettes. As if to give vent to both encomium and satire, two contrasting houses are now usually found in the same novel. There is still the house embodying community and continuity, the "house of life." There is also the "crystal cage," or what Quentin Anderson, borrowing one of James's own titles, calls the "other house," [74] whose "otherness" is created by its soulless inmates.

The Other House (1896) itself provides the most obvious illustration. Here the dying Julia Bream obliges her husband to swear that he will not marry again while their daughter lives, thus creating a macabre situation in which the woman's best friend murders the child to have the father for herself. The stage of this somber drama is confined to two houses in counterpoint: Bounds, the mansion of Tony Bream; and Eastmead, the neighboring house of the innocent but observing Mrs. Beever. Contrasting details accentuate their differences and deepen their import. Bounds, the "other house," the center of evil, is, as Edwin T. Bowden points out, ornate and showy, "a fitting scene, almost in the tradition of Poe, for acts of mystery and terror." Eastmead, on the other hand, is, in James's words, a "great, clean, square solitude," providing as Bowden goes on to note, a background of order and quiet for the growing awareness of evil: "The intrigue and crime find their origin in that ornate house across the river, but are seen only here, in all their incongruity, destroying an atmosphere of simplicity and decency." [75]

The Awkward Age offers a more significant instance of this same counterpoint. Composed dramatically as a series of scenes and dialogues, the novel depicts the fashionable but decadent social set of Mrs. Brookenham, and, with something of the tone and tempo of a rare high comedy, it exposes the match making and fortune hunting, the adulteries, scandals, and intrigue of the new age ambiguously defined by the title. To maintain theatrical verve, James prunes the description of setting to the spare, minimal requirements of stage direction; nevertheless, even here the houses are essential as symbols.

The Awkward Age is unusually complicated in structure for a James novel, just as the number of characters is remarkably large; nevertheless, one basic contrast provides discernible form and meaning—the contrast between the new, self-consciously "modern" social world of Mrs. Brookenham and the traditional world of old Mr. Longdon. Her world—so up-to-date, amusing, and exciting on the surface—is at bottom materialist, tasteless, tense, even sordid; his remains calm, sane, genuinely humane. On the level of plot, this is evident in the contrast between the behavior of Mr. Longdon and Mrs. Brook (as she is called) toward her daughter Nanda: she attempts to maneuver Nanda into a wealthy marriage while scheming to keep Vanderbank, the one man her daughter loves, for herself; Mr. Longdon, on the other hand, is protective and loyal to the girl throughout her predicament. Symbolically, the contrast is embodied in two country houses—Mertle and Beccles: one, a rendezvous for the rootless associates of Mrs. Brook; the other, the ancestral home of Mr. Longdon.

Mertle, like the houses in "The Author of Beltraffio" and "A London Life," is beautiful in itself; what demeans it is the waywardness of its tenants. On her first visit there, Nanda is charmed by its age and loveliness, by "the combination of delightful things—of old rooms with old decorations that gleamed and gloomed through the high windows, of old gardens, that squared themselves in the wide angles of old walls" (*AA*, p. 203). She soon comes to realize, however, that despite this appearance of beauty and order Mertle really represents the vagrant, aimless ways of those in her mother's circle. The house seems to belong to no one in particular; it is merely rented out for brief periods by some anonymous owner to a vague assortment of tenants. During Nanda's stay, it is being rented by Mitchy, the parvenu son of a bootmaker, to amuse himself and others from Mrs. Brook's set. In such a house and in such company it comes as no surprise that Nanda is neglected by Vanderbank or that the Duchess, unlike Mrs. Brook, keeps a strict eye on her own daughter. Mertle is evidently the type of place that a character elsewhere in the novel has in mind when he observes that if London is dangerous for young girls, a "big house in the country is as much worse—with the promiscuities and opportunities and all that" (*AA*, p. 392).

Old Mr. Longdon is inevitably repelled by what he sees at Mertle and is anxious to woo Nanda away from it. Shocked by "this sudden invasion of somebody's—heaven knows whose—house," he wonders what people are "made of that they consent, just for money, to the violation of their homes" (*AA*, p. 219). Nanda, of course, knows only the present, and to give her the chance to experience another mode of existence, Mr. Longdon invites her to "come down to Suffolk for sanity," to his own house of Beccles. "I want to show you what life can give," he tells her, "not, of course, this sort of thing" (*AA*, p. 323).

Beccles is a "temple of peace," to use Mr. Longdon's own words; and there—like so many other of James's characters in similar country houses—Nanda passes through a happy novitiate. One of the charms of the place is that, unlike Mertle, it does provide a sense of genuine continuity and established custom:

> Beyond the lawn the house was before him, old, square, red-roofed, well assured of its right to the place it took up in the world. This was a considerable space—in the little world, at least, of Beccles—and the look of possession had everywhere mixed with it, in the form of old windows and doors, the tone of old red surfaces, in the style of old white facings, the age of old high creepers, the long confirmation of time. [*AA*, pp. 335–36]

Even Vanderbank momentarily succumbs to the spell of Beccles, and Mitchy himself, representative of the modern, is taken with the purity of its effect. "Mr. Longdon," he recognizes, "had not made his house, he had simply lived it, and the 'taste' of the place . . . was nothing more than the beauty of his life" (*AA*, pp. 328–29). And as Nanda lingers there, Beccles takes on a living quality. "Everything in the place," she declares, "is such good company" (*AA*, p. 336).

After this visit, it is true, the novel resumes its complicated pattern: Nanda refuses Mitchy, her mother's choice, and eventu-

ally she loses Vanderbank, her own. Beccles may then seem
peripheral; nevertheless, it remains a moral fulcrum for the
novel. When at the end Nanda may seem to have no place to
turn, Mr. Longdon's request that she join him there again reveals that she is not wholly lost.

What seems a rather obvious antithesis in novels like *The
Awkward Age* elsewhere shifts kaleidoscopically into more perplexing patterns. Both types of houses, it then appears, are problematic: the "other house," though evil, remains a shining edifice
whose bland surfaces and engaging tenants distract even the
morally alert; and the true "house of life" sometimes tempts its
sensitive residents to accept withdrawal and isolation. As in a
fairy tale, either one may seem an enchanting palace magically
brought into being with the stroke of a wand and may be as
swiftly transformed into a mysterious cave or dungeon cell. Both
James's characters and his readers must therefore tread cautiously,
deceived by neither aesthetic appearances nor easy moral schema-
tizations.

The bewitching charm of the "other house" is most notable in
Matcham, which has the distinction of appearing in two major
novels, *The Wings of the Dove* and *The Golden Bowl*, as if by
repetition James wished to make us more aware of the kind of
"otherness" charging the atmosphere of each. Matcham almost
seems the model of a great house, beautiful and courtly, yet
it is attended largely by those in pursuit of status, money, or
illicit love. As its name implies, it is involved with matchmaking
—of, indeed, more than one kind: it provides the meeting
ground for those contemplating respectable but profitable mar-
riages and a dissembling rendezvous for those engaged in respectable adultery.

In *The Wings of the Dove* the first kind of pairing off comes
into view to unsettle the innocent Milly Theale. Maneuvered
into visiting Matcham by Lord Mark and Mrs. Lowder, the
American heiress there experiences a double revelation—both a
sublime aesthetic vision and a poignant moral disillusion. She is
at last introduced to "largeness of style" and *"appointed* felicity":
"The great historic house had, for Milly, beyond terrace and
garden, as the centre of an almost extravagantly grand Watteau-

composition, a tone as of old gold kept 'down' by the quality of the air summer full-flushed, but attuned to the general perfect taste" (*WD*, p. 208). But this discovery is immediately followed by Milly's perceiving the real reason for her invitation to Matcham: she is the object of some transaction between Lord Mark and Mrs. Lowder. And as Quentin Anderson observes, the bargain between the two is reinforced by the metaphor of Mrs. Lowder as a shuttle, weaving him into her design. Although Matcham may offer Milly a vision, it cannot produce the reality. Even her sense of apotheosis before its magnificent Bronzino portrait, as J. A. Ward notes, is "personal and prophetic, rather than social and actual." [76]

In *The Golden Bowl*, Matcham diplomatically connives at extramarital adventures. Of course there is no evidence of assignation, appearances remain what they should be; but in his rather arch description of this house "full of people, of possible new combinations, of the quickened play of possible propinquity," James establishes the moral tone with an unambiguous ironic figure: "What anyone 'thought' of anyone else—above all of anyone *with* anyone else—was a matter incurring in these halls so little awkward formulation that hovering judgment, the spirit with the scales, might perfectly have been imaged there as some rather snubbed and subdued, but quite trained and tactful poor relation . . ." (*GB*, 1 : 330–31). So it happens that when Prince Amerigo and Charlotte find themselves together at Matcham—and for the first time at a distance from Maggie and Mr. Verver, their respective mates—they are safe from criticism and can draw relief from "the easy tradition, the almost inspiring allowances of the house . . ." (*GB*, 1 : 330). Indeed, it is the hostess of Matcham herself, Lady Castledean, who provides the occasion for the actual adultery of the Prince and Charlotte. With all other guests leaving, she detains them because she wishes to keep behind a young lover of her own and cannot very well do so "without spreading over the act some ampler drapery" (*GB*, 1 : 352).

Throughout this sequence bringing the relationship of the Prince and Charlotte to its illicit climax, Matcham is a felt presence, contributing almost cinematically to each nuance of the action. For the Prince himself, the sensuous loveliness of the place—like a Spenserian Bower of Bliss—augments the temptation to surrender to long-suppressed impulse: "Every voice in the great bright house was a call to the ingenuities and impunities of pleasure; every echo was a defiance of difficulty, doubt, or danger; every aspect of the picture, a glowing plea for the immediate . . ." (*GB,* 1 : 332). And the mutual decision of the Prince and Charlotte to go to nearby Gloucester to give themselves to each other—and so to execute perhaps one of the most complicated sets of marital betrayals in fiction—becomes ironically a scene of unexpected lyricism because of the radiance and delicacy of the visual images drawn from their splendid surroundings. Here, with the immediacy and tempo of a finely composed film, dialogue and movement and setting are synthesized in a series of "shots" lasting several pages, as if to create an atmosphere consonant with Edmund Burke's dictum that vice may lose half its evil by losing all its grossness.

The details should be savored. They not only display the novelist's virtuosity and irony, they prepare the reader for a great counterscene that James mounts with equal directorial finesse at Fawns, the foil for Matcham and the home of the Ververs. The scene begins with the Prince strolling the terrace by himself in the April morning and scanning the windows of Matcham. Charlotte appears at her window, and when she smiles down to him, there is the suggestion of a more romantic and courtlier age. "It only wants a moon, a mandolin, and a little danger, to be a serenade," the Prince calls up to her. She in turn flings a white rosebud to him. But the frustrating conventions of courtly love are abandoned. Charlotte comes down to him, and their cadenced movement toward each other against the facade of Matcham seems made for cinema: "Mrs. Verver appeared, afar off, in one of the smaller doorways. She came toward him in silence, while he moved to meet her; the great scale of this particular front at Matcham, multiplied thus, in the golden morning, the stages of their meeting and the successions of their consciousness" (*GB,* 1 : 357–58). From the terrace, the pair can spy the towers of Gloucester—where, it is implied, their visit to the cathedral—like the visit of Emma and Leon to Rouen's cathedral in *Madame Bovary*—will be but the prelude to erotic intimacy.

In *The Golden Bowl*, Matcham, as already noted, has its foil in Fawns. But the result is not an obvious moral equation statically balancing sophistication and innocence. Rather, if Matcham almost disarmingly flaunts the charms of evil, Fawns bears witness to the seductions and jeopardies of virtue. Prominent in both halves of the novel, before and after the visit of the Prince and Charlotte to Matcham, Fawns is a stage reflecting first the ingenousness, then the ordeal, and finally the culmination of Maggie Verver's moral development.

Fawns appears in a different light in each half of the novel. In the first half it is a seemingly idyllic world where, before her marriage to the Prince, Maggie and her father, Adam, live as in another Eden—in fact, the recurring imagery of gold, as J. A. Ward notes, quickly suggests the Golden World itself.[77] Nonetheless, the meaning of Fawns is more complicated than this alone would suggest. Fawns is superior to Matcham; but to take it, in the way Maggie and her father do at first take it, as an ideal of virtue easily achieved and established, is also to be exposed to deceptions and temptations of a subtle kind. Through innocence, the Ververs are oblivious to the "fallen" world beyond their serene abode; they are sheltered, detached, withdrawn from that world. Fawns, James almost Miltonically hints, is the home of "cloistered virtue."

In the second half of *The Golden Bowl*, however, virtue is uncloistered, challenged, tested. Maggie discovers the real relationship between her husband and her friend Charlotte, her suspicions confirmed by their late return from Matcham and the Prince's account of Gloucester. At this point Fawns becomes literally and emblematically the theater for Maggie's full recognition of the evil of her circumstances and of the choice consequently imposed upon her. Again anticipating the technique of the modern film, James dramatizes Maggie's changing consciousness—her insights and decisions—by following her movements within, without, and about the stately mansion. At first Maggie retreats. Watching the intimate family party in the smoking room at Fawns on a summer night, she suffers nervously before

their "conquest of appearances" (*GB*, 2 : 233). Impelled to leave
the room and wander alone on the terrace, she hovers by a long
window and inspects them again. The perspective deepens her
awareness of incongruity. "They might have been—really charming as they showed in the beautiful room," Maggie reflects, "and
Charlotte certainly, as always magnificently handsome and su-
premely distinguished—they might have been figures rehearsing
some play of which she herself was the author." Their plausi-
bility only accents the horror of her discovery—"the horror of
finding evil seated, all at its ease, where she had only dreamed
of good; the horror of the thing hideously *behind,* behind so
much trusted, so much pretended, nobleness, cleverness, tenderness" (*GB*, pp. 235, 237). Fawns, it is now evident, cannot be an
unsullied Eden. Even the "temple" may be desecrated.

For Maggie, however, the discovery of evil is not a defeat, but
only a possible temptation—the temptation of "the straight
vindictive view, the rights of resentment, the rages of jealousy."
This temptation to retaliate is as understandable as the temptation of passion to which the Prince yielded at Matcham, yet to
Maggie it is only a consciousness of what is "horribly possible,"
not a challenge to her authentic self. And her view of the interior
of the house, this time the illuminated but empty drawing room,
is the "objective correlative" of her choice. "Spacious and splendid, like a stage again awaiting a drama, it was a scene she might
people, by the press of her spring, either with serenities and
dignities and decencies, or with terrors and shames and ruins"
(*GB*, 2 : 236). Maggie chooses the "serenities and dignities and
decencies," because, as she recognizes upon looking again
through the window at the group assembled in the smoking
room, she cannot give them up as lost.

Ironically, Maggie's real temptation is to retreat rather than
retaliate, but if she is not to give up the others, she cannot withdraw or remain aloof from action. As Quentin Anderson observes in his analysis of the moral climax of the novel, Maggie,
"the little goddess, descends." [78] She has to accept humanity in
all its wickedness, and to do so she must deny herself. Her two
important encounters with Charlotte demonstrate this self-denial,
and in both, Fawns is the symbolic stage. Indeed, at the very

moment of her decision not to revenge her wrong, Maggie is alarmed by the sudden appearance of Charlotte in the empty drawing room: "The splendid shining creature was out of the cage, was at large" (*GB*, 2 : 239). Maggie defensively takes flight along the terrace, but after Charlotte catches up with her and both return to the drawing room, there is a new deployment of forces. To Maggie, the very look of the room, "with all its great objects as ordered and balanced as for a formal reception," makes it seem "appointed for some high transaction, some real affair of state" (*GB*, 2 : 246). And so it is. There Charlotte asks her overwhelming question: of what wrong does Maggie wish to accuse her? And there Maggie understands what line she must take. "You *have* been quite mistaken," she replies to Charlotte, now finding her own advantage in the ambiguities of appearance. "All I can say is you've received a false impression." From this point, it is Charlotte who is "off in some darkness of space that would steep her in solitude" (*GB*, 2 : 249).

Despite this favorable reversal, however, Maggie does not press her new advantage; she does not abandon Charlotte to isolation. Still compassionate, she is moved to go to the "detached member of the party" (*GB*, 2 : 250) and to give some clear demonstration of support. Only the occasion is wanting, and the one that arises offers an unmistakable parallel and contrast to both Maggie's earlier scene on the terrace at Fawns and the Prince's scene with Charlotte at Matcham. Standing by the window of her room at Fawns and surveying the gardens bathed in an immensity of light, Maggie finds charm "in her seemingly perched position— as if her outlook, from above the high terrace, was that of some castle-tower mounted on a rock" (*GB*, 2 : 306). Here once more, James exploits cinematic elements of movement and light, panorama and close-up. Suddenly Maggie catches sight of Charlotte's umbrella descending the steps below and heading in a kind of flight toward the shaded recesses of the garden. With the pretext of bringing Charlotte the correct volume of the book she is carrying, Maggie decides to follow. The symbolic correspondence with the scene at Matcham is clear. There Charlotte, looking down from her window at the Prince and then descending, yielded to passion; here Maggie, also descending, is performing an act of humiliation in a brave attempt to save Charlotte. Instead of holding her "perched position," Maggie risks herself; no longer "cloistered," virtue is in active pursuit, not to destroy but to rescue.

The pursuit is "a repetition more than ever of the evening on the terrace," as Maggie herself recognizes. "She passed again through the house, unchallenged, and emerged upon the terrace . . . with that consciousness of turning the tables on her friend which we have already noted. But as far as she went, after descending into the open and beginning to explore the grounds, Mrs. Verver had gone still further . . ." (*GB,* 2 : 308). Moreover, in her flight, Charlotte ironically withdraws to a pavilion that, like a distorted mirror, seems to reflect a diminished image of Fawns itself: "This," Maggie perceives, "was the asylum, presumably, that the poor wandering woman had had in view . . . a sort of umbrageous temple, an ancient rotunda, pillared and statued, niched and roofed, yet with its uncorrected antiquity, like that of everything else at Fawns, conscious hitherto of no violence and no menace from the future" (*GB,* 2 : 306). Here Maggie allows Charlotte to save face in a dignified way. Even lying again, Maggie does "all." Uncloistered, she redeems herself and others and Fawns itself.

Finally, it might be said that Maggie's paradoxical victory at Fawns not only sums up the true meaning of the house of life for James, but it also brings to an affirmative climax his recurring theme of withdrawal and return, retreat and counterattack —a motif sometimes misunderstood because of James's own dialectical proclivities or the reader's emphasis on single works apart from others providing contrast or qualification. For example, in *The Awkward Age,* "Flickerbridge," and "The Great Good Place" (whose dream setting seems an amalgam of a country house and a monastery), James does stress withdrawal, indeed withdrawal as something justifiable, even necessary; and the ideal house therein presented is a sequestered, silent, solitary kind of place inviting the Freudian suspicion that what James was really after was a "womb with a view." At times, in fact, James displays an interesting affinity with the poets of the nineteenth century who also responded to the attractions of withdrawal—with Tennyson in "The Lotus-Eaters" and "The Palace of Art," Arnold in "Kensington Gardens," even with the early Yeats. This motif is usually dismissed as escapist, though perhaps a little too easily. If its poetic manifestations are often flaccid and enervating, they at least implied some recognition of contemplative modes of being beyond the busy philistinism of the time. And James's quiet houses—contrasting with the growing hysteria of London and the peopled cages of Mundham and Matcham—assume the need for spiritual sanctuary in a secularized age. In any event, it is not withdrawal in itself that is escapist, but the failure to return.

This James himself recognized. It is not an accident, for example, that the famous nightmare he recorded in *A Small Boy and Others* became for him a paradigmatic crisis of retreat and counterattack repeated in various guises in his fiction. In that nightmare, the reader will remember, the dreaming James, pursued and appalled by some dim malign figure, at first tries to escape by locking himself in a room and holding the barred door against his assailant; but in a sudden moment of "life-saving energy," he finds himself forcing the door outward and rushing forth to witness his pursuer in retreat—"routed, dismayed, the tables turned upon him." Moreover the scene of this triumph, the dreamer discovers, is the glorious hall of the Galerie d'Apollon in the Louvre, another palace of art. The reversal situation of the dream, as Quentin Anderson notes, is clearly repeated in "The Jolly Corner." [79] It receives another variation in *The Sense of the Past,* where Ralph Pendrell, succumbing to the "charm of isolation and enclosure" [80] offered by his newly inherited London mansion, finds his way back into another century only to suffer the horror from which he is saved by Nan's sacrifice. In *The Portrait of a Lady,* the retreat of Isabel Archer to Gardencourt and her decisive return to Italy and the burden of her moral commitments there provides one more instance. But of all James's works, it is *The Golden Bowl* that stages the drama of withdrawal and return to humanity in the setting of the country house itself. Maggie Verver's charitable and courageous *volte-face* in pursuit of Charlotte at Fawns allows the palace of art and the house of life to merge as one.

❧ 2 ❧

Disputed Heritage

THE EDWARDIANS AND THE COUNTRY HOUSE:

Wells, Forster, Galsworthy, Ford

---

*The changing of the old order in country manors
and mansions may be slow or sudden, may have
many issues romantic or otherwise, its romantic
issues being not necessarily restricted to a change
back to the original order; though this admissable
instance appears to have been the only romance
formerly recognized by novelists as possible in
the case.*

Thomas Hardy, Preface to *A Laodicean*

As an American, James found in the country house a kind of platonic archetype which, despite his perceptiveness about the more disquieting actualities of English society, he managed to raise to an imaginative realm of being above the vicissitudes and erosions of history. His younger contemporaries in the Edwardian era, however, possessed a more troubling awareness of historical and social change: for them, the sense of the past was forced to contend with the nagging sense of the present. Novelists like H. G. Wells, John Galsworthy, Ford Madox Ford, and E. M. Forster display, therefore—each in his own way—a genuine sociological concern with the transformations taking place in English institutions, mores, and national character. Indeed, Ford —when discussing his motives for undertaking the series of novels known today as *Parade's End*—stated quite clearly that he "wanted the Novelist to appear in his really proud position as historian of his own time." It is this view of the novelist as social historian in a rather explicit sense that helps to distinguish the Edwardians from Henry James on one hand and the novelists of the twenties on the other; and that explains their impulse for combining, somewhat unevenly, the symbolic and the literal, the satirical and the documentary.[1]

Indeed, while recognizing the obvious differences in personal tone and literary quality, one may note how frequently these novelists converge upon the same contemporary problems and explore themes which, if not actually identical, complement each other in some significant way. In doing so, moreover, they practice what Richard Ellmann considers the typical Edwardian literary tactic of giving "some single unifying event or object, some external symbol" a "public quality" by measuring a whole society in its terms.[2] Consider, for example, the possible correlations between *Howards End* (1910) and some other Edwardian works. Lionel Trilling has called *Howards End* a novel about England's fate, observing that its symbol for England is the house named in the title and that its plot raises the question "Who shall inherit England?"[3] Forster's novel is not singular in this but rather exemplary: the novels of Wells, Galsworthy, and Ford also imply the question, "Who shall inherit England?"—or, at least: "What is England? What has England become? What

should England become?" Nor is Forster alone in employing a
house as the symbolic focus of his theme: Galsworthy, in fact,
titled one of his novels *The Country House* (1907); and Wells
in *Tono-Bungay* (1909) made Bladesover estate the key for understanding the hierarchical structure of English society. More
often than James, however, these novelists saw the house not
above but within the flux of contemporary history, responding
uncertainly to the currents and eddies of the new century.

It was almost inevitable that they should, since the diagnosis
of these forces was a major preoccupation of the period. In 1909,
for example, C. F. G. Masterman, the Liberal politician, published a dismaying social commentary, *The Condition of England,* to remind his readers that they were living in a world
where the "one single system of traditional hierarchy" had
"fissured into a thousand diversified channels . . . and every
variety of vigour, somnolence, and decay." And this, he also
emphasized, raised another problem: namely, "the difficulty of
ascertaining where the essential nation resides: what spirit and
temper, in what particular class or locality, will stand to the
future for twentieth-century England." Today, in fact, Masterman's book reads like an elucidation of the recurring themes of
the Edwardian novelists.[4] Making explicit what Galsworthy,
Forster, and Ford attempt to render through character, situation,
and symbol, Masterman dwells upon the social disorientation
resulting from the triumph of the middle-class ethos, the increasing commercialization and vulgarization of nearly all aspects
of daily life, the shift from a traditional sense of aristocratic
obligation to the pursuit of irresponsible leisure, the passing
away of the English peasantry and the consequent decline of
rural life, the spoliation of the countryside itself through the
encroachment of the suburban villa and the invasion of the new
motor cars from the city.

And among all the symptoms of a changing order, Masterman
dwells most intently upon the decay and sale of the ancient
houses of England. "In many of the home counties," he observes, "the bulk of the older estates have passed into the hands
of the 'new wealth,' the plutocracy which looks for its consum-
mation in ownership of a portion of the land of England." Some
of the new proprietors, he is willing to admit,

are assiduous in rural welfare: some have taken over what remains of the feudal tradition as a "going concern" . . . and exercise the ample bestowal of patronage, and all the manifold energies which flow from the great house into the surrounding countryside. There are some also who introduce a breath of fresh air—even an unashamed Democratic spirit—into the somewhat heavy atmosphere of the remoter regions of rural England.

But to others among these newcomers, he laments,

all this is frankly a toy and a plaything. They have purchased an estate, as they would purchase food and raiment, for the purpose of enjoyment. They convert the house into a tiny piece of the city, transplanted to the happier air of the fields. They entertain themselves and their friends in the heart of England, for whose vanishing traditions and enthusiasms they care not at all.[5]

From Masterman's remarks—and similar ones by others might easily be added—we may conclude that the gravitation of a number of Edwardian novelists toward the country house for their themes and symbolism was neither arbitrary nor coincidental. In a changing world, the country house offered to some, like Wells and Galsworthy, the possibility of dramatizing the failures of a whole social order; for others, like Forster and Ford, it provided an emblem of what might be restored or at least a clue to what might be conserved.

In their response to the historical situation, these Edwardian novelists were actually returning to the more traditional modes of the seventeenth-century poets and eighteenth-century novelists who, prompted by similar motives, also employed the country house to express their apprehensions about radical social change. In fact, Edwardian fiction revives, whether intentionally or not, many of the techniques and motifs found in the literary treatments of the country house during previous periods (see Appendix A). For example, when E. M. Forster in *Howards End* describes how the garage of the Wilcoxes damages the roots of the wych elm tree, he is not only responding to a society in which traditional vital forms are endangered by the mechanizations of finance capitalism; he is also using a motif of "improvements" that can be traced back to Jane Austen and Scott and, beyond them, to Smollett. So, too, when Ford signals the end of an order with the cutting down of the great tree at Groby, he uses a traditional means of indicating the truncation of an organic society. In *Tono-Bungay* even H. G. Wells, perhaps without realizing it, takes up the familiar motif of contrasting houses to illustrate the differences between the old-style gentry and the new. All this is not to deny that the Edwardians faced a critical and far-reaching social crisis but merely to recognize that their intentions and literary strategies were not without precedents.

The general context established, we may turn to their variations.

Of all the Edwardians, Wells was the least interested in symbolism. "I am a journalist," he declared, almost impertinently, to his more literary confreres. "I refuse to play the 'artist.' " [6] And the notorious *Boon,* along with some of the letters exchanged with James, clarifies his distinction with an obtuseness, even a show of bad manners, that makes painful rereading today. Even from a literary point of view, therefore, Wells could not be expected to find in the country house the rich symbolic overtones so appealing to James. Yet for this very reason, perhaps, his portrayal of Bladesover in *Tono-Bungay* is illuminating for the study of the country house in modern fiction. "An anatomist of the Edwardian social order," [7] Wells moves toward the large sociological generalization; thus, in approaching the house, he extends what others assume or suggest.

Moreover, if his impulse for sociology dilutes the possibilities of symbolism, we are always aware that it is the sociology, not of the detached, bloodless observer, but of one profoundly involved with the object he dissects. "Bladesover," we are told by George Ponderevo, the narrator of *Tono-Bungay,* "is the clue to almost all that is distinctively British and perplexing to the foreign inquirer in England" (*TB,* p. 15). But the observation, not remarkably original in itself, acquires emotional force when the evidence to support it is drawn from the mixed impressions of Wells's own boyhood experiences. As Wells admitted in his autobiography, Bladesover is really a picture of Up Park, the aristocratic household where his mother, Sara Wells, was employed as a housekeeper, and where he was permitted to stay off and on in his youth.

From one point of view, Up Park possesses an atmosphere and a history that would have engaged the imagination of James himself. Built in the late seventeenth century to the designs of William Talman, it stands on the Sussex Downs overlooking the Channel and is considered by Peter Quennell one of the most beautiful houses of its kind still existing in England.[8] The ancestral home of the Fetherstonhaughs, Up Park was inherited by Sir Henry Fetherstonhaugh, an aristocrat who might have been drawn by Richardson. As a young blood, he counted among his mistresses a girl who was to become infamous some time later as Nelson's Lady Hamilton; in his later years, he married a pretty housemaid who—like her fictional prototype, Pamela—had apparently resisted his less conventional advances on the backstairs. They had no children, so that after the death of the couple, the great house ironically passed to Lady Fetherstonhaugh's maiden sister, who had been living with them. This other country girl, taking the noble name of Fetherstonhaugh for herself, now reigned alone over stately Up Park. In 1880 she called back Sara Wells, her favorite maid, as housekeeper.[9]

Wells's own experiences at Up Park, however, were hardly those to prompt either a Jamesian nostalgia or a Jamesian irony. The son of a servant, Wells saw the life of the great house from "below stairs." How humiliating and frustrating this was for the individualistic young man the somewhat reticent autobiography never really makes clear; but if we accept Gordon Ray's view of George Ponderevo as "practically Wells's *alter ego*," we can see that he must have constantly smarted under the reminders of his station and "place." This, of course, can be sentimentally overstated, as it is in Horace Gregory's remark that Wells's "place was so 'low' that the loveliest, broadest landscape turned to desert." Peter Quennell is more perceptive when he observes that the early life of Wells in the great house—and "its associations, if not with servitude, at least with the idea of social inferiority and economic helplessness"—probably bred in him a psychological opposition to certain forms of beauty and exaggerated a detectable strain of philistinism: "Symmetry and form were associated in his mind with the vision of Up Park, its graceful portions, its harmonious setting, and what he denied himself, he tended to distrust in others." [10]

On the other hand, to overlook what was of positive value for Wells during his visits to Up Park not only misrepresents the case but may preclude a proper understanding of the function of Bladesover in *Tono-Bungay*. Again, as Wells tells us in the autobiography, the fact that his mother became a housekeeper helped him to make a new start in life by saving him from becoming a draper's apprentice; and the visits with her allowed by Miss Fetherstonhaugh gave him sufficient freedom to take advantage of what Up Park offered to his curiosity. He wandered through its park and grounds, rummaged in an attic housing volumes of Italian engravings, experimented with a telescope, and above all borrowed books from Sir Harry's eighteenth-century library. "For me at any rate," he admits, "the house at Up Park was alive and potent. The place had a great effect upon me; it retained a vitality that altogether overshadowed the insignificant ebbing trickle of upstairs life" (*EA*, pp. 105–06). And, passing from his personal experiences to historical generalization, Wells places the country house exemplified in Up Park among the great cultural institutions of Europe:

Now it is one of my firmest convictions that modern civilization was begotten and nursed in the households of the prosperous, relatively independent people, the minor nobility, the gentry, and the larger bourgeoisie, which became visibly important in the landscape of the sixteenth century, introducing new architectural elements in the towns, and spreading as country houses and chateaux and villas over the continually more orderly countryside. Within these households, behind their screen of deer park and park wall and sheltered service, men could talk, think and write at their leisure. . . . The management of their estates kept them in touch with reality making exhaustive demands on their time. Many, no doubt, degenerated into a life of easy dignity or gentlemanly vice, but quite a sufficient number remained curious and interested to make, foster, and protect the accumulating science and literature, of the seventeenth and eighteenth centuries. Their large rooms, their libraries, their collections of pictures and "curios" retained in the nineteenth century an atmosphere of unhurried liberal inquiry, of serene and determined insubordination and personal dignity, of established aesthetic and intellectual standards. [*EA,* pp. 104–05]

Furthermore, even in its decline the country house remained for Wells, as it did for James, an image of human possibilities. "The new creative forces," he continues,

have long since overflowed these first nests in which they were hatched and for the most part the European country houses and chateaux that were so alive and germinal in the seventeenth and eighteenth centuries, stand now mere empty shells, resorts for week-end gatherings and shooting parties, but no longer real dwelling places, gracefully and hospitably in decay. Yet there still lingers something of that former importance and largeness in outlook, on their walls and hangings and furnishings, if not in their attenuated social life. [*EA,* p. 105]

Such reflections reveal that Wells's relation to Up Park was much more complicated than critics like Gregory and even Quennell seem to suggest and that, in writing *Tono-Bungay,* Wells was drawing upon his experience of a great country house not simply for the raw material of situation and setting but for thematic perspective as well. The novel represents the outrageous career of George's uncle, Edward Ponderevo—provincial chemist, purveyor of quack medicine, and financial adventurer. Yet it is not his story alone. Conceived, in Wells's own words, "as a social panorma in the vein of Balzac" (*EA,* p. 423), *Tono-Bungay* attempts to portray the disintegration of English society resulting from both the disruptive forms of finance capitalism gone wild and the decay of the old landed aristocracy. Bladesover, the house and estate of Lady Drew—obviously embodying the mixed reactions of Wells to Up Park—functions both as a representation of a moribund system and, paradoxically, as a community of values in counterpoint to those of the newly emerging world of Edward Ponderevo.

Consequently, the opening chapters about Bladesover, seemingly digressive at first, are an integral part of the novel. Like the beginning of *Great Expectations*—a novel which *Tono-Bungay* seems to echo at times—they reveal through the humiliations of a young boy the oppressive character of the class system about him; but unlike Dickens's Pip, George, the son of the housekeeper, is not so interested in narrating the immediate experiences of his childhood as in recording his mature reflections about his early social world. The "Bladesover system," he tells us, appeared a "complete authentic microcosm" and enabled him to understand much that would be otherwise "absolutely incomprehensible in the structure of English society" (*TB*, pp. 7, 15). The wide park and the fair large house suggested hierarchical status: "They represented the Gentry, the Quality, by and through and for whom the rest of the world, the farming folk and the laboring folk, the tradespeople . . . and the upper servants and the lower servants, breathed and lived and were permitted" (*TB*, p. 8). The very architectural details reinforced his awareness of social gradations; he remembers the way "the great house mingled so solidly and effectually with earth and sky" and the "contrast of its spacious hall and salon and galleries, its airy housekeeper's room and warren of offices with the meagre dignities of the vicar, and the stuffy rooms of even the post-office people and the grocer" (*TB*, p. 8–9). With some relish for its absurdities, he recalls the sense of rank that made even the servant's hall a replica of the remote world of the masters above stairs. Above all, he remembers the bitterness of his boy's love for little Beatrice Normandy, who, while a guest of Lady Drew, first encouraged and then betrayed him. "The son of a servant," he observes, "counts as a servant" (*TB*, p. 39).

Yet at the same time George does not deny that his familiarity with the house was a fine thing for him. "Bladesover," he admits, like Wells himself, "had not altogether missed greatness." It had at least "abolished the peasant habit of mind" and cultivated the sensibility: "About the park there were some elements of a liberal education; there was a great space of greensward not given over to manure and good grubbing. . . . It was still a park of deer. I saw something of the life of these dappled creatures, heard the belling of stags, came upon young fawns in the bracken." And here, for once, George speaks with an almost Jamesian accent: "There was mystery, there was matter for the imagination . . . it was the first time that I knowingly met beauty" (*TB*, pp. 20–21).

Though Bladesover itself occupies only the first few chapters of *Tono-Bungay*, its image and implications are relevant to the rest of the novel. First of all, Bladesover explains much of what George later encounters in London and elsewhere in England. Walking about the West End, he realizes that with Bladesover in mind he holds the key to the hierarchical layout of the city and to the architecture of its buildings. The great residences and parks reflect the spirit of the country estate; even Victorian middle-class homes, aping the great, also rise over servants' basements. The museums and libraries, George speculates, sprang from the cultured leisure of men of taste. Even when he reluctantly submits to his sweetheart's wish for a "proper" wedding in a London church, he finds the unnecessarily elaborate ritual still another attempt to keep up a Bladesover tradition in an impersonal urban context oblivious to its communal meaning.

Furthermore, as his involvement with his uncle's fraudulent but lucrative enterprises increasingly exposes to him the new social forces displacing the landed ruling class, George seems—in spite of his earlier rebellion—to consider Bladesover as a counter to the irresponsibility and vulgarity of the emerging plutocracy. In London itself, these new forces seem blind forces of invasion, of cancerous growth. The "great stupid rusty iron of Charing Cross station," the factory chimneys smoking right over Westminster, "the huge dingy immensity of London port," all have the effect of "something morbidly expanded, without plan or intention, dark and sinister toward the clean clear social assurance of the West End" (*TB*, p. 98).[11]

More significantly, George sees the moral emptiness of his uncle's inflated dreams in the series of houses he occupies in his swift rise to power. From the shabby provincial lodgings of Camden Town to ornate Crest Hill, each marks a stage of social ascent and moral decline. The big gaunt villa at Beckenham offers only the opportunity of greater social pretension through playing out "with the assistance of novels and illustrated magazines" a surburban version of aristocratic life. The more luxurious Chiselhurst mansion, with its "grounds" rather than mere gardens, becomes a storehouse, which his uncle's new passion for shopping fills with clocks, pictures, and "old things." ("I doubt if Lady Drew and the Olympians did that sort of thing," George muses, "but here I may be only clinging to another of my former illusions about the aristocracy," *TB*, p. 252.) In contrast the next dwelling, Lady Grove, a beautiful, lordly house, with chivalric, Catholic traditions reaching back to the Crusades, still manifests an authentic nobility that makes the presence of his acquisitive uncle, a "man of luck and advertisement" (*TB*, p. 276), absurdly incongruous. To George, the very portraits of its extinguished family—enigmatic, invincibly complacent—seems to reprove: "It was just as though, after all, he had *not* bought and replaced them altogether; as though that, secretly, they knew better and could smile at him. . . ." More in keeping, therefore, with Edward Ponderevo's sense of style, and farthest from the balanced good taste of Bladesover, is of course Crest Hill: This mammoth edifice—hatched in his uncle's brain as a truly "twentieth-century house," ridiculously out of scale with human needs and values, demanding the energies of three thousand workmen yet ironically left unfinished—remains an architectural abortion, a symbol of not only his uncle alone but also the spurious, ignoble ethos he personifies.

Throughout the novel, therefore, Bladesover provides a perspective on the changes in modern society that would otherwise be lacking, since it represents, as Masterman noted in his own references to *Tono-Bungay*, "a civilization which could be approved or condemned, but which at least was a coherent thing— a rule of life, a code of conduct, an organic society." [12] Wells's novel, however, is not a study in static contrasts between the traditional and the modern, between the ordered and the anarchic. As Kenneth B. Newell observes, its basic structure is really based on the idea of change; a dominant metaphor is the life cycle of the organism, of its growth and decline; disease imagery manifests the decay investing all elements of British society.[13] Even the world of Bladesover does not escape this decay. Toward the end of the novel George describes England as "a feudal scheme overtaken by fatty degeneration and stupendous accidents of hypertrophy" (*TB,* p. 396). Beatrice, its feminine embodiment, reappears as "a sick and tired woman," physically and morally empty (*TB,* p. 388). "One gets bored," she explains to George, "bored beyond redemption. One goes about to these huge expensive houses I suppose—the scale's immense. . . . They go about making love. Everybody's making love. I did" (*TB,* p. 383).

Bladesover itself, like the other country houses in the novel, is also rented out to parvenu. And on his last view of the house, George feels that everything seems to have "shivered and shrivelled" at the touch of the new occupants. The brown eighteenth-century volumes are gone from the library, replaced by "new books in gaudy catchpenny 'artistic' covers"; the new mistress "collects" china cats, and a great number of specimens "stand about everywhere in all kinds of deliberately comic, highly glazed distortions." To the reader, it is as though James's Poynton has been turned into Waterbath: "There was the trail of the Bond Street showroom over it all" (*TB,* p. 62).

Nonetheless, ambivalence remains. George's severest judgment is reserved for this "meretricious gentry," and the basis for his verdict is the disparity between them and the true aristocrat:

> It is nonsense to pretend that finance makes any better aristocrats than rent. Nothing can make an aristocrat but pride, knowledge, training, and the sword. These people were no improvement on the Drews, none whatever. . . . I do not believe in their intelligence or their power—they have nothing about them at all, nothing creative or rejuvenescent. . . . They could not have made Bladesover, they cannot replace it; they just happen to break over it—saprophytically. [*TB,* pp. 62–63]

Elsewhere George also claims that "everybody who is not actually in the shadow of Bladesover is as it were perpetually seeking after lost orientations" (*TB,* p. 15). The only new orientation he finds affirmative for himself is science; but the unintentional irony of the conclusion of the novel, as Mark Schorer points out, is that scientific knowledge and power are summed up in a destroyer. Actually, *Tono-Bungay* would have greater structural and thematic coherence if Wells had dramatized more forcibly in his ending the tragedy involved in the decline of Bladesover—not as a social system, but as an embodiment of certain laudable aesthetic and humane values.[14]

About the significance of Bladesover, Wells—or, at least, his narrator—is often explicit to the point of being rather obvious; through George's talk, as Tindall observes, what begins as novel threatens to become essay.[15] In contrast, the house in Forster's *Howards End* functions as a symbol resonant with unstated meanings and attended by such images as tree, hay, motor car, and city flat. In some respects Forster is thus closer to James than to Wells; indeed, certain parallels between *Howards End* and *The Spoils of Poynton* suggest that he may very well have taken a hint from the American novelist: in both novels, not only are houses the major symbols, but a basic plot element involves an older woman, deeply committed to her home as a very special kind of place, finding in a young girl who is a stranger the responsive sensibility that makes her its true spiritual heir and thus justifies her becoming the actual one as well; whatever the differences between Mrs. Gereth and Mrs. Wilcox, between Fleda Vetch and Margaret Schlegel, their positions are remarkably similar.[16]

On the other hand, Forster does resemble Wells in being very much aware of the relation of his house to the specific local circumstances of a changing England, and throughout the novel he too is quite explicit about them in his essaylike asides. True, Howards End is not the patrician estate of Bladesover; but as a traditional home of rural England, it also stands in counterpoint to the commercial and urban forces of disruption. Forster's Wilcoxes, admittedly, are not identical with Edward Ponderevo and his like, with the monopolists and the advertisers; but they move in the same rootless ambience, one of money, social climbing, expensive hotels, and new-bought country houses. This is not to identify *Howards End* and *Tono-Bungay;* rather, it is to recognize that "placing" the two together as Edwardian novels helps to illuminate each one.

In this connection it is of interest that Forster during his early years was also personally involved with the houses that took on profound meaning for him, and that he has given his autobiographical reflections about them. In his life of Marianne Thornton, the great aunt whose bequest of money made Cambridge and a writing career possible for him, Forster significantly presents the biography of a house as well as a person. The house is Battersea Rise, the home of the Thorntons in Clapham Common from the late eighteenth to the mid-nineteenth century. This house became for him, as Trilling notes, "the prototype of all consecrated houses." [17] Though he barely remembers his visit there as a small boy, Forster writes that, to the family, "it was a perfect playground and in after years a sacred shrine." And he adds a pointed observation of his own:

It satisfied in them that longing for a particular place, a home, which is common amongst our upper and middle classes, and some of them transmitted that longing to their descendants, who have lived into an age where it cannot be gratified. There will never be another Battersea Rise, and the modest imitations of it which lasted into the present century and became more and more difficult to staff have also disappeared. [*MT*, p. 5]

Furthermore, when he records the disposition of the family after Henry Thornton's elopement in 1852, he is again autobiographical:

Their outlook wavered; they did not know whether they wished Henry to return at once or after an interval or never. They did not know whether they wished the house to be sold and to vanish off the spiritual face of the earth, or to stand as it was, an empty and dishonored shell. I understand many of their feelings: it has so happened that I have been deprived of a house myself. This will not be understood by the present generation. [*MT*, p. 205]

Finally, he tells us in the same volume of his affection for the Hertfordshire home of his childhood and of his using it as a model for Howards End:

> It certainly was a lovable little house, and still is, though now it stands just outside a twentieth-century hub and almost within sound of a twentieth-century hum. The garden, the overhanging wych elm, the sloping meadow, the great view to the west, the cliff of fir trees to the north, the adjacent farm through the high tangled hedge of wild roses were all utilized by me in *Howards End,* and the interior is in the novel too. . . . I took it to my heart and hoped, as Marianne Thornton had of Battersea Rise, that I should live and die there. We were out of it in ten years. [*MT,* p. 301]

Despite this loss, Forster's boyhood in the Hertfordshire house, like the rather different experiences of young Wells at Up Park, made for a point of view of later consequence to fiction. "The impressions received there remained and still glow," Forster concludes, "and have given me a slant upon society and history" (*MT,* p. 301).

Against this background, his employment of the house as symbol is obviously not fortuitous. Indeed, Howards End itself is simply the most outstanding of a number of houses in his work. As Don Austin has demonstrated in some detail, both Windy Corner in *A Room With a View* and Cadover in *The Longest Journey* also function as symbols of continuity, transferring to responsive members of a new generation the powers of renewal they mystically possess. Windy Corner appears "as a beacon in the roaring tide of darkness"; and it always seems to offer its occupants the possibility of restored communion: "So the grittiness went out of life. It generally did at Windy Corner. At the last minute, when the social machine was hopelessly clogged, one member or another of the family poured in a drop of oil." At Cadover, Stephen Wonham feels a true sense of being at home, even in his uncomfortable attic room: "Here he lived absolutely happy, and unaware that Mrs. Failing had poked him up here on purpose, to prevent him from growing too bump-

tious. Here he worked and sang and practiced on the ocha-
roon." [18]

A later and admittedly slighter work, *England's Pleasant Land*
(1938), surveying a thousand years of history since Norman times,
celebrates the pastoral contentment that once existed when the
manor house, village, and countryside formed one true community. "The Lord is strong," the commentator asserts about
England's great days, "because he has his villages, the villagers
are strong because they have their Lord." Forster finds "a genuine and tragic theme" in the destruction of the countryside
through enclosure, irresponsible squirearchy, impoverishment of
the villager, and the arrival of the automobile. And "The Abinger Pageant" (1952) raises the same issue. "Houses and bungalows,
hotels, restaurants, arterial roads, by-passes, petrol pumps and
pylons," the epilogue asks, "are these going to be England? Are
these man's final triumph?" These last reveal, moreover, how
persistent Forster's preoccupation has been with the deeper
effects of seemingly superficial, newfangled changes. As Virginia
Woolf discerned, he was so inclined to see his characters at the
mercy of those conditions that change with the years that "the
social historian will find his books full of illuminating information." [19]

Among all these English houses of Forster, Howards End is,
of course, the richest symbol. Differences among critics, rather
than cancelling each other, have only helped to establish its
fecundity. Trilling, as we noted above, has identified Howards
End with England; it is that and more. Through its natural
setting, its relation to the surrounding hayfield and lovely old
wych elm, the house also represents "the Earth as a way of life"
and the "vital past of England." As Frederick Crews has noted,
it also "apparently stands for the integrated family life that
was led there by Ruth Wilcox and is to be continued by Margaret." From still another point of view, it suggests the possible
reconciliation between the potentially antagonistic sexual forces
of the masculine and feminine natures: "I suppose that ours is a
female house," Margaret declares early in the novel, but muses
differently later at Howards End: "House and tree transcended

any similes of sex . . . to compare either to man, to woman, always dwarfed the vision" (*HE,* pp. 51, 236). Indeed, there are metaphysical implications as well, if we agree with Crews that Howards End is "an emblem for Forster's ideal of harmony between the spiritual and the physical." [20]

Furthermore, Howards End is a symbol which integrates nearly every component of the novel—its plot, characters, theme, and imagery. The house is named in the very title. Already on the first page, before the story is under way or the characters really introduced, the place is described, "old and little and delightful," in Helen's letter to her sister Margaret (*HE,* pp. 7–8). Forster himself has defined the action of the novel as "a hunt for a home" [21]—and this way of looking at it not only clarifies the entanglements and the coincidences of the plot, but also reminds us that Howards End—the true home, epitomizing social, historical, and cosmic community—remains central even when not immediately present. Structurally, moreover, Howards End is the positive thread in a series of interwoven contrasts that run throughout: between country and city; between an almost Wordsworthian feeling for nature and an Arnoldian sense of the "strange disease of modern life, / With its sick hurry and divided aims"; between the organic world of ancient landscape and the threatening, mechanistic world of motor cars, garages, and telegrams; between rural England, with its stabilizing sense of place and history, and the "nomadic civilization" materializing in early twentieth-century London, with its new flats and "architecture of hurry" (*HE,* pp. 298, 125).[22] Above all, Howards End becomes the criterion for assessing characters representative of contrasting qualities of being.

The major contrast among the characters is, of course, between Mrs. Wilcox and the rest of her family, particularly her husband, Henry. Howards End, even as property, belongs to Mrs. Wilcox; but from her first appearance it is obvious that she, in turn, belongs to the spiritual ambience of Howards End. In Helen's opening letter, Mrs. Wilcox is before the house, first tending the garden and later coming from the meadow, her arms full of hay. She worships the past, we are told elsewhere, and possesses the "instinctive wisdom the past alone can bestow

—that wisdom to which we give the clumsy name of aristocracy" (*HE*, p. 28). In London, conversely, the clever talk of the young alarms her: "It was the social counterpart of a motorcar" (*HE*, p. 86). Still, her deep, intuitive feeling for others prevents Mrs. Wilcox from dividing the generations. "We are all in the same boat, old and young," she confides. "I never forget that" (*HE*, p. 91). And when Margaret is forced to leave her home in Wickham Place, Mrs. Wilcox is almost hysterically sympathetic: "To be parted from your father's house—it oughtn't to be allowed." For behind her emotion is her own profound sense of place: "Can what they call civilization be right, if people mayn't die in the room where they were born?" (*HE*, p. 96).

To the realm of value represented by Mrs. Wilcox and Howards End, the rest of her family remain blindly obtuse. Efficient masters of the world of motorcars and telegrams but imaginatively impoverished, the male Wilcoxes are prototypes —like Galsworthy's Forsytes—of the urban middle classes that have "accreted possessions without taking roots in the earth" (*HE*, p. 171). Really more at ease in a London flat, they regard Howards End simply as property rather than a home. Though shocked by Mrs. Wilcox's last wish to leave the place to Margaret —"they could not know that to her it had been a spirit, to which she sought a spiritual heir" (*HE*, p. 114)—the Wilcoxes decide against keeping it as a family home for themselves and, without any sense of loss, they rent it out. Moreover, even when Henry later traces the history of Howards End for Margaret, he prosaically confines himself to an account of its mortgages and mismanagement (*HE*, pp. 235–36). It is no accident, consequently, that upon returning there with Margaret he should find that he is missing the key or that in its fields he should be plagued with hayfever.

Margaret, on the other hand, the character who comes closest to being the "central intelligence" of the novel, moves from London to Howards End, both literally and metaphorically: first by her brief and intimate association with Mrs. Wilcox and later through her marriage to Henry. Under the influence of the older woman, Margaret begins to see London as "Satanic" (*HE*, p. 98); and when her family home at Wickham Place is destroyed to make room for flats, she appreciates Mrs. Wilcox's sense of place all the more. "Houses are alive," she now tells the practical Henry (*HE*, p. 177). On her first visit to Howards End, moreover, Margaret glories in the spell of the place while it in turn seems to submit to her: when Henry goes off in search of the key, the door opens to her hand; old Mrs. Avery even takes Margaret for Mrs. Wilcox herself. And it is Margaret who points out to Henry the pigs' teeth in the wych elm, which Mrs. Wilcox told her possessed curative powers, but which the rest of the family have never noticed.[23]

Finally, it is Howards End, of course, that brings the novel to a close by serving as the symbolic stage where reconciliations may take place: between Margaret and her estranged sister Helen, between Margaret and her husband.[24] There, too, the remaining imbalances of the story are leveled off: Margaret is to have Howards End after all, just as Mrs. Wilcox intended; indeed, she now learns of that intention. The infant son of Helen and the hapless Leonard Bast, who died under the threat of a sword and beneath a fallen bookcase, will be next in line as its heir. "I feel that our house is the future as well as the past," exclaims Margaret in summation (*HE*, p. 389).

Admittedly, in a novel displaying such intelligence and irony, this ending may seem to leave the scales too evenly balanced for some readers; the conclusion, they may feel with Trilling, offers a "rather contrived scene of busyness and contentment in the hayfield." To do justice to Forster, however, we should take note of his own second thoughts about his early novels. "As for the ends of *The Longest Journey* and *Howards End*," he has recently remarked, "they are certainly unsatisfactory, but perhaps were less so at the time. Then the English countryside, its reality and creative retreat into it, were more plausible than they are today." And in any case, as another critic maintains, the novel does not imply that Howards End itself is an unthreatened shelter; enough is said about the encroaching suburban tides to suggest that it may be only a temporary one. This very precariousness makes Howards End a symbol that remains apposite to the present age: it is a "fortress against forces which are always in danger of swamping the values which it protects." [25]

Passing from Wells and Forster to Galsworthy, the reader is stuck by the way parallels and differences jostle each other for his attention. The parallels, it is true, essentially result from the preoccupation of these authors with the problems of a changing society; the differences are often large: differences in temperament, imagination, and literary quality; but such differences along with the parallels make them instructively complementary.

Resemblances between Galsworthy and Forster are mainly resemblances in theme or at least intention.[26] Certainly, what Galsworthy expressed about his aims might apply to Forster's. His subject was, he noted, the "spiritual limitation" of the upper classes. "I have no animus against any class," he went on, "except that unconscious and most potent of all animi which inhabits every mind which longs to understand and feel with all other minds, and chafes against barriers and humbug and the manifold forms of Pharisaism." [27] Affinities between Galsworthy and Wells are even stronger. Both of them saw the novel not primarily as an aesthetic form but as a vehicle for rather explicit social criticism. Though with less grasp of the workings of society than Wells, Galsworthy also attempted his own Balzacian panorama and pathology. Rather schematically, he produced a series of novels—including *The Man of Property* (1906), *The Country House* (1907), and *The Patricians* (1911)—with the intention of diagnosing, as their respective titles indicate, the middle class, the gentry, and the aristocracy. They are uneven novels at best; but taken together, they do form a social composite analogous to that found in Wells's book. More important for our purposes, all three—like *Tono-Bungay* and *Howard's End*—bring the reader back to the country house as a center of focus.

Paradoxically, Galsworthy, who was probably more at home in the country-house world than other Edwardian authors, often found there much more to criticize and far less to admire. Again, the explanation is mainly biographical. Though his portrayal of the Forsytes inevitably associates him with prosperous middle-class London, his personal background reveals other social ties relevant to his fiction. Son of a solicitor and grandson of a merchant, Galsworthy—like his Forsytes—traced his paternal forebears to small farmers who had lived in Devon since the sixteenth century. On the other hand his mother, Blanche Bailey Bartlett, was—in his words—"absolutely of the provincial squire class." [28] His boyhood home was not in London but in Surrey, where his father had built Coombe Warren, a solid Victorian house looking across the North Downs toward the Epsom grandstand, which could just be seen. Coombe Warren—or at least the setting and the grounds—was in fact Galsworthy's model for Robin Hill, the country place built by Soames Forsyte. Moreover, despite the fact that his family might be termed *nouveau riche,* Galsworthy himself was educated in the conventions of more securely established members of the English upper class. A rather typical public school boy at Harrow and a foppish undergraduate at Oxford, he became a guest at various country houses. He knew, as Edward Garnett's criticism of *The Patricians* once forced him to insist, a good many English noblemen. Throughout his life, his personal tastes and habits remained those of an English country gentleman—simple leisure, sports, riding, uncomplicated enjoyment of the natural landscape.[29]

For all his criticism, therefore, Galsworthy's unconscious sympathies responded to this world. Indeed, he was aware of his own divided loyalties: his books, as he once candidly admitted to Garnett, were not really "social criticism" at all but "spiritual examination"—simply "the criticism of one half of myself by the other half, the halves being differently divided according to the subject." [30] Unfortunately, however, this ambivalence did not lead Galsworthy to anything like the transcendent symbolism of James or the broad social perspective of Wells. It simply remained something personal. Today the primary reason for this is more clearly understood: Galsworthy had only one basic complaint against society that involved his whole being, and that was the needless suffering that its hypocritical codes and pitiless divorce laws inflicted upon his wife Ada and himself before they could be married. Galsworthy fell in love with Ada while she was married to his cousin, Arthur Galsworthy, whom she found incompatible. Out of consideration for John's father they did not elope but were forced to carry on a clandestine love affair. Only after his death did they expose themselves to the then inhuman proceedings of a divorce trial. This near-traumatic experience helped to transform young Galsworthy from a fox hunter and clubman into a liberal-minded novelist with a genuine subject. Indeed, it provided what was to become the basic plot of his major novels. Imaginatively limited, Galsworthy, as Woodburn O. Ross has pointed out, "learned to ring changes, for the most part, on one situation, the marriage-triangle in which one partner had some justification for infidelity." [31] Apart from this personal motive for social criticism, Galsworthy really did not have very much to say, despite the ambitious literary project he set for himself. The plot situation he repeatedly and sentimentally derived from his own experience lacked the powdercharge that the declared range of his fiction required.

All this is particularly evident in *The Country House*, an almost documentary treatment of the squire in his local habitat.[32] Life at Worsted Skeynes, the ancestral home of the Pendyces, is explicitly described as representative, "Nothing out of the common; the same thing was happening in hundreds of country houses throughout the 'three kingdoms'" (*CH*, p. 53). If Henry James seems charmed by the beauty of the country house in solitary repose, Galsworthy is equally taken by the folkways of the gentry. A typical shooting party, Sunday breakfast and churchgoing, a horse race, and a country dance are presented with an almost anthropological thoroughness. His obvious intention is to satirize the unthinking conformity to ancient custom. "At Worsted Skeynes," he declares, "there was but one set of people, one church, one pack of hounds, one everything" (*CH*, p. 136). But mixed with the anger is a good deal of relish, all the same. The open-air world of horses and dogs, the amenities of dining room and smoking den, the moods of the house itself with its almost conscious reflection of the changing times of the day—all seem to survive the irony to make an appeal of their own.

The plot itself, however, never really copes with this ambivalence. Turning on the commonplace love affair between George Pendyce, the heir of Worsted Skeynes, and the unhappily married Helen Bellew, then concentrating on the reactions of his father and various country types to the threatened scandal of divorce, the novel pursues an increasingly narrow course and one not always clearly relevant to any broad assessment of the country-house milieu introduced at first. True, the unsympathetic response of the squire to his son's romance is shown to be a reflex action, manifesting a mindless conservatism and a distrust of emotion often typical of the provincial gentry; but the temperamental reaction of the old man in this one family crisis does not by itself totally discredit him or his system, though Galsworthy explicitly and repeatedly insists that it does. Actually a number of the squire's positive values—which Galsworthy appears willing to admit though he never quite comes to terms with them—make the novelist's excessive, one-sided sympathy for the son seem schematic and sentimental. The squire, for example, is allowed to reveal a genuine sympathy for dumb animals, a code of duty, industry, and a deep-rooted, almost Forsterian sense of place. "The efforts of social man, directed from time immemorial towards the stability of things," Galsworthy even comments, "culminated in Worsted Skeynes. . . . There was another feeling in the squire's heart—the air and the woods and the fields had passed into his blood a love for this, his home and the home of his fathers" (*CH*, p. 141). In all this, however, the reader becomes aware of a good deal of inconsistency rather than a genuine, compelling ambivalence.

This confusion is also a reason why Galsworthy only half succeeds with one of his most interesting characters—Mrs. Pendyce, the squire's wife, whom even D. H. Lawrence, perhaps the best and certainly the severest critic of Galsworthy, found "lovable." [33] Remarkably similar to Mrs. Wilcox in some ways, Mrs. Pendyce is sensitive, maternal, curiously self-sufficient, endowed with the instinct of a lady: "So elastic and so subtle, so interwoven of consideration for others and consideration for herself, so old, so very old, this instinct wrapped her . . . like a suit of armour of the finest chain" (*CH*, p. 215). Like Mrs. Wilcox, she serves as a foil to her husband, whose unfeeling stubbornness she defies by leaving his house and going to the assistance of her son in London. It is her personal quality alone, moreover, that finally persuades Mrs. Bellew's husband to break off his divorce proceedings. "You're the only lady I know," he submits in explanation (*CH*, p. 196).

And yet in this characterization of Mrs. Pendyce, Galsworthy is still inconsistent or at least obscure. Unlike Mrs. Wilcox, who stands in a meaningful contrast to her husband because each represents a different class and a defined style of life, Mrs. Pendyce belongs to the same class Galsworthy would indict. It is true that toward the close of the novel he attempts to establish a social distinction between her and the squire by noting that she was originally a Totterbridge, an old family with an ancient home in Warwickshire. In her family line, we are told, "there was some freer strain, something non-provincial." The Pendyces, on the other hand, are decidedly a "county family"—"provincial in their souls" (*CH*, p. 227). But this interesting and perhaps valid gradation, introducing subtleties Galsworthy ignores elsewhere in the novel, comes to mean very little. In any event, by the close of *The Country House*, Mrs. Pendyce is happy to return to Worsted Skeynes. The solution of her son's problem and the avoidance of a scandal allows the novel to conclude. Nowhere does Galsworthy really intimate, as do Wells and Forster, that the country house is menaced by anything more unsettling than a son's romance and a divorce suit.

Ascending the social scale, Galsworthy next considered the aristocracy itself in *The Patricians*. Its house is, therefore, the considerably more stately mansion of Monkland Court, seat of the titled Caradocs, where the stables, the reader is told, are as large as many country houses. The very elevation of this stratum of power and authority might seem to promise that great social themes are to be now more thoroughly explored. The son of the house, Eustace Caradoc, Viscount Miltoun, is an aristocrat on the Disraelian pattern, who visualizes an England swept of "slums and plutocrats, advertisements and jerry-building, of sensationalism, vulgarity, vice, and unemployment . . . where every man from noble to labourer should be an oligarch by faith and a gentleman by practice" (*TP*, p. 79). He is contrasted on one hand with old Lord Dennis, who has little belief in any regeneration of the country by any means but kindly feelings between the classes, and on the other with a young radical named Courtier, who finds in the great house a "hopeless insulation from the vivid and necessitous sides of life" (*TP*, p. 173).

But in the end this novel's engagement with such serious choices and commitments turns out to be largely spurious. Like *The Country House, The Patricians* toys with the problems of society and then turns to a small domestic issue. Their plots are fundamentally the same: Lord Miltoun falls in love with a woman caught in a loveless marriage and his parliamentary career is threatened by scandal. When he gives her up because he cannot give up politics, it is explicitly stated that his choice reveals—in the words of Lord Dennis—"something dried up in all our caste" (*TP*, p. 317). True or not, this says very little about the larger issues the novel introduced; and in this small dénouement Monkland Court, some of whose virtues even the skeptical Courtier admitted, passes out of sight.

The plot of the marital triangle is found once again in the better-known novel *The Man of Property*, which was originally intended as a novel complete in itself and only later extended as *The Forsyte Saga* (1922). This time, the woman is Irene Forsyte, who, mismated with the middle-class Soames, finds herself in love with young Bosinney, his architect. Here, however, the familiar plot, too meager for carrying the burden of social meaning intended in the other novels, is highly suitable for the dissection of the middle class. Focusing on the husband as well as the lovers, the novel finds in the situation a revealing correspondence between the proprietary instinct he displays toward his own wife and the acquisitive ethos of a whole social class; indeed, Soames's sexual possession of his wife against her will unmasks the middle-class reduction of everything, even emotions and human beings, to the category of property.

In *The Man of Property*, therefore, the satire largely succeeds and Galsworthy lives up to his claim of having embalmed the upper middle class and preserving the sense of property in its own juice.[34] The customs of the Forsytes, documented with precision, becomes a definite source of irony and symbolism. Ritual dinners of champagne and mutton served under candle chandeliers bespeak their affluence and philistinism. Their table conversation, when not concerned with shares and furnishings, turns compulsively to the topic of health and doctors, giving hint—

like the disease in Mann's *Buddenbrooks*—of ebbing social power. Aging Forsytes crowd the pages, and the death of old Aunt Ann and the solemn funeral that concludes the first part of the novel seems to presage the end of the bourgeois epoch.

In this novel, too, the house plays a more definite symbolic role. Robin Hill—not a traditional country house at all but built to order like Crest Hill in *Tono-Bungay*—nonetheless becomes an image of value in contrast to the Forsyte world. Not as rich a symbol as Howards End, it has about the same function and for almost the same reasons. Much like the Wilcoxes, the Forsytes are most at home in the urban world of London. The "whole spirit of their success" is embodied in their townhouses, strategically deployed around Hyde Park, watching "like sentinels, lest the fair heart of London, where their desires were fixed, should slip from their clutches." But their urban achievements imply spiritual failure. Originally from farming stock in Dorsetshire, they have divided feelings about their country ancestors. "Yeoman—I suppose very small beer," old Jolyon surmises. Although an early Forsyte was a stonemason by trade and rose to be a master builder, "their inherited talent for bricks and mortar" now finds an outlet in acquisition rather than construction (*MP*, pp. 15–16). When young June, tired of London, asks her uncle why he cannot build country houses, he replies: "Buying land—what good d'you suppose I can do buying land, building houses? I couldn't get four per cent. for my money!" (*MP*, p. 41).

It is significant, therefore, that planning and building the house at Robin Hill forms the narrative backbone which joins the major characters and themes. Typical of his class, Soames Forsyte inhabits a pretentious London dwelling. Almost inexplicably, however, he begins to consider a country house. There is an interesting complex of motives: he wishes to take his wife away from people that only deepen her "subdued aversion" toward him; a true Forsyte, he also recognizes the possibilities of a first-class investment. But something more curious is at work, something atavistic that seems expressed in the painting he collects: "They were all landscapes with figures in the foreground, a sign of some mysterious revolt against London, its tall houses, its interminable streets, where his life and the lives of his breed and class were passed" *(MP,* 49).

Ironically, however, by building the house Soames creates a situation which, first of all, repeatedly exposes his ingrained obsession with money over every other value and which, finally, brings about the loss of his wife. He hires June Forsyte's fiancé, Bosinney, to design the house, believing that the obscure young architect will be pliable to terms. The house thus becomes a battleground between property and art: the man of business haggling over costs, the architect devoted "to the image of the house he had conceived and believed in" *(MP,* p. 98). Aesthetic values occasionally triumph over material interests. Soames does agree, despite the unintended expense, to the beautiful site chosen by Bosinney—one with a great ancient oak that recurs throughout the *Saga.* But when Robin Hill is actually completed —a splendid, original dwelling—Soames proves unyielding and sues Bosinney for going beyond the estimated cost. Soames discovers, moreover, that during the process of its construction his wife has fallen in love with Bosinney, and here there is no means of reclamation even after the architect's death in the fog. The house is left empty and ownerless, and thus becomes a symbol— albeit a simple one—of values beyond the comprehension and sympathy of the philistine.

This is further evidenced by what becomes of the house before the conclusion of *The Man of Property.* Along with the story of Soames, Irene, and Bosinney, a story of dissolution, there is the counterplot of old Jolyon and his son, a story of reconciliation. Like Bosinney, young Jolyon is an artist of sorts, a watercolorist; he too in his early years defied the Forsyte conventions by leaving his wife because of his love for a governess. His father broke with him, only to find that years of estrangement involve a loneliness the Forsyte philosophy cannot relieve. The "figurehead of his family and class and creed," he grows "older and older, yearning for a soul to speak to" *(MP,* p. 31). Through the course of the novel old Jolyon follows his impulse and heals the rupture, and the renewal of the family bond is manifested in his decision to give up living alone in London and take the vacant house at

Robin Hill where he may live with his son and grandchildren.

Thereafter, in the other novels of the *Saga,* Robin Hill continues to suggest a different order of feelings from that which characterizes the more typical Forsytes. In the interlude, "Indian Summer of a Forsyte," old Jolyon finds new life there. "I'm glad to have washed my hands of London," he admits, and finds "plenty of occupation in the perfecting and mellowing of the house" (*MP*, pp. 294, 286).[35] While there, he is moved by compassion for Irene's plight and assists her. There, too, he dies quietly under the old oak. By the *In Chancery* volume, the house has passed to another generation and already kindles a sense of continuity. Seated under its great oak, young Jolyon admires "the dignity Bosinney had bestowed upon it" and wonders if Robin Hill "might even become one of the 'homes of England'—a rare achievement in these days of degenerate building" (*IC*, pp. 364–65). In the house he now and again catches "a moment of communion with his father" (*IC*, p. 377) and realizes that there is "a smack of reverence and ancestor-worship (if only for one ancestor) in his desire to hand this house down to his son and his son's son" *IC*, p. 365). And when Jolyon marries Irene and brings her back to Robin Hill, there is, momentarily at least, further sense of another harmony restored.[36]

Unfortunately, however, in the final volume, *To Let,* the symbolic quality of the house is beclouded by defects of characterization and plotting. This novel opens in the early twenties, so that at first Robin Hill appears to suggest something permanent that has survived not only the changing generations but the holocaust of the war. Continuity seems assured by the fact that Jolyon's son Jon, amiable and imaginative like his father, will inherit the house. But once again Robin Hill becomes the stage for a struggle with the Forsyte world of Soames. Quite by accident Jon meets Soames's daughter, Fleur; neither one knows anything of the old bitterness between the families, and they fall in love. The implications of their possible marriage cause dismay to the older generation, especially to Irene and Jolyon. But Galsworthy's resolution dismays the reader because symbol, theme, and characterization work at cross-purposes. On one hand, the union of Jon and Fleur, bringing the *Saga* back full circle to the conflict of *The Man of Property* and resolving it, would be consistent with the symbolic meaning of Robin Hill as an abode of harmony and reconciliation. Needless to say, however, this would be pure sentimentality, considering all that has passed before. And with his daughter as mistress of the house he originally built, Soames would know a kind of final vicarious triumph, as he himself recognizes in his speculations about the "poetic justice" of it (*TL*, p. 778).

To defeat Soames and expose his philosophy, the two young people must be torn apart. Jolyon's death-bed letter to Jon discloses Soames's brutal treatment of Irene and makes the boy's marriage to Fleur impossible. The meaning Galsworthy intends here is clearly formulated by Beach: "the ugly working of the sense of property in one generation brings about the grievous frustration of love in the following generation." At the end of the *Saga*, the vacated Robin Hill is "to let"; the symbolic counterweight to the grasping world of the Forsytes becomes, in Mottram's phrase, "an empty habitat of murdered emotions." [37]

Now if all this could be taken seriously, *The Forsyte Saga* would remain a profound indictment of the defeat of community by property. But this ending obviously has its own sentimentality. The characters poised against Soames—indeed, the occupants of Robin Hill themselves—seem no better than he. As D. H. Lawrence astutely perceived, Irene and Jolyon are "meaner and more treacherous to their son than the older Forsytes were to theirs." If Fleur is "having" and thus a true daughter of the "man of property," they seem equally possessive in preventing her from marrying Jon. Apparently discomfited by this himself, Galsworthy defended the ending in his preface by calling such an interpretation "hypercriticism of the story as told." [38] But the rebuttal suggests that he himself mistook his own story as told. In particular, he did not really grasp all the symbolic implications and possibilities of Robin Hill. To have done so, of course, Galsworthy would have had to transcend personal limitations and be a novelist of a different stature altogether.

Superficially, Ford Madox Ford might seem to resemble Galsworthy; actually, of course, his strongest affinities are with James and, to a lesser degree, Forster. It is true that the contemporary English novel that might seem closest to *The Forsyte Saga* as a social chronicle is *Parade's End;* but when the two are really compared, as Richard A. Cassell observes, Galsworthy's family history "seems pale, limited in imagination, extremely traditional in manner." [39] What Ford and Galsworthy share in these two works—even though they are completed in the twenties—is the Edwardian preoccupation with "the condition of England." A measure of what separates them is Ford's appreciation of James, an appreciation of both his fictional techniques and his quest for ideal social forms.

Like James, Ford was in his own way an outsider of sorts in England. Son of a naturalized German father, reared in "the hothouse atmosphere of Pre-Raphaelism," [40] he looked upon English society with a Jamesian kind of ambivalence, quite different from the mixed feelings of even the less complacent members of a world circumscribed by public school, university, and London club. Like James and to some extent Wells, Ford was as an outsider more perceptive and searching than Galsworthy about the realities of English society and, paradoxically, more prompted to find the most satisfying embodiment of his own values in the old ways of some ideal feudal England. (Indeed, Ford's "snobbery," his inveterate posing as an "old boy" from Malvern or Eton, was a self-dramatization that, like James's dining out and country-house visiting, finds a more serious counterpart in his fiction.) In fact, in his own study of James— written, as he ironically reminds us, by "a Tory mad about historic continuity"—Ford responds to just this complexity in the novels. James, he insists, gave a truthful picture of English society and really asked if the leisured life depicted—the "life of the West End, of the country house, of the drawing room, possibly of the studio, and of the garden party"—was worth living.[41] On the other hand, Ford recognized elsewhere that what James was seeking in this world was some kind of ideal community: "It was possible," he observes,

that James never wanted to live outside tea-parties—but the tea-parties he wanted were debating circles of a splendid aloof-

ness, of an immense human sympathy, and of a beauty you
did not find in Putney. . . . It was his tragedy that no such
five o'clock ever sounded for him on the timepieces of this
world. And this is no doubt the real tragedy of all of us—of
all societies—that we never find . . . our ideal friends living
in an assured and permanent republic.[42]

In consequence, it is not surprising that Ford has much the
same feeling for houses as James. "For me," he remarked, "houses
always seem to be alive, listeners, watching the ways of men
with sardonic eyes."[43] As a matter of fact, he wrote a little
morality play entitled *A House* (1921), in which a family home
speaks as an allegorical figure with lines not unlike those opening Eliot's "East Coker":

> All, all the houses beneath the far-stretching sky
> Shall have the same fate as I
> And they that dwell in me.
> All shall mark the pressing of generations
> On the heels of preceding generations.
> ....
> . . . having stood too long;
> So they go down to the ground.
> The circle comes round
> All over and over again.[44]

And since he admired *The Spoils of Poynton* and acclaimed *A
Passionate Pilgrim* as "the apotheosis of the turf, the deer, the
oak trees, the terraces of manor houses,"[45] Ford undoubtedly
had James in mind as a model when he too employed houses
symbolically in his own fiction. This is particularly evident in
Ford's best novels, *The Good Soldier* and *Parade's End,* where
the country house provides the theme with a symbolic extension
that would otherwise be missing.

In *The Good Soldier* the country house functions in several
ways reminiscent of James. The ironic story of Edward Ashburnham, "Captain, Fourteen Hussars, of Branshaw House,
Branshaw Telegraph," is more than the story of an individual

involved in passionate and complicated adulteries: it is, as Kenneth Young observes, "a subtle picture of the downfall of a class"—even possibly, as another critic speculates, a diagnosis of a whole epoch on the brink of the Great War.[46] With the action presented by the narrator, the American Dowell, in a series of time shifts, *The Good Soldier* does not yield its subtleties and ambiguities to brief discussion; but admitting this it is possible to note how Branshaw Manor, the ancestral home of Ashburnham, is brought into relationship with the follies, bickerings, infidelities, and suicides among representatives of the English gentry and leisure-class Americans abroad. At first the house is employed for ironic effect, as in James's "A London Life," with the emphasis on the incongruity of smooth, charming surfaces and the strange discords concealed behind them. "The beautiful, beautiful old house," Dowell comments. "It was unbelievable that anything essentially calamitous could happen to that place and those people. I tell you it was the very spirit of peace" (*GS*, p. 20).

Though only a small part of the action occurs there, Branshaw Manor takes on greater importance in the lives of the four major characters as the novel progresses. Edward Ashburnham, the owner, is deeply attached to the estate and generous with his tenants, but he loses personal control of the property to his Anglo-Irish wife, Leonora, who shrewdly takes advantage of his costly weakness for women. Indeed, the payment of exorbitant blackmail to an unscrupulous husband who threatens the scandal of divorce proceedings after the discovery of his wife's infidelity, plus an expensive interlude with a grand courtesan, would leave Ashburnham impoverished, were it not for Leonora's coldly efficient management of the estate through increase of rents and curtailment of customary charities. The proud Leonora, in turn, determined to reestablish herself at Branshaw in the future whatever happens to her husband, forces him to settle the property in her name and puts the house up to let, even though this affects him with a "feeling of physical soiling" (*GS*, pp. 167–68). At the same time Dowell's wife Florence, also an American, has her own designs upon Branshaw. Descended from an English family that had owned Branshaw before the Ashburnhams, Florence

entertains hopes, until her suicide, that her affair with Edward
may bring about her return as its mistress. Finally, after the passions of these others are spent, Dowell settles there himself.

Thematically, furthermore, this quadruple relationship with
Branshaw is not without moral and social overtones. Insofar as
Ashburnham himself is a tragic and not an ignoble figure—as
Meixner suggests—a major source of his tragic stature is his commitment to his own tradition. Ashburnham's "really trying lia-
bilities," as even the superficial Dowell recognizes," are in "the
nature of generosities proper to his station" (*GS*, p. 58). In contrast, his wife Leonora—coming from "a family of small Irish
landlords—that hostile garrison in a plundered country"—is
coldly efficient without any redeeming sense of *noblesse oblige.*
As Ashburnham puts it to himself, "his own traditions were entirely collective, his wife was a sheer individualist" (*GS*, p. 146).
Even his refusal of Nancy is, we may agree with Cassell, a victory of the generous emotions over the selfish ones.[47] On the
other hand the Dowells—rich Americans whose wealth is significantly based on abstract capital rather than the stable feudal relation to land—are self-exiled from their native country; with
"no attachments, no accumulations," they pursue the rootless,
leisured existence of affluent tourists—wanderers, as Dowell himself remarks, "upon the face of public resorts" (*GS*, p. 21). Florence can imagine herself as a country lady in the home of her
ancestors, but even this superficial dream of status is frustrated
by her selfish, adulterous intrigues.

At the close, as Dowell himself settles down at Branshaw, he
turns this center of age-old loyalists and obligations into a chilling house of isolation. "I don't like society—much," he tells us.
"I am that absurd figure, an American millionaire, who has
bought one of the ancient haunts of peace. I sit here, in Edward's
gun-room, all day and all day in a house that is absolutely quiet.
No one visits me, for I visit no one. No one is interested in me,
for I have no interests. . . . So life peters out" (*GS*, p. 254).
Thus the fate of Branshaw Manor is another symbolic index of
theme, like the similar fate of Bladesover in *Tono-Bungay* or,
to cite another's comparison, like the more absurd fate of Tony
Last's estate in Waugh's *Handful of Dust* being converted into a

kennel for foxes.[48] An old order changes and yields not so much to a new order as to a barren, anarchic individualism.

In *Parade's End*, Ashburnham and Branshaw Manor, representatives of the old "feudal" traditions, have more fully realized counterparts in Christopher Tietjens and Groby estate, his ancestral home.[49] Tietjens is described as "the last English Tory"; more properly, he is the ideal English Tory—not, as Auden observes, a political reactionary or a social snob—but a gentleman of honor.[50] ("Principles," he asserts, "are like a skeleton map of the country—you know whether you are going north or south," *PE*, p. 144). And if he is at times rather literal and even naïve in his commitment to his code ("Other men get over their schooling. I never have," he confesses. "I remain adolescent," *PE*, p. 490), his absurdities ironically expose others more often than himself. Moreover, he is considerate with animals, sensitive to the English landscape, cultivated enough to enjoy seventeenth-century poetry, and so concerned with the well-being of his men in the trenches that they think he is a promoted ranker. There are even moments when he aspires to Anglican sainthood, so that Cassell is undoubtedly correct in his observation that the symbolism of Tietjens's first name—Christopher—must be taken quite seriously: "He is 'the Christ-bearer,' the living embodiment of the conscience of his nation and race."[51]

It is important to recognize that Tietjens's values are not personal or arbitrary but rooted in the way of life of Groby, "a rambling Yorkshire manor house" (*PE*, p. 43). Curiously, Groby is rarely present in any immediate physical sense, but throughout the cycle of novels allusions and recollections transform it into a spiritual setting, one of those "countries of the mind"— to use Robert Liddell's term—which fictional characters often carry about with them, in memory, fear, hope, or desire, as a second background.[52] Tietjens, we note, is repeatedly identified —in fact, identifies himself to himself—as Tietjens of Groby: "He was . . . Tietjens of Groby; no man could give him anything, no man could take anything from him" (*PE*, p. 556). Indeed in a half-serious, half-ironic interval, Tietjens imagines the whole Christian cosmos patterned after the model of Groby. He conceives the Almighty as

on a colossal scale, a great English Landowner, benevolently
awful, a colossal duke who never left his study and was thus
invisible, but knowing all about the estate down to the last
hind at the home farm and the last oak; Christ, an almost too
benevolent Land-Steward, son of the Owner, knowing all about
the estate down to the last child at the porter's lodge, apt to
be got around by the more detrimental tenants; the Third
Person of the Trinity, the spirit of the estate . . . the atmosphere of the estate, that of the interior of Winchester cathedral just after a Handel anthem had been finished, a perpet-
ual Sunday, with, probably, a little cricket for the young men.
[*PE,* pp. 365–66]

And though here his mood is tongue-in-cheek, the image of
Groby nonetheless remains the center of his moral universe.

Even the sexual code of Tietjens is founded on this sense of
Groby. The major personal problem of Tietjens is a marital
one: he is a cuckold. But unlike Soames Forsyte, he indulges in
neither self-pity nor egocentric possessiveness toward his wife. A
cuckold himself, he despises cuckolds. "A certain discredit," he
asserts, "has always attached to cuckolds. Very properly. A man
ought to be able to keep his own wife" (*PE,* p. 10). The founda-
tion for this impersonal attitude toward his own predicament
is that Tietjens sees sexual matters as continuous with the whole
structure of social relationships exemplified in Groby. This is
clearly revealed in his observations on the coolness shown by
the county toward another betrayed husband: "We felt Groby
and the neighborhood were unsafe. . . . It wasn't rational or
just. But that's why society distrusts the cuckold, really. It never
knows when it mayn't be driven into something irrational and
unjust" (*PE,* p. 11). Furthermore, Tietjens is against what he
calls "lachrymose polygamy" and its "polysyllable justification by
love"; he stands for monogamy and chastity—"And for no talking about it," and for its converse—"Of course if a man who's a
man wants to have a woman he has her. And again, no talking
about it" (*PE,* p. 18).[53] Tietjens will not divorce his wife because a gentleman does not inflict the ordeal on a lady and because his wife is a Catholic. For the sake of his son, whom he

suspects may have been fathered by another, he is willing to keep up appearances. Despite his ardor for Valentine Wannop, he is not inclined to seduce her; and when at last he does consider making her his mistress, he realizes he must give up living at Groby. An example has to be set for the tenantry: "You could not have a Valentine Wannop . . . not a lady, the daughter of your father's best friend! They wanted Quality women to *be* Quality and they themselves would go to ruin" (*PE*, p. 635).

However, if Groby provides a stabilizing center for Tietjens himself, this does not mean that Ford ignores the historical changes that threaten this house and its prototypes. Quite the contrary: believing the novelist should "appear in his really proud position as historian of his own time," [54] Ford made the personal story of Tietjens the story of the cataclysmic decade of the Great War; and he incorporated so many of the familiar motifs of change and dissolution that *Parade's End* now seems the apotheosis of the "Edwardian" novel we have been considering. The very title evokes the passing of ritual ceremony, the end of an epoch, as do the closing pages of *Tono-Bungay* and *The Forsyte Saga*.[55] Again, disease functions symbolically —with Tietjens's amnesia, his loss of memory, bespeaking a loss of tradition; and the self-inflicted paralysis of Mark Tietjens implying the incapacity of the ruling class. Once more, contrasting values are epitomized in the antitheses of the rural and the urban, the organic and the mechanical.[56]

Moreover, Groby itself, like other houses in Edwardian fiction, is shaken by the shifting tides of history—from the past as well as the present. Indeed, Tietjens sees the house as being under a curse ever since its Roman Catholic owners were dispossessed by the first Tietjens who came over with Dutch William in the late seventeenth century. Only Groby's return to Papists, he continues to feel, will make up for this sacrilege. Significantly, therefore, the closing novel of the cycle, *The Last Post*, revolves around the question of inheritance in much the same manner as does *Howards End*. Mark Tietjens, the oldest son, is the actual heir of Groby; but tired of the estate and the tenantry, he recognizes in Christopher the true spiritual heir and wishes to bequeath it to him. Christopher himself refuses Groby because of his liaison with Valentine; and choosing to live in a cottage and sell old furniture, he gives the house to his wife Sylvia.

Thereupon, Groby also must suffer the familiar fate of so many country houses: it is rented out to a wealthy American couple, the Bray de Papes. Mrs. Bray de Pape—by her husband's admission "the most active woman from here to Santa Fe"— decides to cut down Groby Great Tree, and in the process manages to topple the side of the house as well. Ironically, unsettling as this is to Christopher, it has the effect of lifting the curse. Sylvia relents in her persecution of Christopher and yields him to Valentine. With the estate passing to Christopher's Catholic son—who is legitimate after all—the sacrilege is over. Christopher and Valentine will settle down to a pastoral life of their own, and it may even be that their son will eventually become master of Groby.

Thus Ford's novel concludes with something of the same attempt at affirmation as *Howards End;* and revealingly, it has brought forth much of the same mixed criticism. None other than William Carlos Williams found in the destruction a phoenix symbol promising rebirth. "This is not the 'last Tory,' " Williams proclaims, "but the first in the new enlightenment of the Englishmen." On the other hand, John A. Meixner finds there "elegiac lament, not spiritual assurance." Calling the ending of *The Last Post* "a sentimental indulgence," he notes that Ford himself did not like the book and asserts that "it was a fairy tale, a wish, the symbolization of something he wanted to be. But in his heart he did not believe it." [57] Even if we agree with Meixner, what remains significant is that the country house, whatever its historical destiny, remained for Ford one "symbolization of something he wanted to be." And it is this that associates him with James, his master, and with elegists who were still to come.

⚜ 3 ⚜

Shattered Glass and Toppling Masonry

Shaw, Huxley, V. Sackville-West,
Lawrence, Waugh, Isherwood

I see barns falling, fences broken,
Pastures not ploughland, weeds not wheat.
The great houses remain but only half are
*   inhabited.*
Dusty the gunrooms and the stable clocks
*   stationary.*
Some have been turned into prep-schools . . .
Others into club-houses for the golfe-bore
*   and the tope-hole.*
> W. H. Auden and Christopher Isherwood,
> *The Dog Beneath the Skin*

As the curtain falls upon the last act of Shaw's *Heartbreak House,* unseen and unidentified aircraft drop bombs upon an English garden and one member of a weekend party plays "Keep the Home Fires Burning" on a flute. Thus did Shaw, with a compound of familiar levity and unexpected grimness, make his own ambiguous contribution to the literature of the country house and at the same time provide the coda for one era and the overture to the next. *Heartbreak House*—conceived in 1913, completed during the war, but not produced in England until 1921—was not received with open arms by audiences that had just survived four years of actual hostilities; in retrospect, nonetheless, this fantasia, still one of the most haunting and visionary of Shaw's plays, decidedly marks a place between one generation and the next. For while its social diagnosis recalls the preoccupations of the more serious Edwardians, its satirical flute may be said to have sounded one of the major keys in which the postwar writers would play variations on the country-house theme. Though not necessarily influenced by Shaw, novelists like Aldous Huxley, Victoria Sackville-West, the early Waugh—even D. H. Lawrence and Christopher Isherwood—descended upon the stately home, equally intent on exposure and demolition. The apparent doom of the country house, which elicited from others a poignant nostalgia and even tragic sense of loss,[1] became for them the occasion of mordant comedy. If their typical hero is often a laughable "antihero," so their typical house is usually an "antihouse," a foolish parody of the community it once was or still pretends to be. When placed together, such novels as *Crome Yellow* (1921), *Lady Chatterley's Lover* (1928), *The Edwardians* (1930), *The Memorial* (1932), and *A Handful of Dust* (1934), though highly individual works in themselves, make an illuminating configuration that might as justifiably be captioned "Heartbreak House" as Shaw's drama.

The Shavian mode, of course, was not the only one: the poet Yeats, an even more visionary Anglo-Irishman, sang of the country house in contrasting but equally vibrant tonalities. In a number of poems of the postwar period, Yeats looked upon the world of the great house not without irony but with a susceptibility to its emblematic overtones that reminds us of Henry

James. "Ancestral Houses" finds in the rich man's flowering lawns, peacock and old terraces, great chambers and long galleries, images suggesting the human possibilities of which poets dream. As will be discussed in the next chapter, his other poems on Coole Park and the aging Lady Gregory are elegies to a vanishing order that rebuke the anarchy and rootlessness of the present.

If Shaw's *Heartbreak House,* in a manner of speaking, announced the theme of a new generation of satirists, Yeats's lyrical celebrations of the great house might be said to have sounded the countertheme another group of novelists were ready to develop. During the years between the wars, particularly as one war passed from memory and another threatened, writers like Elizabeth Bowen, Virginia Woolf, Joyce Cary, Henry Green, and Evelyn Waugh turned to the house with a new seriousness. Satire gave way to elegy: the era that opened with *Heartbreak House* and *Crome Yellow* (1921) closed with *Brideshead Revisited* (1945). Indeed, Waugh's fiction in particular reminds us that, with respect to the country house, satire and elegy do not of necessity exclude each other; such is the complexity of feeling involved that these extremes often meet and convenient distinctions blur. For the sake of emphasis and coherence, we shall consider the satirists and the elegists separately, while recognizing that they often lean toward one another. In fact, even *Heartbreak House* itself becomes all the more haunting by defying the tidy classifications of the literary purist.

Shaw called *Heartbreak House* "A Fantasia in the Russian Manner on English themes," and cited such plays as Chekhov's *Cherry Orchard* and Tolstoy's *Fruits of Enlightenment* as his models. Still, it also seems evident that *Heartbreak House* has affinities with English literary modes as well; and to lose sight of them is to miss something of the play's spirit and meaning. The very title—whether Shaw intended any allusion or not—brings to mind the similarly devastating alliterations of Peacock's *Headlong Hall* and *Crotchet Castle* as well as the more somber connotations of *Castle Rackrent* and *Bleak House.* Much of the comic extravagance of the play—including the impossible names of the characters—reveals something of the wild, farcical inventiveness that runs through a line of English fiction from the eighteenth century. The main setting, in particular—the room fantastically designed to resemble the stern gallery of an old-fashioned sailing ship—is not an example of the late nineteenth-century realism deriving from Ibsen but of the comic expressionism in which Dickens delighted—and may very well be borrowed from Smollett's *Peregrine Pickle,* as Grant Webster suggests.[2] Throughout Shaw's play, furthermore, the country house functions both metaphorically and literally as it does in the novels of James and Forster.

The very opening sentence of Shaw's famous preface to the drama emphasizes at once the symbolism involved in the title. *Heartbreak House,* Shaw declares, is not merely the name of the play: "it is cultured, leisured Europe before the war." Nor does the symbolism stop with the title and setting: on the contrary there are, according to the count of Martin Meisel, "at least thirty pregnant allusions, great and small, to 'the house,' which give cumulative reminder of its emblematic character."[3] In fact, it is the house, we might add, that provides unity of structure and theme in a play which, on the surface at least, seems even more discursive than Shaw's other dramas. What plot there is in the conventional sense turns upon situations familiar enough in country-house literature: a family reunion and visits by outsiders. These stock devices are, of course, given new life through typically Shavian transfusions. The return of Lady Utterwood to her father Captain Shotover and her sister Mrs. Hushabye becomes the comic antithesis of any sentimental renewal of family ties. More important, Shaw chooses both occupants and guests to present a cross section of the Edwardian establishment— gentry, capitalist, old colonial—and to expose a ruling class given over to misrule.

As in country-house literature generally, Shaw's characters reveal themselves in their attitudes toward the house. Interestingly enough, their reactions are often more complicated, even more ambivalent, than most readings of the play manage to note. To be sure, the indictment implied in the title and specified in the preface is dramatically rendered in the irresponsible ways of the house and its occupants; the lack of good form and the ignorance of common social decencies suggest a breakdown of order, as even the eccentric Captain Shotover insists. At the same time, there is much to be said for the place: its informality, absence of ceremony, candor, even camaraderie have an appeal of their own. Whether we take the house to be England, society, or universal home, these qualities bespeak community as well. Indeed, the true occupants of the house are quick to detect humbug and meanness in their most complacent guests. "You are beneath the dome of heaven in the house of God," Captain Shotover reminds the capitalist Mangan. "What is true within these walls is true outside them" (*HH,* p. 65). And even Hector warns him against posing: "In this house we know all the poses: our job is to find the man under the pose" (*HH,* p. 117).

Characters who find fault with the house are not always intelligent or sympathetic. Lady Utterword despairs of her father's home because she finds on her return "the same disorder in ideas, in talk, in feeling" (*HH,* p. 46) that she knew upon leaving years before; yet her own superficiality is exposed by her preference for a "horseback hall," where "the stables are the real centre of the household" (*HH,* p. 125). Again, Boss Mangan, who arrives from London with something of the same cocksureness of Edward Ponderevo in *Tono-Bungay,* soon finds that the house he calls "crazy" has him unmasked and at bay. In contrast, the more attractive characters like Captain Shotover and Ellie Dunn are profoundly involved with the house and torn by their feelings for it. Ellie is disillusioned by almost everything that happens there; but she is also saved from a misalliance with Mangan and is cherished by Captain Shotover. The Captain himself is at once its gloomiest critic ("Youth! beauty! novelty! They are badly wanted in this house," *HH,* p. 48), its quickest defender ("What! the numskull said that there was something wrong with my house!" *HH,* p. 124), and its readiest counselor.

Finally, the haunting last act reveals that Shaw intended from the beginning to bring these recurring motifs of the house to a kind of musical crescendo. A beautifully modulated, almost poetic sequence presents the responses of the various characters to the house in a series of revealing counterpoints. It begins with this exchange between Mangan and Ellie:

MANGAN: Ever since I came into this silly house I have been made to look like a fool, though I'm as good a man in this house as in the city.

ELLIE (*Musically*): Yes: this silly house, this strangely happy house, this agonizing house, this house without foundations. I shall call it Heartbreak House. [*HH*, p. 134]

And it closes with the voices of the others:

HECTOR: Do you accept that name for your house?

CAPTAIN SHOTOVER: It is not my house: it is only my kennel.

HECTOR: We have been here too long. We do not live in this house: we haunt it.

LADY UTTERWORD (*heart torn*): It is dreadful to think how you have been here all these years while I have gone around the world. I escaped young; but it has drawn me back. I felt sentimental about papa and Hesione and the old place. I felt them calling me. [*HH*, p. 134]

Thereupon, the ship-house-society metaphor suggested by the major setting takes the ascendancy, and issues not unlike those raised by Howards End, Bladesover, and Groby are made explicit. "And this ship that we are all in?" cries Hector to Captain Shotover, "This soul's prison we call England?" The Captain replies that she is about to go on the rocks unless Englishmen like Hector learn their business: "Navigation. Learn it and live; or leave it and be damned" (*HH*, 138–39). But the answer provided by the whole dramatic context seems much more ambiguous. Hector has barely received his instruction when, without warning, bombs from the sky explode around the house. In what seems a moment of apocalypse, the earth reels and glass falls, bringing to mind the "shattered glass and toppling masonry" of the Circe chapter in Joyce's *Ulysses* and the "falling towers" of Eliot's *Waste Land*. It seems too late now for Captain Shotover's counsel.

Curiously, however, the play does not end in the sinister darkness others have found there. The occupants of the house survive untouched; only the two outsiders, the two intruders—Mangan and the burglar, "the two practical men of business"—are killed hiding in the gravel pit. "The ship is safe," the Captain himself declares (*HH*, p. 142). Yet we may wonder about this ending. How are we to take those who, like Hesione and Hector, find in the violence merely an aesthetic thrill? Ellie hopes for the return of the bombers. Is this a death wish or the desire for some purification by fire? Is the house a phoenix that will rise from its own ashes after all? Does the playing of Randall's flute—the last sound we hear—support or deflate such affirmation?

With *Heartbreak House*, we are in the world of the twenties, where potential tragedy modulates disturbingly into farce.

Crome Yellow by Aldous Huxley displays, so to speak, a "heartbreak house" that has survived the Great War but has not on that account emerged purified and reborn into a new life of purpose and responsibility. Quite the contrary: ancient Crome of the title plays host to another Peacockian assemblage of eccentrics talking, posing, and flirting in an atmosphere of disenchantment and futility not unlike Shaw's. Ironically, one apparent difference is the very lack of the sense of urgency that occasionally breaks through the farcical business of Shaw's play and awakens even the most shallow denizens of the house to their confused drifting. "Since the war we wonder at nothing," is Mr. Scogan's chilling comment on contemporary horrors even more frightful than those adumbrated by Shaw's last act (*CY*, p. 159).

Nevertheless, *Crome Yellow* remains the most genial of Huxley's satires. Brief and mellow, the account of the young poet Denis Stone's ineffectual visit to Crome seems imbued, as most readers have felt, with the special quality of a pastoral idyll, so that even disenchantment becomes enchanting. Moreover this charm, as Angus Wilson suggests, is connected with the physical setting— the old country house and the farmyard near by. The story progresses with pleasing casualness simply by following the familiar, comfortable routines of country-house guests in perfect summer weather—the easeful loveliness of the surroundings giving piquancy to their misadventures and frustrations. Even the grotesqueries prove amusing rather than sinister, and the same effect results from the queer architecture of Crome and the correspondingly bizarre history of its family. Indeed, perhaps nowhere else does Huxley indulge so lavishly what one critic has called his "voluptuous feeling for landscape and architecture" [4] as in this first novel.

There is, in fact, evidence to show that Crome is a carefully designed composite of actual houses that Huxley scrutinized as both a connoisseur and a satirist. The model for Crome has usually been thought to be Garsington Manor, the house near Oxford which Lady Ottoline Morrell made the rendezvous for English literati during her occupancy from 1915 until the mid-twenties. Peter Quennell, for one, points out that Lady Ottoline has long been recognized by some in Huxley's satirical portrait of Priscilla Wimbush, the eccentric mistress of Crome; and he surmises that the place described in the novel owes a great deal to her Garsington household.[5] Apparently, however, Garsington is not the only prototype of Crome. L. P. Hartley—who recalls paying his first visit to Lady Ottoline's in the company of Huxley —has suggested to me that *Crome Yellow* really describes another house called Beckley Park, also in the vicinity of Oxford.[6] In fact, a comparison of Crome with these two houses leads to the conclusion that Huxley copied what he wanted from each and, as we should expect, added a few imaginary properties of his own.

Crome resembles Garsington mainly in its landscape and garden. Cycling his way there, the poet Denis climbs a high slope to reach the house, enters through a gate opening into a great courtyard, and finds a terraced garden bordered by yew hedges. All these details match those of Garsington. Even the stone-brimmed swimimng pool at Crome, formerly a fishpond, seems an obvious reproduction of the narrow one at Garsington where, as Quennell recalls, favorite guests were occasionally emboldened to swim. However, the odd exterior of the house at Crome appears to be inspired by Beckley Park. The impression the building first makes on Denis is graphically presented: "The facade with its three projected towers rose precipitously from among the dark trees of the garden. The house baked in full sunlight;

the old brick rosily glowed. How ripe and rich it was, how superbly mellow! And at the same time, how austere!" (*CY*, p. 11). But this is an impression Beckley would make, not Garsington. Beckley is also a red brick house, while Garsington is gray; more important, Beckley has the unusual architectural feature of three massive towers, imposing in their height and angularity. Moreover, it is surrounded by three medieval moats, now filled in, similar to those which were the outlet for the fantastic privies built atop the great towers of Crome by Sir Ferdinando.[7]

Indeed, Huxley probably copied these peculiar features of Beckley because they very well suited one of the satirical themes of his novel: the deflation of a modern tendency to seek an escape in a romanticized past. His Henry Wimbush, the proprietor of Crome, is an antiquarian who has spent nearly thirty years compiling a history of his house and his ancestry. A parody of the stuffier chronicles of other noble seats, his account of book-lined privies in the ancient towers and the unfortunate dwarf Sir Hercules constantly diverts us; but it also exposes, as one commentary notes, his attempt to find in the past a substitute order for the chaos of the present.[8] "Give me the past," Henry tells Denis. "It doesn't change; it's all there in black and white" (*CY*, p. 287). It is obvious that in Huxley's view this is not a Jamesian sense of vital continuity with the past but a dispirited retreat from actuality. "If all these people were dead," Huxley has Henry comment at his own party, "this festivity would be extremely agreeable. Nothing would be pleasanter than to read in a well-written book of an open-air ball that took place a century ago. . . . But when the ball takes place today, when one finds oneself involved in it, one sees the thing in its true light" (*CY*, p. 289). Furthermore, Henry's history of Crome itself reveals the past's own barbarism, duplicity, and folly by recording the brutality of Ferdinando toward his dwarf father, the hypocrisy of the three sisters who practice asceticism in public while gorging themselves in the privacy of their rooms, not to mention the "two suicides, one violent death, four or perhaps five broken hearts, and a half a dozen little blots on the escutcheon in the way of misalliances, seductions, natural children, and the like" (*CY*, p. 119).

For all the charms of its halcyon atmosphere, *Crome Yellow* is, therefore, something more than an idyll. From one point of view, it is rather a swan song. For Huxley, the English country house—which often evokes the best of the past—will itself disappear. Shaw may seem to grant a reprieve to Heartbreak House. Huxley, as a rather deliberate passage toward the close of the novel makes clear, coolly prophesies its doom:

> At breakfast that morning Mary found on her plate a picture postcard of Gobley Great Park. A stately Georgian pile, with a facade sixteen windows wide; parterres in the foreground; huge, smooth lawns receding out of the picture. . . . Ten years more of the hard times and Gobley, with all its peers, will be deserted and decaying. Fifty years and the countryside will know the old landmarks no more. They will have vanished as the monasteries vanished before them. [*CY*, p. 249]

In *Crome Yellow* the poet Denis, alone in the old house, amuses himself by wandering from room to room as though he were "exploring a dead, deserted Pompeii." What sort of life, he asks himself, "would the excavator reconstruct from these remains; how would he people these empty chambers?" (*CY*, p. 13).[9] It is in just this vein of satirical archaeology that Victoria Sackville-West composed *The Edwardians,* a novel about another and even more patrician "Heartbreak House"—the great mansion of Chevron. For as her title makes clear, the novel is not about the postwar world at all but undertakes instead a reconstruction of the country house in its last great heyday of power and elegance—from the irreverent vantage point of the twenties. Out of the conflict of Sebastian, the young duke and heir of Chevron, with the high social world to which he is bred, she designs a museum piece, deliberately suffused with the rather airless, almost lifeless atmosphere of the exhibition room. The rituals of prewar aristocracy are documented with anthropological exactitude; the characters themselves appear intentionally formalized—so many waxwork figures, costumed sartorially and morally according to the conventions of period; even the style itself, cool and a trifle mannered, augments the sense of distance. Yet here the remembrance of things not long past but nonetheless irrevocable begets not a pensive nostalgia, only a studied archness and suave irony. Composed *après le deluge, The Edwardians* assumes a perspective which leaves no room for either moral earnestness or antiquarian sentimentality.

This is not to say, however, that Victoria Sackville-West is quite so detached as Huxley about the fate of the country house. She hardly could be: born at Knole Park, one of the most illustrious estates in England, she was educated to its traditions from childhood; as mistress of Sissinghurst Castle after her marriage to Harold Nicolson, she was preoccupied with the country house throughout her life. Indeed, in her book *Knole Park and the Sackvilles* (1923), she not only describes the great Jacobean mansion and its variegated history but beautifully conveys the profoundly personal meaning the place has for her:

> One looks down upon the house from a certain corner in the garden. . . . The house lies below one in the hollow, lovely in its colour and its serenity. It has all the quality of peace and permanence; of mellow age; of stateliness and tradition. It is gentle and venerable. Yet it is . . . gay. It has the deep inward gaiety of some very old woman who has always been beautiful, who has had many lovers and seen many generations come and go, smiled wisely over their sorrows and their joys, and learnt an imperishable secret of tolerance and humor.[10]

She stresses, also, that Knole "is, above all an English house. It has the tone of England . . . ":

> It is not an incongruity like Blenheim or Chatsworth, foreign to the spirit of England. It is, rather, the greater relation of those small manorhouses which hide themselves away so innumerably among the counties, whether built of the grey stone of southwestern England, or the brick of East Anglia, or merely tile-hung or plastered like a cottage. It is not utterly different from any of these.[11]

In a later volume, *English Country Houses* (1941), she says much the same thing but with an emphasis that is close to E. M. Forster's. The true house, she observes, is "essentially part of the country, not only in the country, but part of it, a natural growth. Irrespective of grandeur or modesty, it should agree with its landscape and suggest the life of its inhabitants past or present." The "soul of the house," she insists, "the atmosphere of a house are as much part of the house as the architecture of the house, or the furnishings within it. Divorced from life, it dies." [12]

In *The Edwardians,* therefore, Victoria Sackville-West inevitably displays an ambivalence that gives her satire an affinity not so much with Huxley as with James—at least, say, the middle James of *A London Life* and "The Death of the Lion." Indeed, *The Edwardians* sometimes reads like a novel of a minor James —a less subtle James, to be sure, but one with the master's satirical relish for documenting country-house custom, and with greater candor about its polite infidelities and scandals. Like James, Victoria Sackville-West allows us to see the great house from more than one perspective. She gives the point of view of Leonard Anquetil, the arctic explorer and social lion of the hour, but she goes further, complementing this with the view of the insider, that of Sebastian, the heir of Chevron. In fact, it is the conflict of these two points of view that gives thematic substance to the novel.

The Edwardians opens with Sebastian literally standing on the leads of the vast roof of Chevron and enjoying his high, free view of the house, garden, and park spread out before him.[13] It closes with his riding to the coronation of George V in the musty family coach—which, he discovers, has no handle on the inside of the door and a window too firmly stuck to be opened. The two scenes embody the contrast between Sebastian's view of Chevron and Anquetil's. For Sebastian does appreciate the life of Chevron, not the superficial life of his mother's parties and guests, but "the whole community of the great house." To him, the hum of its work and routines, the estate business, the immediate relations with craftsmen and tenants—"an order of things which appeared unchangeable to the mind of nineteen hundred and five"—means "warmth and security, leisure and continuity" (*TE,* pp. 39–40). On the other hand, Anquetil sees the world of Chevron and its traditions as a stifling prison which a young man like Sebastian should determine to escape.

This is not a simple black-and-white contrast, since both points of view are presented with a complicating irony. At Chevron, Anquetil, the guest of the duchess herself, is in the beginning alternately bored, critical, and sardonically amused. The whole magnificent place, he feels, is "a dead thing, an anachronism, an exquisite survival." Under the influence of Sebastian, however, Anquetil—for all his "democratic instincts" (*TE*, p. 58)—almost succumbs to the spell of Chevron and the past. Indeed, he has to force himself to resist much that he finds dignified, elegant, and gracious; and he becomes determined to show Sebastian that he "*ought* to rebel against the oppression of the past" (*TE*, p. 69). "A place like Chevron," he warns the young duke, "is really a despot of the most sinister sort: it disguises its tyranny under the mask of love" (*TE*, p. 75). Thereupon, he invites Sebastian to leave Chevron and join his expedition to the Arctic: "Learn another point of view. This is your opportunity" (*TE*, p. 79).

This lower-class counsel of perfection hardly endears the explorer to the young duke. Sebastian promptly refuses the invitation, but the admonishment is not forgotten; in fact, it plagues him throughout the rest of the novel. In spite of the fact that his sense of "silent communion with Chevron" (*TE*, p. 231) seems to Sebastian a profoundly worthwhile experience in comparison to his superficial love affairs with a titled lady, a middle-class housewife, and an artist's model, he can no longer be at ease there. Even his sister Viola, now educated to Anquetil's point of view, presses him hard about his vested status. "Your love for Chevron isn't pure," she tells him. "It includes the whole system on which Chevron is run. It includes . . . the carpenter's shop, and the forge, and the wood-cutters; and it includes your relationship to them" (*TE*, p. 222). Their extended debate in the fifth chapter is not unlike the debate which is at the center of James's *Princess Casamassima*, where the country house of Medley functions in a way analogous to Chevron. And it is a genuine debate because it evidently reflects the divisions of the author herself. Indeed, she has to cut a Gordian knot to conclude her novel. After his experience in the stifling coach, Sebastian encounters Anquetil once again, and receives another invitation to explore the world. Still hesitating because of Chevron, he is supplied with the perfect motive. "You'll be a better master to Chevron," the explorer tells him (*TE*, p. 314). This time, Sebastian does go with Anquetil, but he leaves the basic dilemmas of the novel unresolved behind him. In this respect, a comment of Yeats on *The Edwardians* is, in fact, both relevant and characteristic. "Miss Sackville-West," the poet wrote in a letter, "sees only the futility of her own class—and all that is admirable; but O those radical critics O that Arctic explorer. . . . It is not true that it is easier to live a profound life in an Arctic hut than in Knole, unless the Arctic hut means the ascetic's contemplation. . . . I said I hate the book, yet I admire it immensely." [14] As inconclusive as *Heartbreak House*, *The Edwardians* survives mainly as satire rather than as sociology.

Heartbreak House and *The Edwardians,* portraying the country house on the eve of war, imply an ambiguous prognosis by hindsight. *Crome Yellow,* looking into the future, leaves no doubt about its ultimate fate. Both *Lady Chatterley's Lover* and *A Handful of Dust,* however, show the country house come to grief in the immediate present. Indeed, allowing for all the differences between Lawrence and Waugh, we cannot help noting that the basic plot situations in these two novels are remarkably similar. Both novels return to one of the major motifs of modern fiction: the cuckolded husband. Moreover, like the line of novels from Flaubert and Tolstoy down to Galsworthy and Ford, they both employ the familiar triangle not for itself alone but to make a social comment: to reveal the failure of a class through the inadequacy of one of its male representatives who must discover that his wife is being unfaithful to him with an objectionable outsider. [15] Clifford Chatterley of Wragby Hall and Tony Last of Hetton Abbey, whatever their individual differences, suffer a similar doom; and in each novel the manorial seat is more than a setting: it embodies the moral collapse of the stately home and its traditions.

That Lawrence should have concerned himself so directly with the country house may seem uncharacteristic at first. Of all the writers we have considered, he might be expected to seem the least knowledgeable about it. A collier's son, who from birth to early manhood knew only the world of the mining village, Lawrence was even more remote from the actuality of the country house than H. G. Wells, who, through an outsider, was at least familiar with its atmosphere and regimen. Yet as a sensitive observer who rose from his own class without ever adopting the allegiances of another, Lawrence became extraordinarily perceptive about social matters. His later personal experiences in the country-house world, combined with his profound sense of things English—of, above all, "Old England"—that he assimilated from his reading, gave him what he needed to understand the archetypal nature of the country house.

What direct contact Lawrence had with the country houses may have been limited; but as a novelist on whom nothing was ever lost, he made the most of his familiarity with those he did know. Two houses did, in fact, play an important part in his life. The first was Lamb Close, a mansion in the vicinity of Eastwood, where Lawrence grew up. Belonging to the estate of the Barbers, a mine-owning family, it was, according to Harry T. Moore, a house of rather recent growth: originally a farmhouse that the owner (Matthew Lamb) turned into a shooting box in the eighteenth century, it was bought by the Barbers and elaborately rebuilt. Lawrence, Moore observes, gave no indication that he was ever inside the house; but he often walked or cycled past and caught sight of the young squire on horseback, and there is one account of his being ordered off the property while crossing through it. In any case, the Barbers apparently came to epitomize for Lawrence the type of gentry who lose touch with the land around them and live by mechanically exploiting its resources. Moreover, Lamb Close itself appears frequently in Lawrence's fiction—as High Close in *The White Peacock;* Shortlands, the home of the Criches in *Women in Love;* Shottle Home in *Aaron's Rod.* Even Chatterley's Wragby Hall, Moore notes, looks strangely like Lamb Close.[16] Wragby is described as "a long low house in brown stone, begun about the middle of the eighteenth century." And, much like Lamb Close, Wragby stands "on an eminence in a rather fine old park of oak trees" and looks out upon the smoke and steam of the colliery pit lowering over the "raw straggle of Tevershall village [Eastwood?], which began almost at the park gates" (*LCL,* p. 11).

The other house was the far more distinguished Garsington Manor, which we have already mentioned in relation to *Crome Yellow.* Lawrence knew this one better than any other because of his close, though short-lived, relationship with Lady Ottoline Morrell. Both the house and his hostess made a profound impression upon him, as his letters reveal. If Lamb Close was for Lawrence a manifestation of what was ugly and blighting in the English class system, Garsington's beauty, graciousness, and hospitality gave him an almost Jamesian sense of other possibilities. "Here," he wrote in 1915, "one feels the real England—this old house, this countryside—so poignantly." [17] Indeed, for a time he fell almost completely under its spell and even saw Garsington as the possible seat of a new community that he, Lady Ottoline, Bertrand Russell, and others might form to save England. "We must have some meetings at Garsington," he wrote to Lady Ottoline:

> Garsington must be the retreat where we come together and knit ourselves together. Garsington is wonderful for that. It is like the Boccaccio place where they told all the Decamerone. That wonderful lawn, under the ilex trees, with the old house and its exquisite old front—it is *so* remote, so perfectly a small world to itself, where one can get away from the temporal things to consider the big things. We must draw together.[18]

Indeed, the spell of Garsington evidently became so seductive that Lawrence, rather like the fictional Anquetil in *The Edwardians,* had to force himself to resist. "It was jolly to be at Garsington," he wrote, this time to Lady Cynthia Asquith:

> it is in its way so beautiful, one is tempted to give in, and to stay there, to lapse back into its peaceful beauty of bygone things, to live in pure recollection, looking at the accomplished past, which is so lovely. But one's soul rebels.[19]

It is not that the country house caused any irritation to a democratic conscience as it did with James: Lawrence had no a priori objection to aristocracy as such; in fact, he once wrote sympathetically of Hardy's country-house novel *A Laodicean,* because he found the *predilection d'artiste* for the aristocracy "rooted deeply in every imaginative being." [20] No, for Lawrence Garsington was to be resisted because its day was over:

> This place is so beautiful, so complete, and so utterly past, bygone, reminiscent, that it seems like a dying man seeing the whole of his past life in a flash, as he dies.[21]

In a curious, visionary passage, Lawrence takes up this image of the drowning man; and identifying himself with the house, with England, with the English past, he follows the cycle of a day which at dawn leads him out of the house toward life but which eventually brings him back to the house—and death:

> Shafted, looped windows between the without and the within, the old house, the perfect old intervention of fitted stone, fitted perfectly about a silent soul, the soul that in drowning under this last wave of time looks out clear through the shafted windows to see the dawn of all dawns taking place, the England of all recollection rousing into being. . . .
>
> Coming home . . . to the stone, old three-pointed house with its raised chimney stacks, the old manor house lifting its fair, pure stone amid trees and foliage, rising from the lawn, we pass the pond where white ducks hastily launch upon the lustrous dark grey waters.
>
> So to the steps to the porch, through the doorway, and into the interior, fragrant with all the memories of old age, and of bygone, remembered lustiness.
>
> It is the vision of the drowning man, the vision of all that I am, all I have become, and ceased to be. It is me, generations and generations of me. . . . And oh, my God, I cannot bear it. For it is not this me who am drowning swiftly under the last wave of time, this bursten flood.[22]

Garsington, with its almost uncanny spell and ambiguous symbolic overtones, evidently became for Lawrence a kind of Spenserian Bower of Bliss. He was in danger of being lured from

what he considered his true and appointed path, and he apparently steeled himself not to succumb to the appeal of the
country house so gracefully represented there. Indeed, *Women in
Love* shows him turning his experiences at Garsington into
material for satire, lampooning some of the very same people
Huxley caricatured in *Crome Yellow* but in a manner rather less
genial. Hermione Roddice, it seems generally agreed, is a rather
cruel portrait of Lady Ottoline herself.[23] And though the country house of Breadalby is not physically modeled on Garsington
Manor (Breadalby is described as a Georgian house; Garsington is
Tudor), Lawrence intensified his more negative reactions toward
what it represented in the impressions of Birkin. Attracted by
the past and the "house, so still and golden, the park slumbering
its centuries of peace," Birkin nevertheless concludes: ". . . what
a snare and a delusion, this beauty of static things—what a horrible dead prison Breadalby really was, what an intolerable confinement, the peace!" [24]

It is not surprising, therefore, that when he came to write
Lady Chatterley's Lover a decade later, Lawrence chose to forget
what was distractingly beautiful at Garsington and to select a
more suitable model for the dismal Wragby Hall in the Lamb
Close he remembered glowering over Eastwood, though peopling
it with some of the more thin-blooded, cerebral types he met
through Lady Ottoline. Wragby had to symbolize all that was
deadening in the upper classes of contemporary English society,
and there was no place for the kind of lighting that subdued and
qualified the portrait with allusion to past beauty and graciousness. The past and the old hierarchical system even at its worst,
Lawrence was willing to admit, had a sense of "togetherness"
lacking in the present. "In the old England," he wrote in "A
Propos of *Lady Chatterley's Lover*," "the curious blood-connec-
tion held the classes together. The squires might be arrogant,
violent, bullying and unjust, yet in some ways they were *at one*
with the people, part of the same blood-stream. We feel it in
Defoe and Fielding." On the other hand, he maintained, the
individualism of the cultivated classes today destroyed this, and
the growing sense of apartness and class-consciousness became

"thoroughly unpleasant, English in the bad, mean, snobbish sense of the word." [25] Wragby Hall, consequently, had to be shown as "thoroughly unpleasant" in just this sense.

To fail to emphasize this function of Wragby is to neglect both the social dimension of *Lady Chatterley's Lover* and its symbolic form as well. The novel's structural design, as Julian Moynahan points out, is really a spatial one: "the most enduring meanings of the novel are inextricably bound up with the arrangement of its locations—the manor house, the industrial village, and the wood." Indeed, comparing the three texts of the novel, Mark Schorer has noted that the most obvious development from one version to another is Lawrence's increase in the description of both the mechanical world and the wood of the Chatterley estate. Wragby Hall, presented first, embodies the world into which Connie has married and which she must eventually reject.[26] A "warren of a place without much distinction," the family seat of the Chatterleys stands physically close to the raw, straggling mining village from which its wealth is drawn; but the house and its occupants remain aloof and isolated from the community around them. "There was no communication between Wragby Hall and Tevershall village," Connie is made to recognize. Not even the vestiges of the old order survive: "No caps were touched, no courtseys bobbed. The colliers merely stared" (*LCL*, pp. 11–13).

The condition of the house, moreover, is metaphorically the condition of Clifford Chatterley, Connie's husband.[27] "He was not in touch with anybody, save, traditionally, with Wragby" (*LCL*, p. 15). And even this relation is rather insecure. He is not the true heir of Wragby: he is only a second son become heir through the death of his older brother during the war. "Now he was heir and responsible for Wragby," he reflects. "Was that not terrible? And also splendid and at the same time perhaps purely absurd?" (*LCL*, p. 9). Moreover, he himself has been crippled by the war; paralyzed from the waist down, he must go about the estate in a mechanical chair. What is worse, he is sexually maimed as well and thus cannot provide an heir for Wragby. In a word, he is the last of the Chatterleys. Clifford consequently attempts to find in his obsessive sense of property a substitute for a more vital sense of connection and continuity. Ironically, this is brought out most pointedly in a scene in the great wood of the Wragby estate, which comes to mean so much to Connie after she meets Mellors. "This is the old England, the heart of it," Clifford tells Connie, "and I intend to keep it intact." But it becomes clear that he is talking merely from a sense of possession rather than a genuine aesthetic-historical awareness. "I want nobody to trespass in it" (*LCL*, p. 47). And this abstract sense of relationship allows him to propose that Connie might provide an heir for Wragby by having a child by another man.

Even more important is the effect of the lifeless, shut-in atmosphere of Wragby on Connie herself. Though she is its mistress, she has no sense of any real intimacy with the place. Lawrence's imagery stresses the cold efficiency of the life she finds there: "All these endless rooms that nobody used, all the Midlands routine, the mechanical cleanliness and the mechanical order! . . . No warmth of feeling united it organically. The house seemed as dreary as a disused street" (*LCL*, p. 16). She cannot call Wragby "home"—"it was a warm word to use for that great, weary warren" (*LCL*, p. 70). Before she meets Mellors, her only moments of contentment are those away from the house in the solitude of the great wood.

In *Lady Chatterley's Lover,* Wragby functions in a way almost diametrically opposite to those country houses of James and Forster and Ford which, by evoking a sense of a living tradition or an organic relation with the natural landscape, affirm community. Wragby is, instead, the negative pole of the novel; the great wood beyond from which it is dissociated becomes the positive. It is in this mysterious, sacred wood that Connie first sees Mellors—significantly a gamekeeper *and* a kind of natural gentleman; and it is the wood that provides the symbolic background for the transformation that takes place in Connie through sexual relationship with him. This symbolic function of the wood has been clearly described by others;[28] what should be emphasized here is that this profound development of Connie in the natural world of the wood makes her even more alert and sensitive to the decay of the social world around her.

Indeed, if the description of Connie's sexual awakening with

Mellors carries the burden of Lawrence's psychological theme, the brilliant narrative sequence of Connie's trip through the Midlands, in chapter 11, provides a vivid sociological document of great power. Plowing through the squalid mining village, her car passes the dark ruins of Worsop Castle, idles in Stakes Gate, with its new "works" and "model dwellings," and rolls out into the country uplands, where another country house reminds her of the changes overtaking England:

> It had once been a proud and lordly county. In front, looming against and hanging on the brow of the sky-line, was the huge and splendid bulk of Chadwick Hall, more window than wall, one of the most famous Elizabethan houses. Noble it stood alone above a great park, but out of date, passed over. It was still kept up, but as a show place. "Look how our ancestors lorded it!" [*LCL*, p. 183] [29]

It is a sharper vision of England than she has ever had—of the past and the present, of the radical discontinuity between the past and the present.

> England, my England! But which is *my* England? The stately homes of England and make good photographs, and create the illusion of connection with the Elizabethans. The handsome old halls are here, from the days of Good Queen Anne and Tom Jones. But smuts fall and blacken on the drab stucco, that has long ceased to be golden. . . .
>
> Now they are pulling down the stately homes, the Georgian halls are going. Fritchley, a perfect old Georgian mansion was even now, as Connie passed in the car, being demolished. It was in perfect repair: till the war the Weatherleys always lived in style there. But now it was too big, too expensive, and the country had become too uncongenial. The gentry were departing to pleasanter places, where they could spend their money without having to see how it was made. [*LCL*, p. 185]

The climax of this trip is her visit to Shipley, a Georgian mansion, truly superior to Wragby: "It was much lighter, more alive, shapen and elegant. . . . Even the corridors managed to be ample and lovely, softly curved and full of life" (*LCL*, p. 186).

The Lawrence of the early Garsington mood seems to be speaking; but Shipley, like Wragby, is also being smothered by the collieries crowding its park. Its squire, Leslie Winter, who once felt "in a good-natured but quite grand way lord of his own domain and of his own colliers" (*LCL*, p. 187), now has the sense of being shoved out by the spirit and will of an alien population. Moreover, Connie learns with his death that Shipley itself has come to an end. The heirs gave the order for demolishing the house, then denuded the park of its timber, divided the estate into lots, and sold them for semidetached villas. With Shipley gone, the doom of the country-house world seems final.

For the social collapse embodied herein, Connie has her own private solution: she will join Mellors in a farmer's cottage. Like Connie, Lawrence himself sought his own individual solutions; but from another point of view, he was not an individualist in any anarchic sense. His basic instinct was, as he said himself, a "societal instinct," [30] an impulse toward community. Therefore, not the least impressive aspect of *Lady Chatterley's Lover* is his almost documentary account of the dissolution of the great country houses and his understanding of the broad social implications for the nation:

> One England blots out another. The England of the Squire Winters and the Wragby Halls was gone, dead. The blotting out was only not yet complete.
> What would come after? [*LCL*, p. 189]

Despite the bitterness of these pages of the novel, however, something remains of the ambivalence Lawrence felt about Garsington. He finds the old aristocratic order dead or at least dying, but at the same time he is objecting to the failure of its best representatives to resist the industrial, mechanical forces he found ugly and dehumanizing. Wragby Hall is indicted not so much for what it is as for what it is not. Paradoxically, Lawrence's indictment of the country house implies a kind of lament for lost opportunities.

There are resemblances to be found between *A Handful of Dust* and *Lady Chatterley's Lover*. Indeed, from one point of view Waugh's novel might be taken as a parody of Lawrence's. Here again, a country gentleman preoccupied with his ancestral home is married to a woman who, bored with his house and his company, betrays him with a man not a member of their own class but a stranger, an outsider—one farcical difference being, of course, that in *A Handful of Dust* the other man, John Beaver, is not in the least like Mellors but the rather dreary, seemingly sexless, parasitic son of a high-society decorator. To be sure, Tony Last, the husband, is a more sympathetic character than Clifford Chatterley—foolish perhaps but decent. His absurd fate, however, is no less exemplary; and his house, Hetton Abbey, like Wragby Hall, epitomizes the delusions and losses of a social order.

These resemblances, seemingly fanciful at first, are rooted in deeper ones. Despite the fact that Lawrence and Waugh are two modern writers whom we are not very likely to associate, they are in several respects concerned with the same problems. Waugh is in his own way also preoccupied with the frustration of what Lawrence called the "societal instinct" and the quest for community. To be specific, the London scenes in his earlier fiction do, for all their unpretentious levity, expose the breakdown of authentic relationships in modern society by satirizing the pseudocommunity of modern partygoing with its forced, hysterical togetherness ("Masked parties, Savage parties, Victorian parties, Greek parties, Wild West parties, Russian parties, Circus parties, parties where one has to dress as someone else, almost naked parties in St. John's wood, parties in flats and studios and ships and hotels and night clubs . . . all that succession and repetition of massed humanity. . . . Those vile bodies").[31] Furthermore, like Lawrence and his other contemporaries, Waugh also developed his own countersymbols of community. Throughout his novels, as Frederick J. Stopp observes, "symbols of allegiance to a group"—a home, a city, a club, a *civitas*—become increasingly prominent. Buildings, of course, recur most frequently. Waugh's characters, as Stopp adds, are often seeking "to preserve or create a local habitation"; in their fantasy life, the "country of their desire is symbolized by some architectural structure, some sign of human occupancy." The major symbol of this kind in Waugh's fiction is the country house. Admittedly, Waugh's penchant for stately homes is not unalloyed with a certain snobbery; nevertheless, its more serious historic and aesthetic side must also be credited. Waugh himself has called the country house England's chief national artistic achievement, and in a Jamesian tone he has spoken of these ancient buildings as "monuments to the living past." In the words of Eric Linklater, Waugh obviously finds in "the integrated and purposeful existence on a nobleman's estate" a dramatic foil for the chaos of modern life. Indeed, with the exception of Henry James and possibly Elizabeth Bowen, no other novelist has so consistently employed the country house as a symbol in one work after another.[32]

This is not to say, however, that Waugh has presented the country house in a monotonous or solemn manner. As Stopp himself comments, "the contrast, change, and vandalistic rebuilding of these structures reflects the theme of each story," but the actual tone may be "comic, tragic, or burlesque." [33] In the early novels, particularly, the tone is just as satirical as that of Shaw or Huxley. The reader is presented with crumbling ancestral seats, often bizarrely redecorated in a style alien to the dignity of the original, or serving a function absurdly incongruous with the graciousness and order of their past. In *Decline and Fall,* for example, Llannabba Castle, which from one vantage point seems a "model of medieval impregnability," is not feudal at all but only redone in Victorian Gothic, and it now operates as a fifth-rate public school. In the same novel, moreover, Kings Thursday, an unspoiled Tudor mansion, when sold to Margot Best Chestwynde, is torn down and rebuilt as "something clean and square" by an architect best known for his design of a chewing gum factory. Again, in *Vile Bodies,* old Doubting Castle is turned into the setting for an all-talkie, super-religious film story of John Wesley.

In *A Handful of Dust,* one of Waugh's best novels, Hetton Abbey is used for all it is worth to produce a double-edged satirical effect. On one level, Hetton represents the traditional order of landed England and thus offers the familiar contrast with the shallow, anarchic world of fashionable London. The quiet

seclusion of the estate, with its mildly ceremonious tempo, com-
pares favorably with the frenetic partygoing of Lady Cockpurse's
circle. ("I don't keep up the house," Tony explains, "to be a
hostel for a lot of bores to come and gossip in," *HD*, p. 19).
Moreover, rather like Howards End, Hetton stands as a symbolic
counter to the city flat, which to Waugh as much as to Forster is
a manifestation of the nomadic rootlessness and discontinuity
of contemporary life. It is not an accident, therefore, that Tony,
the fond master of the Abbey, is betrayed by his wife Brenda in
a tiny maisonette designed by Mrs. Beaver herself, a specialist in
the new tastes of the well-to-do. ("What people want, she said,
was somewhere to dress and telephone," *HD*, p. 52). Indeed, it
is significant that Tony's humiliating downfall has its origins in
Brenda's boredom with her country home and her self-centered
preference for the trivial excitements of the West End.

At the same time, however, both Hetton and its master are
themselves objects of Waugh's satire. The "madly feudal" Tony
is a good man in his way, but he is also naïve and rather absurd.
As Walter Allen remarks, he may not get what he deserves, but
certainly what he must expect: "he is betrayed as much by the
nature of his illusions as by his wife."[34] The house, as we see
from the first, epitomizes these illusions. Despite Tony's attachment to every glazed brick and encaustic tile, Hetton, "formerly
one of the notable houses of the country," but "entirely rebuilt
in 1864 in the Gothic style," is, as the local guide book coolly
informs us, "now devoid of interest." Besides, simply as a
dwelling, it is ridiculously uncomfortable: quarter chimes from
the central clock tower disturb all but the heaviest sleepers; an
ecclesiastical gloom pervades the great hall; and the antiquated
heating apparatus gives off blasts of hot air or leaves a cavernous
chill (*HD*, pp. 13–14).[35]

Obviously, Hetton Abbey is not meant to stand for any authentic living tradition. On the contrary, its battlements, towers,
groined ceilings, and stained glass windows are all sham Gothic
of the nineteenth-century revival. As Richard Wasson shows in
his perceptive essay on the novel, Waugh has intentionally made
Hetton a ludicrous embodiment of the picturesque medievalism
of those Victorians who, in their attempt to patch up and disguise

the broken tradition bequeathed to them by the Renaissance, revived the trappings of a once vital past without any genuine awareness of their spiritual substance.[36] Within its make-believe crenellated walls. Tony lives out a fantasy inherited from his Victorian forebears and their literature and so has lost touch with the realities of the contemporary society around him.

Indeed, Tony's absurd doom is forecast and mirrored by Hetton itself. With the bedrooms named preposterously after the knights and ladies of Arthurian legend, Hetton becomes a parody of ancient Camelot. Brenda's sleeping alone in "Guinevere" portends from the beginning a cuckold's fate for the "madly feudal" Tony. His own room, "Morgan le Fay," which has been his since childhood and which still houses "a gallery representative of every phrase of his adolescence" (*HD*, p. 15) reflects the boyish immaturity incapable of coping with Brenda's duplicity. At each stage of Tony's downfall Hetton plays its part. Though he lives for his house and for keeping it up, Tony sacrifices needed repairs to give Brenda a flat in London and thus unwittingly assists her infidelity. Soon after the death of John Andrew, his only son and heir to the family seat, Tony learns of his wife's relationship with Beaver when she writes that she will not return to Hetton and wishes a divorce. To ease her divorce, he goes through a staged adultery in a seaside hotel that serves as a humiliating contrast to the quiet decency of Hetton. And his most painful disillusionment comes when Brenda admits to him that she expects Hetton to be sold to meet her demands for alimony: "A whole Gothic world had come to grief . . . there are now no armour, glittering in the forest glades, no embroidered feet on the greensward; the cream and dappled unicorns had fled" (*HD*, p. 209). Of course the final irony is that, with Tony believed dead in a Brazilian jungle, though actually trapped there by the eccentric Mr. Todd, who wants a companion to read Dickens aloud to him, Hetton is correspondingly reduced to a breeding farm for silver foxes.

Tony Last, as his symbolic name obviously portends from the start, is, like Clifford Chatterley, the last of his line, and Hetton Abbey, like Wragby Hall, sums up in its own way the inadequacies of a class and the failure of a tradition. It is true, of course, as Frank Kermode points out, that "Hetton, within the limits of Tony's understanding, is an emblem of the true City"; but what *A Handful of Dust* mercilessly renders is "the limits of Tony's understanding." Like Huxley's antiquarian Henry Wimbush in *Crome Yellow,* Tony is so oriented to the past that he is crippled in his dealings with the present. In other words, he lacks a genuine historical sense, which, as T. S. Eliot noted, involves "a sense of the timeless as well as of the temporal and of the timeless and temporal together," so that one is able to be "acutely conscious of his place in time, of his own contemporaneity." [37] Waugh himself returns to the country house and the possibility of a more vital orientation toward the past in *Brideshead Revisited* and *Sword of Honour,* which we shall consider in the next chapter. The Hetton Abbey he designed for *A Handful of Dust,* however, belongs with the "heartbreak houses" of his fellow satirists.

 Chronologically falling between *Lady Chatterley's Lover* (1928) and *A Handful of Dust* (1934) is Christopher Isherwood's early novel *The Memorial* (1932), which pronounces its doom upon the country house by combining, so to speak, the mood of Lawrence with the manner of Waugh. Like Lawrence, young Isherwood was determined to document the malaise which spread through England after the war. His novel, as he explains in *Lions and Shadows,* is about the war, "not the War itself, but the effects of the idea of 'War' " on his generation. "I was out to write an epic," he admits; but it was to be one deliberately deflated in form: "a potted epic; an epic disguised as a drawing room comedy." [38]

 The war theme is announced in the title: the memorial is a war memorial to the fallen dead of a Cheshire village; and its dedication in 1920, a major event of the novel, ritualistically brings together characters whose lives have been so changed and blighted by the war that the official clichés of the public ceremony produce ironic effects reminiscent of Flaubert's agricultural fair in *Madame Bovary.* The memorial is not the only symbol, however. Equally central in establishing a sense of dissolution is Vernon Hall, the nearby country house, whose young heir is one of the commemorated dead. Indeed, *The Memorial* is essentially the story of the decline of Vernon Hall and the people associated with it through several generations; and once this is recognized, the spare economical construction and the relativistic time scheme employed become even more meaningful. Abandoning continuous narrative and chronological sequence, Isherwood presents four limited periods of time: 1920, 1925, 1928, and 1929. Beginning *in medias res* with 1928, he returns to the earlier years. The novel is, in his own words, "an epic in an album of snapshots"; [39] each of the four sections gives a particular "snapshot" of the house in a revealing moment of its recent history, and their juxtaposition dramatizes through contrast the progressive stages of its degeneration. Moreover, the perspective afforded by this relativistic time sequence is augmented by a correspondingly relativistic handling of the point of view. Vernon Hall is seen through the eyes of several different characters, each one providing his own distinctive colorations.

In the first part (1928), the dominant point of view is that of Mrs. Vernon, the widow of Richard Vernon, heir to the Hall. It is evident that her world has been thoroughly swept away: her country home is "shut up and empty, in the hands of caretakers" (*TM*, pp. 26–27); and she is now living alone in a London flat. Yet she remains neurotically fixed in the past, still keeping up the role of a wife bereaved by the war and pursuing antiquarian interests in the company of Major Charlesworth, a Prufrockian bachelor, who is charmed by her "reactionary romanticism" (*TM*, p. 29). The second part, turning back to 1920, pictures the Hall in moods of nostalgia and apprehension aroused by the war's immediate aftermath. A friend of the dead Richard Vernon, Edward Blake, a tortured homosexual, coming back to the Hall once more, remembers a perfect holiday there, when "spellbound by the aged silence of the house, the garden and the woods," he found it "the only place where he could have lived forever, untormented by his restlessness" (*TM*, p. 133). Here, too, Mrs. Vernon sentimentally recalls the halcyon days of the Hall before the war—"a beautiful, happy world, in which next summer would be the same, and the next and the next" (*TM,* p. 87).

But these wistful glances backward ironically accentuate the changes which are overtaking the Hall in 1920 and which will reduce it to the moribund state already depicted in the first part of the novel. Mrs. Vernon, like Lawrence's gentry, shudders anxiously and uncomprehendingly at the new brick villas crowding the park gates. Her father-in-law, John Vernon, the squire, has become a paralytic, slobbering old man, tucked into his carriage like a great naughty child and stared at by curious newcomers. His daughter Mary, seeing him through their eyes, suddenly realizes that the world of Vernon Hall is now an anachronism: "Landowners were becoming obsolete. The vehicle he sat in was obsolete. The animal which drew it was nearly obsolete" (*TM,* p. 124). And Mrs. Vernon's son Eric, burdened with his mother's fixation on the past and with a nervous stammer, finds no meaning in the possibility of his eventually inheriting the Hall and comes to hate its suffocating atmosphere. In consequence, the third part (1925) presents an open break between Eric and his mother over Vernon Hall. "You care more for this house than you do for human beings," he tells her. "When it's mine . . . I shall have it pulled down" (*TM,* pp. 202–03).

Finally, in the closing part of the novel (1929), Vernon Hall suffers the familiar ignominious fate of many another country house: it is sold to a Midlands manufacturer. It will never be restored, as Mary Vernon recognizes upon an impromptu visit before the new owners, the middle-class Rambothams, take over. "How extraordinary," she then thinks, "that real live people have lived here. For now the house was quite dead. It had died of neglect. It was a show place, like all the others. Mrs. Ramsbotham would probably not bring it back to life. She would like it better dead. She would have garden parties here and houseparties from the south. She was a climber" (*TM,* p. 246).

Furthermore, it was obvious once again that the fate of Vernon Hall, like the fate of other ancestral houses already discussed, is to be taken as representative. For Isherwood as for Huxley and Lawrence and Waugh, the demise of the country house dramatizes the material, social, and moral bankruptcy of the old order in a new era. Indeed, in a manner reminiscent of Lawrence in *Lady Chatterley's Lover,* Isherwood makes a point of supporting and extending the symbolic implications of the decline of Vernon Hall by showing what has happened to other great houses as well. In the very beginning of *The Memorial,* for example, there is a passage that describes the coming dismantlement of a house chosen for one of the archaeological excursions of Mrs. Vernon and Major Charlesworth. Here, through detail and tone, Isherwood, leaving no doubt that this sort of demolition has become typically routine, prefigures what is in store for other places. The passage brings to mind one cited earlier from *Crome Yellow* and almost echoes another from D. H. Lawrence. Simply to quote it is to sum up the postwar decade's satirical prognosis about the English country house:

> They met, that afternoon, in the grounds of the house they had come to visit, an old mansion in the far western suburbs— the country residence of a family which was just about to relinquish it. In a few months the low white building with its Ionic portico, its Queen Anne windows, its long vista of shaven lawns between high elms which did not quite hide a steady stream of cars and buses along the distant road, would be sold, the house pulled down, the land used for building, for allotments, for playing fields. The boards were already up at the drive gates, and the old caretaker who received them seemed bowed with the sense of impending disaster. The whole spirit of the meeting was tactful and hushed. Permission to view had been obtained as a special favour. There were three Lelys in the long gallery and a landscape by Cotman. They would be sold at Christie's. Some wonderful Jacobean furniture. The family had been driven into hotels, on to chicken farms, away to the south of France. The caretaker was alone, waiting for the enemy. [*TM*, p. 28]

❦ 4 ❧

Setting the House
in Order

THE COUNTRY HOUSE IN A TIME OF TROUBLES:

Yeats, Bowen, Green,
Woolf, Cary, Waugh

O, But I saw a solemn sight;
Said the rambling, shambling, travelling man;
Castle Dargan's ruin all lit,
Lovely ladies dancing in it.
    What though they danced! Those days are
        gone,
Said the wicked, crooked, hawthorne tree;
Lovely lady or gallant man
Are blown cold dust or a bit of bone.
    O, what is life but a mouthful of air?
Said the rambling, shambling, travelling man;
Yet all the lovely things that were
Live, for I saw them dancing there.
             William Butler Yeats,
     The King of the Great Clock Tower

        In succession
Houses rise and fall, crumble, are extended,
Are removed, destroyed, restored . . .
        T. S. Eliot, "East Coker"

Satire, to be sure, was not the only response to the eclipse of the country house during the years between the wars. Almost in symphonic counterplay, there were statements of nostalgia, veneration, and lament. Even in the early twenties, when the satirists reigned, literary obeisance was still being paid, so that within a year or two after *Heartbreak House* and *Crome Yellow*, we find such works of appreciation as *Earlham* (1922), Percy Lubbock's beautiful reminiscence of childhood in an East Anglian country house, and *Knole and the Sackvilles* (1922), V. Sackville-West's gracious account of her famous home and its history. Indeed, both of these books, though autobiographical and historical, are singularly imaginative in their rendering of the attractions of the great house and might very well seem to be designed as ripostes to the prevailing mockery. Rather Proustian in its pensive recapture of the past, *Earlham* creates the ambience of the old hall named in the title not through narrative but by nuance of mood and cherished image. *Knole and the Sackvilles*, in turn, manages to give the ancient mansion a living identity that somehow transcends the fluctuations of its own history. Each in its own way thus anticipated the theme and tone of what was to come.[1]

After the twenties these counterthemes—introduced, so to speak, in a minor key—shifted to the major. As the frivolities of one decade yielded to the anxieties of another, the friendlier, if ambivalent, attitude of earlier writers toward the country house became dominant once again. During the late thirties, in the charged atmosphere of crisis, dislocation, and violence, the satirical preoccupation with the absurdities attending the decline and fall of the great house gave way to a rather sober concern with the meaning and value of what was falling. Just as any one of the novels discussed in the previous chapter might have been suitably called *Heartbreak House* after Shaw's play, the title of Evelyn Waugh's *Brideshead Revisited* might be said to express the later mood of genial retrospection and generous reassessment. With the threat and finally the outbreak of war, the country house recovered its former potency as a symbol of order and continuity. Satire now modulated into elegy.

Actually, as mentioned in the previous chapter, the elegiac sense of the house as a lost community had already been expressed during the twenties in the poetry of William Butler Yeats. While *Lady Chatterley's Lover* and *The Memorial* were appearing in England, Yeats was composing "Ancestral Houses" and his eulogies to Coole Park. Nor was Yeats alone in his response. After the civil war and the ravages of "the Troubles," other writers in Ireland also concerned themselves with the "Big House" and made its passing the theme of fiction and drama. Indeed, such works as Padraic Colum's *Castle Conquer* (1923), Lennox Robinson's *The Big House* (1928), and several of Sean O'Faolain's short stories grow out of much the same mood as "Ancestral Houses" and might very well be taken as the gloss for Yeats's lyrical meditations.

Undoubtedly, the difference in literary response among Irish writers was due in good part to the difference in the actual fate of the house in England and Ireland. The English country house experienced the indignity of being taxed out of existence, sold to profiteers, turned into school or clubhouse, or casually demolished by contracted wreckers. At best it survived as a lifeless museum for tourists. In Ireland, however, the end of the "Big House" was more dramatically linked with revolutionary social change: the house passed away with the Anglo-Irish establishment. During the Troubles, the house was usually burned down and as a charred ruin became a monument to a vanished order. Even when it was not actually destroyed there was a sense of finality lacking in the decline of the house in England—a finality that gave a certain dignity, even tragedy, to its demise. Paradoxically, dying as a social actuality, the house was reborn, transfigured as a symbol. Divorced from the nagging injustices and complexities of its local history, the house came to represent a humane order of culture and civility, a state of community beyond the circumscriptions of nation or class.

In this, moreover, the revolutionary Ireland of the early twentieth century—a microcosm of the modern world, in many ways—was once again a portent of what was to come elsewhere. Torn by the passionate intensities of ideology and the politics of violence, this Ireland revealed in advance the more fiercely aggravated conflicts that would sweep the larger stage of Europe, and her writers often prefigured the imaginative reactions as well. At least the reaction of Yeats and others in Ireland to the fate of the Big House during the anarchy and terror of the twenties anticipated the change in mood that the English novelists of the thirties and forties display when they come to face parallel disorder and violence.

Indeed, of all the works written between the wars, several magnificent poems of William Butler Yeats in *The Tower* (1928) and *The Winding Stair* (1933) best epitomize this change and therefore provide a suggestive link between the appreciation of the great house found in the novels of James and the nostalgia expressed later in *To Be a Pilgrim* and *Brideshead Revisited*. To look back first, it should be emphasized that Yeats is, in fact, remarkably similar to James in his awareness of the symbolic possibilities of the house—and for quite similar reasons. Like the novelist, he had his own sense of separateness or "otherness" and therefore an almost identical need for some image of ideal community that would fulfill his notions of ceremony and grace. Like James, Yeats also entered the aristocratic household as a guest, as an outsider; and what he experienced there from this vantage point of intimacy and detachment took on the quality of discovery, of revelation, so often expressed by James and dramatized in his novels. "Ancestral Houses"—which Lionel Trilling finds an illuminating companion piece to *The Princess Casamassima* [2]—makes the great house an embodiment of the same human possibilities to which James aspired; and the familiar opening lines easily bring to mind the freedom and plenitude of being evoked by the mellow description of Gardencourt at the beginning of *The Portrait of a Lady*:

> Surely among a rich man's flowering lawns,
> Amid the rustle of his planted hills,
> Life overflows without ambitious pains;
> And rains down life until the basin spills,
> And mounts more dizzy high the more it rains

> As though to choose whatever shape it will
> And never stoop to a mechanical
> Or servile shape. . . .

If Yeats found in the house an emblem of the "great good place,"
he was also, like James, able to do so without necessarily yielding
his ironic awareness of evident incongruities. Indeed, another
stanza of "Ancestral Houses" sums up a recurring Jamesian
theme—namely, the disparity between the greatness of the house
and the smallness of its occupants:

> Some violent bitter man, some powerful man
> Called architect and artist in, that they,
> Bitter and violent men, might rear in stone
> The sweetness that all longed for night and day,
> The gentleness none there had ever known:
> But when the master's buried mice can play,
> And maybe the great-grandson of that house,
> For all its bronze and marble, 's but a mouse.[3]

The reason for this ambiguous compound of eulogy and satire
is, furthermore, basically the same in both instances. For Yeats,
as for James, the great house is at once a historical actuality and
a literary symbol. In Ireland before 1916, as T. R. Henn points
out, the Big Houses still remained the centers of hospitality, of
country life and society. But they were not necessarily all alike:
some made their wealth and security the basis for cultured
leisure; others produced the familiar hard-riding country gentleman who rarely opened a book.[4] Yeats did not blink these differences, as his irony reveals; but since he himself was intimate
with some of the finest of the Irish houses, they became the
source of his symbolism.

"At my grandmother's house," Yeats remembered of his boyhood, "I had learnt to love an elaborate house, a garden and
trees, and those grey country houses, Lissadell, Hazelwood
House and the far rarely seen Tower of Markree had always
called to my mind a life set amid natural beauty."[5] As a young
man in Sligo, Yeats came to know Lissadell through its charming
daughters, Constance and Eva Gore-Booth. In Galway, he was

✣ Illustrations ✣

Up Park, Sussex, model for Bladesover in H. G. Wells's *Tono-Bungay*. Photo by the author.

E. M. Forster and his mother in front of Rooksrest, Hertfordshire, model for Howards End. Reproduced by permission of Harcourt Brace Jovanovich from *Marianne Thornton, A Domestic Biography, 1797–1887,* © 1956, by E. M. Forster and Edward Arnold, Ltd.

Busby Hall, model for Groby in Ford Madox Ford's *Parade's End*. Photo courtesy of G. H. Marwood.

Beckley Park, Oxfordshire, model for Aldous Huxley's Crome Yellow. Photo courtesy of *Country Life*.

Garsington Manor, Oxfordshire, home of Lady Ottoline Morrell and model for Breadalby in D. H. Lawrence's *Women in Love*. Photo by the author.

Knole, Kent, home of Victoria Sackville-West, her model for Chevron in *The Edwardians,* and Virginia Woolf's model for the great house in *Orlando*. Photo courtesy of Aerofilms Ltd.

Coole Park, County Galway, Ireland, the home of Lady Gregory. Photo courtesy of Irish Tourist Photo, Bord Failte Photo.

Penshurst Place, Kent, home of the Sidney family and inspiration for Ben Jonson's poem "To Penshurst." Photo courtesy of *Country Life*.

the guest of Edward Martyn at Tulira Castle, and he also went
to Roxborough, the home of Lady Gregory's family, nearby. In
England, moreover, Yeats—like Aldous Huxley and D. H. Lawrence—visited Garsington during the great days of Lady Ottoline Morrell; indeed, the fountain and the straying peacocks of
"Ancestral Houses" were probably inspired by what he saw at
this lovely old manor house in Oxfordshire.[6]

Above all, of course, there was Lady Gregory's Coole Park—
the house that Yeats "came to love . . . more than all other
houses." For Yeats, Coole Park was, indeed, the fulfillment of a
symbolic quest not unlike that of Henry James. "I found at last,"
he wrote, "what I had been seeking, a life of order and of labour,
where all outward things were an image of an inward life."
Lady Gregory herself nourished his sense of what a great house
might be. In the manner of those maternal women of E. M.
Forster and Virginia Woolf, she became hostess, adviser, friend,
"centre of peace." It was Lady Gregory, moreover, who first read
to Yeats Castiglione's *The Courtier,* which further helped to
cultivate his notions of an ideal aristocracy and which even provided some of the attendant images—"the unperturbed and
courtly images"—of a number of poems.[7]

Such images would have undoubtedly appealed to James himself; however, the very titles of the poems in which they occur—
"The People" or "Meditations in Time of Civil War"—remind
us that Yeats was forced to be much more concerned than James
with the historical forces transforming contemporary society and
threatening the great house. James, to be sure, witnessed and
recorded what he sometimes called the *déchéance* of his time,
and, by his own declaration, he possessed the "imagination of
disaster"; nevertheless, he was still able to view society at large
within the comparatively stable framework of the late nineteenth
century. Yeats, in contrast, had to face the anarchy and unmasked
violence of the twentieth. The outbreak of World War I appalled James—indeed, in August 1914 he spoke prophetically of
"this abyss of blood and darkness"; but the holocaust came at
the close of his life. The loosened "blood-dimmed tide" flooded
Yeats in mid-career. Ireland and the great house, too, were
literally going up in the flames of the general conflagration. In

consequence, Yeats shows an affinity not only with James but with later novelists like Elizabeth Bowen and Evelyn Waugh, who because of similar historical circumstances commemorated the highest values of the great house, making them a measure of our modern losses and a reproach to the time.

Even one of the earliest poems Yeats wrote with Coole in mind, "Upon a House Shaken by the Land Agitation," is a response to the historical situation, as its title indicates. But instead of indulging in any kind of sentimentality, the poem boldly asserts the merits of the great house—its "high laughter, loveliness, and ease"—and challenges its would-be despoilers by asking:

> How would the world be luckier if this house,
> Where passion and precision have been one
> Time out of mind, became too ruinous
> To breed the lidless eye that loves the sun?
> And the sweet laughing eagle thoughts that grow
> Where wings have memory of wings, and all
> That comes of the best knit to the best?
>
> [p. 93]

From 1916 through the desperate, unsettling years of the twenties, this challenge is repeated. In a number of poems, images derived from the great house and its customs become symbols of order in a time of trouble. Of Ballylee itself, the ancient tower which he bought and furnished as a home, Yeats could grandly assert:

> I declare this tower is my symbol; I declare
> This winding, gyring, spiring treadmill of a stair
>   is my ancestral stair . . .
>
> [p. 233]

Moreover, with all its other symbolic overtones, Ballylee Tower becomes a kind of miniature of the nobler houses Yeats has known. The poems emanating from the tower are often ritual attempts to preserve against the ruined world outside some traditional sense of community through stylized gesture, commemoration, even prayer. Consider, for example, "Meditations in Time of Civil War," "In Memory of Eva Gore-Booth and Constance Markiewicz," "In Memory of Major of Robert Gregory," "A Prayer on Going into My House," or "A Prayer for My Daughter." Indeed, the closing stanza of this last poem sums up a theme underlying them all:

> And may her bridegroom bring her to a house
> Where all's accustomed, ceremonious;
> For arrogance and hatred are the wares
> Peddled in the thoroughfares.
> How but in custom and in ceremony
> Are innocence and beauty born?
> Ceremony's a name for the rich horn,
> And custom for the spreading laurel tree.
>
> [p. 187]

At Ballylee, furthermore, Yeats remained close to Coole Park and meditated upon the fate of Lady Gregory and her house. Coole was spared during the Troubles, but its mistress was aging and the place was no longer hers. Though she lived out her years there, the house and the great woods were sold in 1927 to the Irish Land Commission. These circumstances occasioned two poems—"Coole Park, 1929" and "Coole Park and Ballylee, 1931"—which, for all their inherent sadness, are not so much lamentations as strong-fibered eulogies to what was passing. In the earlier one, Yeats praises the creative harmony he found at Coole:

> Great works constructed there in nature's spite
> For scholars and for poets after us,
> Thoughts long knitted into a single thought,
> A dance-like glory that those walls begot.
>
> [p. 238]

And he celebrates at the same time the powerful character of Lady Gregory herself, who generously provided others and himself with "A scene well set and excellent company." In "Coole Park and Ballylee, 1931," an even finer poem, Yeats does more: he converts the home of Lady Gregory into a symbol. Bringing a few clear, familiar images to a new crystallization in the last stanzas, he not only magnifies the import the great house of tradition has for him and others to come but also transforms what might seem conventional eulogy into cogent social criticism by rebuking the dislocation and rootlessness of modern life:

> Beloved books that famous hands have bound,
> Old marble heads, old pictures everywhere;
> Great rooms where travelled men and children found
> Content or joy; a last inheritor
> Where none has reigned that lacked a name and fame
> Or out of folly into folly came.
>
> A spot whereon the founders lived and died
> Seemed once more dear than life; ancestral trees,
> Or gardens rich in memory glorified
> Marriages, alliances and families,
> And every bride's ambition satisfied.
> Where fashion or mere fantasy decrees
> We shift about—all that great glory spent—
> Like some poor Arab tribesman and his tent.
>
> [pp. 239–40]

Yeats identified Coole with Lady Gregory. "When she died," he wrote later, "the great house died too." [8] Moreover, this personal loss and the awareness of the interdependence of house and occupant is still evident in later works of Yeats. "The Curse of Cromwell" and *Purgatory* (1939) are informed by the again rather Jamesian recognition that the quality of the house finally rests on the quality of its people and its surrounding society. In *Purgatory* the house is but a ghastly, burnt-out ruin, sharply in contrast with the noble, sunlit mansions of the earlier poems. This dark image, however, as if a film negative, implies by such reversal an equivalent meaning. As the Old Man of the play reveals to the bastard son he has brought there, the ruin was once a great house. The collapse came with the marriage of its heiress to a loutish stable groom who, after exploiting the estate for his own pleasures, burned down the house while he was drunk. The Old Man, the offspring of this misalliance, killed his father in the ruins and thereafter wandered the roads as a peddler. This bleak drama—presenting the reenactment of this terrible past by the

spirits of the dead and ending with the Old Man's murdering his
own son out of a wish to stop the cycle of pollution—has more
than one meaning. On one level, the implications are obviously
sociological: as John Heath-Stubbs points out, the ruin of the
great house suggests the failure of both the Anglo-Irish aristocracy
and the newly-risen bourgeoisie to preserve the best traditions of
the past.[9] Indeed, the lines of the Old Man, like Yeats's poems
about Coole, recall the great days of the house:

> Great people lived and died in this house;
> Magistrates, colonels, members of Parliament.
> Captains and Governors, and long ago
> Men that had fought at Aughrim and the Boyne.
> Some that had gone on Government work
> To London or to India came home to die,
> Or came from London every spring
> To look at the may-blossom in the park.

They also reprimand its despoilers:

> to kill a house
> Where great men grew up, married, died,
> I here declare a capital offence.[10]

Purgatory offers Yeats's last words on the Big House but not the
last Irish word. As noted earlier, other writers in Ireland of varied
political hues also considered its fate in drama and fiction, aug-
menting the poet's quintessential images with more prosaic but
richly heaped details of their own. Like Yeats, they were also
aware that the passing of the stately home was an important and
even possibly a tragic theme, and some even reveal an ambivalence out of keeping with their personal allegiances—a point particularly worth noting when the peculiarity of Yeats's idea of aristocracy and the ancestral house is insisted upon. In fact, the works
of the more sensitive on both sides of the Irish conflict often
remarkably dovetail by doing justice to the pathos and irony that
transcend the simplifications of politics and ideology.

On one side, Padraic Colum in his novel *Castle Conquer* (1923)
chronicles the familiar struggles of impoverished villagers with
the landlord in the ancient house above them, but ends his story

of their final triumph by softening the hard, justifiable pride of victory with unexpected magnanimity toward the losers. For while the defeat of British rule is signaled by the hoisting of the tricolor on the tower of the outcast landlord, one of the native Irish onlookers who has fought to achieve this moment is now able to look back on both sides with compassion: "Then it seemed to him that he had known all who had gone this highway, and knowing them, had sorrow for them all—for those who had gone proudly by in grand coaches, and for those who had lain in the ditches, watching them . . . all, all were alike held in the memory of the land, and one for the sake of the other." On the opposite side, Lord Dunsany, with a similar lack of hostility, portrays in his novel *The Curse of the Wise Woman* (1933) a middle-aged man, self-exiled from Ireland, recalling his boyhood on his father's estate before and during the Rebellion. Though he remembers how his father was forced to flee the house during a raid, he nonetheless looks back, unembittered and nostalgic, to the days when the mysterious bog and hunting the wild geese attached him to the land and its people. "If the scenes of those days be allowed to be quite lost," he muses, "the world will miss a memory of a beautiful and happy country, and be the worse for that. Or was it a sad and oppressed country, as some say? I don't know. It didn't seem so to me." [11]

Equally notable for the absence of rancor but much more searching is *The Big House* (1928) by Lennox Robinson. Set during the Great War and the Troubles, this play dramatizes key moments in the lives of the Alcocks, a cultivated, well-intentioned Anglo-Irish family living at Ballydonal House. The climax comes with the burning down of their ancestral home; but no time is wasted on either recrimination or nostalgia. Instead, there is a cool-tempered diagnosis of the vanishing order—of the stupidities of its worst representatives, of the imperceptions as well as the decencies of the best. Ballydonal House itself is depicted as the exception rather than the rule: the manners, culture, and good will of its occupants are made to stand in bold contrast to the ignorance, dissipation, and brutishness depicted as more typical of the landowning class in Ireland. Yet for this very reason Ballydonal House—like Yeats's Coole Park—comes to represent an order of values that may survive its physical destruction, as Kitty Alcock—the daughter of the house and, so to speak, its conscience —finally recognizes. "We were ashamed of everything," she admonishes her dispossessed parents, "ashamed of our birth, ashamed of our good education, ashamed of our religion, ashamed that we dined in the evenings and that we dressed for dinner, and, after all, our shame didn't save us or we wouldn't be sitting here on the remnants of our furniture." And no longer ashamed herself, Kitty decides to remain in Ireland and restore the house. "I'll build it with my own hands if I'm put to it," she announces, "I believe in Ballydonal, it's my life, it's my faith, it's my country." [12]

Again, from the point of view of the native Irish, two stories of Sean O'Faolain—"Midsummer Night Madness" and "A Broken World"—explore similar ambiguities. The first opens with an I.R.A. man on his way to billet at Henn Hall, a marvelous old house which he wondered at during childhood and whose owner, a half-mad libertine, he recalls with an abstract hatred. "He was one of the class that had battened for too long on our people," he reflects. "I was pleased to think that if he lived he lived only in name; that if he had any physique left now he would need it all to attract even the coarsest women. . . . Perhaps the travelling tinker women would have to suffice?" But his recollection of the loveliness of the place also involves a disturbing ambivalence all the same: "Thinking of the big Red House, with its terraced lawns, and its cypresses and its yews, and its great five-mile wall, all built by the first Henn . . . I could not believe that even such a house would fall so low." While billeting at the hall, he makes some unsettling discoveries about both the other side and his own. In the alcoholic, rheumy-eyed old Henn he finds the remnants of an ancient courtesy and sense of bitter frustration with the Irish that he had never anticipated: "I saw for the first time how deep the hate on his side could be, as deep as the hate on ours, as deep and as terrible." And in one of his own I.R.A. men he comes to see a coarse sensualist and political fanatic who bullies old Henn into marrying a tinker girl he himself has ruined. The story concludes with ironic admissions on both sides. "She's as good as the next, and better than some, even though she *is* only a tinker's daughter," old Henn submits. And the I.R.A. man, reversing his earlier wish, admits that this grotesque coupling is too painful to think about.[13]

In "A Broken World" another narrator, traveling by train through a wintry countryside, listens to a priest's reflections on a vanished Ireland. The priest, recalling his own poor parish of mountain farmers and the big houses in the valley where the gentry used to live, finds in that past a sense of unity missing from the present: "They in their octagon and we in our lighted cabins, I mean to say, it was two halves of a world." And when the narrator argues "But now that the gentry are gone, won't the people, the mountainy people, and so on, begin to make a complete world of their own?" the priest can only shake his head and shrug his shoulders. The narrator, later walking the cold streets of the city and noticing the few chilled, shrouded people abroad, muses on the moment in the train: "What image, I wondered, as I passed through them, could warm them as the Wicklow priest had warmed us for a few minutes in that carriage. . . . What image of life that would fire and fuse us all, what music bursting like the spring, what triumph, what engendering love. . . ." [14]

Of course, among contemporary writers in Ireland who lived through the "broken world" of the Troubles and their aftermath, it is Elizabeth Bowen who has the most memorably identified herself with the Big House. Throughout her fiction, from *The Last September* (1929) to *A World of Love* (1955), she has made the Anglo-Irish household a haunting setting and a vibrant symbol. And in *Bowen's Court* (1942), as well as in essays like "The Big House" (1942), she has also illuminated the complexities of its condition and fateful influence. Her abiding preoccupation with the great house entitles Elizabeth Bowen to a place not far from James, Yeats, and Waugh.[15]

Like these others, Elizabeth Bowen comes to the house as both celebrant and critic. Indeed, as she reveals in autobiographical moments, her relationship with the house of tradition is at once more intimate and more ambivalent than theirs. James and Yeats bring to the house the susceptibilities and the detachment of the outsider; Miss Bowen speaks from within. The touchstone of her symbolism is Bowen's Court, the Italianate country house her ancestors built near Cork in the eighteenth century. From her summer visits there as a girl down through her occupancy as its mistress, she grew familiar with its customs and possessed by its moods. "The house," she has confided in *Bowen's Court*, "stamps its own character on all ways of living: I am ruled by a continuity that I cannot see" (*BC*, p. 449). More inevitably than James or Yeats, she therefore turns to the great house as an emblem for a style of life. "As on a ship at sea," she remarks elsewhere, "there is a sense of community"; and as if combining a Conradian feeling for its regimen with a Jamesian sense of its past, she continues: "This is, I suppose, the element of its spell. The indefinite ghosts of the past, of the dead who lived here and pursued the same routine of life in these walls add something, a sort of order, a reason for living, to every minute hour." [16]

At the same time, however, Elizabeth Bowen ignores none of the incongruities involved with the great house—particularly one in Ireland. An Irish estate, she has admitted, is often "something between a *raison d'être* and a predicament." Considering Moore Hall, the family seat of the novelist, before it was burned down, she remarks that "while it stood, classic and bare and strong, the house embodied that perfect idea of living that, in actual living, cannot realize itself." [17] And one reason for these disparities, as she recognizes because of her own background, is the historical position of the Anglo-Irish ruling class descending from Cromwellian forebears in relation to the natives of Ireland. "My family," she confesses, "got their position and drew their power from a situation that shows an inherent wrong" (*BC*, p. 452). Paradoxically, therefore, the Big House may become a symbol of isolation as well as community. And in *Bowen's Court*, she dwells on just this peculiarity of Anglo-Irish households:

Each of these family homes with its stables and farms and gardens deep in trees at the end of long avenues, is an island, a world. Sometimes for days together a family may not happen to leave its own demesne. . . . Each member of these isolated households is bound up not only in the sensation of living here. . . . Each of these houses with its intense, centripetal life is isolated by something much more lasting than the physical fact of space: the isolation is an affair of origin. It is possible that Anglo-Irish people, like other children, do not know how much they miss. Their existences, like those of other children, are singular, independent, and secretive.

[*BC,* pp. 19–20]

Placing this emphasis on Bowen's Court, we must not, however, reduce her fiction to reportage: this would mistake her method and intention. In her own comments on setting in the novel she observes that fictitious places must "take on something from the at once simplifying and concentrated imagination which has created them—one may notice a sort of poverty in the atmosphere of a scene which the novelist has no more than 'copied.'" And there are undoubtedly literary influences at work as well. An admirer of Henry James, Elizabeth Bowen surely responded to the symbolic eminence of the country house in his work. With James, she has also shown a certain attachment to the more sophisticated branch of the Gothic tradition: the novelists of the nineteenth century, like Wilkie Collins and Sheridan Le Fanu, she has taken pains to note, saw "the possibilities of the country house from the point of view of drama, tension, and mystery." In her judgment, Collins wrings the last drop of effect from the forbidding mansion in *The Woman In White;* and Le Fanu's *Uncle Silas,* by dividing the scene between two houses—one civilized and comfortable, the other lugubrious—makes the contrast an element of the drama. Nonetheless, it is obviously Bowen's Court that remains paramount for her imagination. Speaking of what conditions the novelist, Miss Bowen has testified that for herself "the influence of environment is the most lasting" and "operated deepest down." [18] And in her remarks on the relation of *Uncle Silas* to Le Fanu's Anglo-Irish experience, she might very well be referring to herself and providing a program note to several of her own novels:

> *Uncle Silas* has always struck me as being an Irish story transposed to an English setting. The hermetic solitude and the autocracy of the great country house, the demonic power of the family myth, fatalism, feudalism and the "ascendancy" outlook are accepted facts of life for the race of hybrids from which Le Fanu sprang. For the psychological background of *Uncle Silas* it was necessary for him to *invent* nothing. Rather, he was at

once exploiting in art and exploring for its more terrible implications what would have been the norm for his heredity.[19]

Certainly, the atmosphere herein described—the "psychological weather," to use Miss Bowen's own phrase—pervades *The Last September*, her novel about the predicament of the Anglo-Irish gentry during the Troubles. Danielstown, a lovely, lonely house —which the author admits derives from Bowen's Court [20]—functions as both stage and symbol. The novel opens with Sir Richard and Lady Naylor, the owners of Danielstown, and their young niece Lois receiving guests on the steps outside; it closes with the house burning down after a raid. The phases of the action are marked off by the arrivals and departures of visitors, and throughout the novel the mansion, with its expressive rooms and brooding landscape, remains a constantly felt symbolic presence.

The tone of the novel is unusually ambiguous: while carrying on its familiar, comfortable routines, the house gives off an air of isolation, even unreality. The Naylors, trying to remain indifferent to the political conflict and violence in the sinister Ireland around them, keep up the conventions of hospitality and civilized form. But seated formally together at dinner, they and their guests seem, in contrast to the immutable family portraits above them, "unconvincingly painted, startled, transitory" (*LS*, p. 36). In the evenings, the menacing sound of lorries and patrols just beyond the demesne intrudes upon the polite conversation on the terrace. This ambiguity is sharpest for young Lois. Despite herself, Lois lingers at Danielstown because she is struggling with her own personal sense of separateness, of adolescent exclusion from the world of adults. "I like to be in a pattern," she confides to her friend Marda. "I like to be related; to have to be what I am. Just to *be* is so intransitive, so lonely" (*LS*, p. 137). On the surface, Danielstown seems to offer her the desired pattern, but Lois discovers there only the reflection of her own plight. Looking down at Danielstown from an enclosing mountain, she wonders why the occupants are not afraid:

> Their isolation became apparent. The house seemed to be pressing down low in apprehension, hiding its face, as though it had her vision of where it was. It seemed to huddle its trees

close in fright and amazement at the wide light unloving country, the unwilling bosom whereon it was set. [*LS*, pp. 93–94]

And after every return, Lois feels that "she and these home surroundings still further penetrated each other mutually in the
discovery of a lack" (*LS*, p. 229).

The ambivalence of Lois, moreover, is not the only symptom
of the uneasy tenor of life at Danielstown. Other characters display their own inadequacy, passivity, and frustration. One guest,
Mr. Montmorency—an ineffectual man who might once have
made a new life in Canada but never went—returns nostalgically
to Danielstown for consolation. Ironically, he spends his time
uxoriously combing his wife's hair and, later, entertaining an
erotic fantasy about a departed guest. Lois's cousin Lawrence, an
Oxford undergraduate, a materialist but moneyless, stays on for
very practical reasons. "I have to eat somewhere," he admits. But
he too is bored all the same: "I should like something else to
happen, some crude intrusion of the actual. I feel all gassy from
yawning. I should like to be here when this house burns" (*LS*,
p. 63). Young Gerald Lesworth, a pleasant English lieutenant
garrisoned in Ireland, represents the "actual" and is, therefore,
an "intrusion." Falling in love with Lois, he is callously hu-
miliated by her aunt's inquiries about his financial and social
eligibility and is finally made to realize that his feelings are not
really returned. Consequently it is no accident that "his earthy
vitality" is numbed by the glacial atmosphere of the drawingroom
at Danielstown; or that his last, confused talk with Lois before
his death takes place in the shadowed wood of the demesne,
"where constricted by firs, thought and movement were difficult"
(*LS*, p. 261).[21]

For all its loveliness, Danielstown is revealed as a world of
divisions and separations—between the conventional and the
actual, the accepted and the excluded, the private life and the
political. Ironically, personal and historical destinies do finally
meet in an act of violence: the house is burned down by the
Irish rebels, and at the end we are told, "The door stood open
hospitably upon a furnace" (*LS*, p. 283).

It would be a mistake, however, to oversimplify *The Last September* as an indictment or a pathology, ironic and unsentimental as it is. There is no implication that the burning of Danielstown is in any way justified; indeed, its destroyers—described as "executioners bland from accomplished duty" (*LS*, p. 283)—are also presented ironically. And the sentence quoted above—"The door stood open hospitably upon a furnace"—may be taken as having more than one prong. Although the imperceptions and disabilities of Danielstown are candidly considered, there lingers—as in the other Irish works mentioned above—an ungrudging sense of loss, of muted elegy. In a preface to a later edition of the novel, Elizabeth Bowen herself seems to be reminding the reader of this by calling attention to the title. *"The Last September,"* she emphasizes, "takes its pitch from the month of the book's name." [22] Certainly the novel is imbued with an autumnal vision of decline and decay; but September itself is Janus-faced, as the closing pages of the novel attest. "Every autumn," says a last visitor to Danielstown, "it strikes me this place really looks its best" (*LS*, p. 282).

A novel of dispossession, *The Last September* never suggests that what has been destroyed did not represent certain values worth preserving. Indeed, in the other novels and short stories that Elizabeth Bowen published between the Troubles and World War II, the social and moral vacuum left by the destruction of the great house ironically brings it back to mind as an inviting image of community and order, embodying "that perfect idea of living that, in actual living, cannot realize itself." Though not always a major setting, the great house still remains an important reference point for orienting the reader to Miss Bowen's symbolic landscape; an off-stage thematic fulcrum, it serves—if only through allusion—to extend a meaning, accent an irony. In her first novel, *The Hotel* (1927), as Barbara Seward has noted, the family homestead has already been abandoned; but this does not grant its heroine, Sydney Warren, the kind of liberation young Lois anticipated in *The Last September,* for she comes to see her little English colony in Italy as unreal and weightless—governed not by any real attachment but by "some funny law of convenience."

Again, in *To The North* (1932), the destruction of a great house becomes an elaborate metaphor for Cecilia Summer's state of grief and dislocation after the death of her husband.[23]

In her later fiction, moreover, Elizabeth Bowen—rather like Forster and Waugh—finds her symbols of isolation and rootlessness in townhouses, city flats, provincial villas, and forlorn hotels—places which, divorced from any human past and suggesting only transience, call up the country house as counterfoil. In *The House in Paris* (1935), for example, the wealthy London home of Karen Michaelis and the *petit-bourgeois* establishment of Mme Fisher—one an impersonal museum, the other a forbidding jail—connote, as Sister Sharp observes, greater austerity and isolation than Danielstown ever did. In *The Death of the Heart* (1938), the servant Matchett says of the chilly London mansion of the Quaynes, "No, there's no past in this house," providing by indirection a contrast with the traditional country house and preparing the reader for the inhumanity of its residents toward the orphaned Portia.[24] In the late short story "Ivy Gripped the Steps" (1945), an ostentatious villa by the seaside becomes the setting for the emotional betrayal of a small son of the poorer gentry.

Furthermore, this sense of the great house as an emblem of human community—implied but unaccented in the fiction that Elizabeth Bowen published between the wars—was poignantly sharpened by her experience of World War II. Living in London through the worst of the bombing, she witnessed the violence that had once swept away the world of Danielstown return with traumatic intensity. History had come full circle: there was greater need than ever for some perspective on the past, for some sustaining image of a viable future. Once more, Elizabeth Bowen returned to her roots: during the early part of the war, she wrote *Bowen's Court,* not to satisfy a nostalgic wish to escape into the past but to reappraise the significance of the landed tradition for the chaos of our time. "In my beginning is my end," she might have said—as did T. S. Eliot in "East Coker" (1940), a wartime poem motivated by much the same need and, incidentally, opening with the image of a house.

A labor of love, *Bowen's Court* belongs, from one point of view, with those other "biographies" of houses—*Earlham, Knole and the Sackvilles, Marianne Thornton*—which, characteristically produced by British novelists, nourish our social imagination by conjuring up a spirit of place and illuminating a style of life. From another point of view, it might well be associated with several English novels of the war period—*Between The Acts* (1941), *To Be A Pilgrim* (1942), *Brideshead Revisited* (1945) —which are informed by the same impulse to reassess the relation of the historic past to the contemporary world by focusing upon a country house. In any case, it is evident that Miss Bowen herself, while composing her chronicle, was explicitly working out themes that were later given fictional form in *The Heat of the Day* (1949), her own novel about wartime England. By her own account, the very paradox involved in writing about one house when all homes were threatened and many destroyed, provided illumination. "I have taken the attachment of people to places," she wrote in the book's afterword, "as being generic to human life, at a time when the attachment is to be dreaded as a possible source of too much pain. . . . But all this—the disparity or contrast between the time and the subject—has only acted to make it more important to me. I have tried to make it my means to approach a truth about life" (*BC*, p. 454).

This truth involved, among other things, the recognition of both the perilous relationship between fantasy and action and the possibly salutary one between power and property. Her ancestors, Elizabeth Bowen perceives, often lived out their lives in subjection to some social or personal fantasy; and here she finds a parallel with the ideological conflicts of the present. "While I have studied fantasy in the Bowens, she observes,

> We have seen it impassion race after race. Fantasy is toxic: the private cruelty and the world war both started in the heated brain. Showing fantasy, in one form or another, do its unhappy work in the lives of my ancestors, I have been conscious at almost every moment of the nightmarish big analogues of today.   [*BC*, p. 454]

Her people, she goes on, were also infatuated with the idea of power; but here there is a difference between the past and the present. Her family and their associates, Miss Bowen maintains, were forced to practice a certain restraint because their power was mostly invested in property: "One may say that while property lasted the dangerous power-idea stayed, like a sword in its scabbard, fairly safely at rest. At least, property gave my people and people like them the means to exercise power in a direct, concrete and therefore limited way" (*BC*, p. 455). Indeed, it is in the lack of property, she argues, that danger may lie, rather than in property itself:

> Without putting up any plea for property—unnecessary, for it is unlikely to be abolished—I submit that the power-loving temperament is more dangerous when it prefers or is forced to operate in what is materially a void. We have everything to dread from the dispossessed. In the area of ideas we already see more menacing dominations than the landlord exercised over land. The outsize will is not necessarily evil: it is a phenomenon. It must have its outsize outlet, its big task. If the right scope is not offered it, it must seize the wrong. We should be able to harness this driving force: at present a minor society makes its own major enemies. [*BC*, p. 455]

The values with which Elizabeth Bowen set out, therefore, remained constant—"accentuated rather than changed by the war" (*BC*, p. 453).

In opposition to the nightmares of a material void, she places the "concrete and therefore limited" world of Bowen's Court. "Yes," she writes, "here is the picture of peace—in the house, in the country round." Like all pictures, she admits, it does not quite correspond to any reality; but in her eyes this incongruity does not diminish the value of the big house as a symbol: "Bowen's Court was, in essence, a family home; since 1776 it had been a symbolic hearth, a magnetic idea, the focus of generations of intense living" (*BC*, pp. 457–58). Moreover, this idea, as she emphasizes elsewhere, is above all a social idea—of good manners, good behavior, and easy, unsuspicious intercourse. In the Big House of the past, "society—or, more simply, the getting together of people was meant at once to be a high pleasure and willing discipline, not just an occasion for self-display." In the present, Miss Bowen insists, the Big House still recalls the social idea to mind: " 'Can we not,' big half-empty rooms seem to ask, 'be, as never before, sociable. Cannot we scrap the past, with its bitterness and barriers, and all meet, throwing in what we have?' " [25]

That the writing of *Bowen's Court* strengthened Miss Bowen's feeling for the great house as a symbol of community is further confirmed by *The Heat of the Day*. In this novel about wartime England, two contrasting houses symbolically extend the crisis in values dramatized by the love affair between Stella Rodney, who has lost her position in the landed gentry through divorce, and Robert Kelway, a lower middle-class Englishman, whose susceptibility to fascism has turned him into a spy. One house is Holme Dene, the pretentious, almost manorial suburban home of Robert Kelway's family; the other, Mount Morris, the old country house in the south of Ireland bequeathed to Stella's son Roderick by the cousin of his dead father.

Holme Dene is, to use the phrase from *Bowen's Court*, "materially a void." As Stella observes to herself on a visit, "You could not account for this family by simply saying that it was middle class, because that left you asking the middle of what? She saw the Kelways suspended in the middle of nothing" (*THD*, p. 109). This distinction between Stella and the Kelways, as William Heath observes, is not a snobbish one: rather, it is meant to reveal that Holme Dene is still another house of isolation—rootless, lifeless, empty of feeling.[26] Though antique in appearance, the place is not actually old—even the oak beams are imitation. Its unsettled atmosphere and denial of emotional attachments are summed up in the fact that it is permanently up for sale and yet no one really minds. "Oh, but there will always be somewhere else," Robert asserts. "Everything can be shifted, lock, stock, and barrel . . . like touring scenery from a theatre" (*THD*, p. 116). Significantly, Holme Dene is fatherless and husbandless; it has become the "projection" of Robert's mother, an incommunicative, obsessed woman, who rules over her domain like the evil spirit of a "bewitched wood" (*THD*, p. 104). It is no accident, therefore, that when Robert attempts to justify his treason he should allude to Holme Dene. "I was born wounded; my father's son," he confides to Stella, "Unwhole. Never earthed in. . . .

Not only nothing to hold, nothing to touch. No source of anything in anything" (*THD*, pp. 263–64).

Mount Morris, in contrast, gives Stella's son, a soldier in the
war, something to hold, something to touch. Though he has
never seen the house nor met the cousin who has left it to him,
Mount Morris bestows on him the sense of community Robert
Kelway so pathetically lacks:

> It established for him, and was adding to day by day, what
> might be called an historic future. The house came out to
> meet his growing capacity for attachment; all the more, per-
> haps, in that geographically standing outside the war it ap-
> peared to be standing also outside the present. The house,
> non-human, became the hub of his imaginary life. [*THD*,
> p. 47]

To be sure, Mount Morris is involved with its own ironies: as
the setting for the honeymoon of Roderick's parents, it was ar-
guably inauspicious, since their marriage was broken by divorce;
moreover, Stella, on her visit there as her son's emissary, recalls
how Cousin Nettie, the last mistress, went mad within its walls.
Nonetheless it becomes clear that Stella also comes to find in the
house the hopeful possibility of renewal—through and for her
son, if not herself. Her own generation, Stella admits, broke the
link between the past and future. However, "that her own life
could be a chapter missing from this book need not mean that
the story was at an end; at a pause it was, but perhaps a pause
for the turning point?" Her dead cousin's "egotistic creative
boldness" may have requisitioned Roderick for the future of
Mount Morris; but the bequest also reveals to her a "man of
faith." Roderick has not been victimized, Stella reflects in a
passage that recalls the plight of Robert Kelway: "he had been
fitted into a destiny; better, it seemed to her, than freedom in
nothing" (*THD*, pp. 167–68).

This does not mean, of course, that Miss Bowen wishes to depict Mount Morris as a kind of Eden; what she implies rather is
that the house may be the means of establishing some viable
human order, "in a direct, concrete and therefore limited way."
And here a comparison with *The Last September* may be in-

structive. In the early novel, young Lois, also seeking "pattern," eventually reacts against the confinement and isolation of Danielstown. In *The Heat of the Day*, Stella's son is no less aware that he has been made the object of "the unapprehendable wills of the dead." One winter night, on his first visit, the house summons him like a visionary presence:

> It could be that nature had withdrawn, leaving everything to be nothing but the identity of Mount Morris. The place had concentrated upon Roderick its being: this was the hour of the never-before—gone were virgin dreams with anything he had of himself in them, anything they had had of the picturesque, sweet, easy, strident. He was left possessed, oppressed, and in awe. [*THD*, pp. 301–02]

Yet it is also evident that the hard commitment demanded of him may involve, as his mother discerned, a better destiny than "freedom in nothing." While "followed by the sounds of his own footsteps over his own land," he contemplates, with an almost religious sense of transcendence, the kind of relation between the past and the future that the whole "idea of succession" inspires; and he then recognizes that, despite the impossibility of any final achievement, it is "a matter of continuing." After such a night, he is ready to accept the commonplace, practical tasks required to restore Mount Morris after the war—to nourish, as Eliot writes at the close of "The Dry Salvages," the "life of significant soil."

In *A World of Love*, her next novel after *The Heat of the Day*, Elizabeth Bowen, still preoccupied with the theme of continuity and renewal, made the Big House in Ireland the major setting and symbol as she did in *The Last September*. In fact, there are revealing correspondences and contrasts to be found between the early novel and the late one. Like Danielstown in *The Last September*, the house in *A World of Love* also suggests the inadequacies of a class but goes farther by embodying its collapse. From the first page, the modest but once stylish mansion of Montefort is described as a decayed house—an emblem, like Gerontion's, for the listless condition of its older generation of inmates, who, as victims of their own "toxic fantasies," their own crippling fixations on the past, live on there in a kind of emotional limbo. It almost seems suggested that Montefort— with its moss, rust, felled trees, out-of-date calendars, defective clocks, and general "air of having gone down" (*WL*, p. 9)—is what Danielstown might have become if it had survived, untended and unloved.

Even its proprietorship is ambiguous. The present occupants, Fred and Lilia Danby, do not possess Montefort; and they cannot really be called tenants or caretakers. Guy, its onetime owner, who died as a soldier in World War I, made no will, though engaged to Lilia. Montefort was therefore left to his cousin Antonia, who arranged a marriage between Lilia and Fred Danby and then allowed them to occupy it. Two daughters, Jane and Maud, are born of the marriage; but with the two women of the older generation still in love with the memory of Guy, the house remains gloomily oriented to the past, its people bound by animosity rather than affection.

Moreover, Jane, like young Lois in *The Last September*, is also on the threshold of life; but as the novel opens she seems less ready to cross over. Having grown up amid extreme situations and "frantic statements," she wishes an emotional equilibrium— with "no particular attitude toward the future" and only an "instinctive aversion to the past." In her eyes, Montefort is therefore neither a jail to escape from nor a haven to escape to: "The passions and politics of her family so much resembled those of the outside world that she made little distinction between the two" (*WL*, p. 48).

For all this, however, Montefort does not suffer the fate of Danielstown. There is always the possibility of renewal. The affirmation evident in *The Heat of the Day* becomes, as Barbara Seward points out, considerably more pronounced in its successor.[27] The "ghost" of Guy, called up by Jane's discovery of his love letters, is finally exorcised, bringing about a new orientation toward the future, not unlike Roderick's. Lilia and Fred find the hardness between them beginning to dissolve, and this provides them with a feeling of redemption: "Survival seemed more possible now, for having spoken to one another had been an act of love" (*WL*, p. 156). The tolling of Big Ben over Maud's wireless restores the world of time to Montefort. Antonia herself looks to the future as the one thing left. And Jane goes forth to find her real lover exiting from a plane at a modern airport. Like its predecessor, *The Heat of the Day, A World of Love* affirms continuity through acceptance and adaptation through commitment. Again, the Big House survives.

The title, theme, technique, and setting of *The World of Love,* as William York Tindall observes, recalls Henry Green's *Loving* (1945), the novel about wartime Ireland written a decade earlier. Here is another Anglo-Irish house that has managed to survive or, to use the novelist's more ominous phrase, has "yet to be burned down." Here, too, the house, with its peacocks, doves, and disappearing ring, functions as a symbol, much as it does in the novels of Elizabeth Bowen, James, and Forster—again, for much the same reasons. Like these novelists, Green has also been concerned, as John Russell observes, with "situations of communion and isolation within and across the boundaries of social class." [28] Like Miss Bowen in particular, moreover, Green knows the great house as an insider and finds there an index to the state of his class and its ambiguous relations with the world outside.

As Green himself reveals in the autobiographical *Pack My Bag* (1940), an important part of his boyhood was spent at Forthampton Court, in Gloucestershire. Tewkesbury Abbey could be seen from the lawn, he poetically remembers, and "always at any time the pealing bells would throw their tumbling drifting noise under thick steaming August air and over meadows between, laying up a nostalgia in after years for evenings at home." What is more significant, during World War I the house served as a hospital, and young Green's association with wounded officers whose lack of manners belied their rank and betrayed their origins proved a social education. "I began to learn the half-tones of class," he testifies. "The effect of this on a child of my class was to open before his feet those narrow, deep and echoing gulfs which must be bridged." [29]

These "echoing gulfs" reverberate through Green's symbolist

fiction. Just as in *Party Going* (1939) the fogbound railway station with its steel-shuttered posh hotel and vast waiting crowd
suggests the class divisions and resultant alienation plaguing
modern society, so Castle Kinalty, the Anglo-Irish household in
Loving, evokes a similar state of separation and discontinuity.
As Tindall reminds us, the fact that it is called a castle, "an enclosure of refuge and defense in hostile surroundings," implies
isolation—both from England at war and encircling, resentful
Ireland.[30] Almost entirely shut up, without electricity, its great
rooms unused and dust-sheeted, Kinalty has not only lost touch
with the present, it no longer maintains a true relation with any
vital past. True, its miniature Greek temple, the tall windows
with Gothic arches, the dovecote modeled on the tower of Pisa,
and the Marie Antoinette furnishings call to mind the great classical, medieval, and renaissance traditions; but thus conglom-
erated as scaled down and gilded shams, they parody the lost
grandeur they invoke. There is not much to suggest that Kinalty
transcends time and change in any positive way, as do some of
the houses of James and Elizabeth Bowen. On the contrary, its
future seems dubious, as the narrator keeps insinuating with his
allusions to the possibility of its being burned down. Furthermore, human relations within the castle are far from what they
should be. The young mistress is unfaithful to her husband off
in the war; her mother-in-law distrusts the servants; and the
servants are suspicious of each other. Kinalty decidedly seems a
house of dissolution and decadence.

All the same, however, the place does cast a spell. The novelist himself describes Kinalty as "a shadowless castle of treasures." And, as Edward Stokes perceives, the references to its
"obsolete, functionless, prodigal splendour" are not always negative: [31] indeed, aided by allusion to fairy tale and romance, the
castle also becomes a palace of enchantment (*L,* pp. 116–17).
Surely it seems so to Edith and Kate, the two lovely young house-
maids who, bringing their own warmth and vitality to its deserted ancient rooms, are given radiance by the splendor surviving from another age. Indeed, Green's description of the two
girls waltzing together in the closed ballroom is indefinably entrancing:

They were wheeling, wheeling in each other's arms heedless at the far end where they had drawn up one of the white blinds. Above from a rather low ceiling five great chandeliers swept one after the other almost to the waxed parquet floor, reflecting in their hundred thousand drops the single spark of distant day, again and again red velvet panelled walls, and two girls, minute in purple, dancing, multiplied to eternity in these trembling pears of glass. [*L*, p. 65]

And similar moments—Edith playing blind man's buff with the children in the Greek sculpture gallery or appearing at the close attended by peacocks and doves—are rendered with equal charm.

Furthermore, it is against the background of the castle with its erotic statues and doves that the flirtation of Raunce and Edith develops into love. There is even a hint, perhaps, as Russell surmises, that they and the other servants really come to "possess the mansion and what joys and tribulations of the hearth it might entail." Below stairs, while their masters are away, the servants do cohere at times into a sort of family around their own table. Eventually Raunce and Edith make the world upstairs their own; in fact, it is while seated comfortably at tea in the Red Library that Raunce first proposes marriage to her. Perhaps the capacity for authentic love is passing from decadent mistress to vital servant, as seems implied by Mrs. Jack's gift to Edith of the silk scarf written over with the words "I love you I love you" (*L*, p. 120). At least, the novel which opens with the death of one butler crying to an unseen woman ends with the elopement and marriage of his successor to a woman who is very much alive. If Green does sense dissolution in the charade the Tennants have made of traditional living, he may also be reaching back, as Russell concludes, "to the inception of a civilized tradition . . . arising from man's natural fecundity and occasional ability to sacrifice." [32] Kinalty Castle may portend both the end of community—and the beginning.

The function of the Big House in the poetry of Yeats and the fiction of Elizabeth Bowen finds its parallel in several English novels of the period of World War II. The reason is not hard to find. Just as the violence and anxieties of the Troubles in Ireland made the Big House attractive as an emblem of order and civilized life, so the greater violence and apprehension of the late thirties and forties helped to dissolve the satirical view prevailing during the previous years and prompted writers like Virginia Woolf, Joyce Cary, and Evelyn Waugh to undertake the kind of reorientation and reassessment found in the elegies to Coole Park or *Bowen's Court*. Indeed, three novels by these writers—*Between the Acts, To Be a Pilgrim,* and *Brideshead Revisited*—form a kind of triptych, and one all the more revealing because, of course, unintentional.[33] Written under the threat of war or during the war, all three novels not only make the country house a paramount symbol but explore its complex, three-dimensional relationship to the English historic past, to the precarious present, and to the uncertain future. In all three, in fact, the house—like Forster's *Howards End*—seems to become a symbol of England and English civilization itself.

Virginia Woolf, to be sure, is not apt to be associated with the country house as readily as James or Forster or Waugh. Born at Hyde Park Gate, a denizen of Bloomsbury, an inveterate promenader of great and populous streets, she calls up London instead. "That is my England," she said of the city during the bombing of 1940, specifying what the imagery of novels like *Mrs. Dalloway* had poetically conveyed. Yet we know from both her books and her friends that Virginia Woolf also possessed a strong feeling for the other, older England beyond the town. "She loved the country," writes her friend E. M. Forster, "the country that is the countryside, and emerges from the unfathomable past." Victoria Sackville-West—whose family history and ancestral home, Knole, inspired *Orlando*—also recalls that "old families and great houses held a sort of Proustian fascination for her . . . and satisfied her acute sense of the continuity of history, English history in particular." Moreover, a number of places outside London played their part in her life and her fiction. The summers spent in Cornwall at St. Ives during her childhood obviously made lasting impressions and left a store of images for her novels. Later on, Asheham, a lovely old house in Sussex which Virginia Woolf turned into a retreat for herself and her friends had its effect. David Garnett, who was himself very much struck by the individuality of Asheham and the "curiously dream-like character" of its facade, has dwelt on the significance of this house for Virginia Woolf. "Places explain people," he remarks. "They become impregnated with the spirit of those who have been happy in them. For a full understanding of Virginia, who spent her holidays and week-ends there for several years after her marriage, Asheham would greatly help." And after Asheham there was Monks House, also in Sussex, which became another sanctuary for many summers and probably colored the writing of *To the Lighthouse* and *Between the Acts,* two novels completed there.[34]

Therefore, while the house admittedly does not have the same prominence in the fiction of Virginia Woolf that it has in that of Henry James and Elizabeth Bowen, it does understandably re-cur; and in several works, early and late, it has a symbolic reso-nance not unlike theirs. In "A Haunted House," the sketch first published in *Monday or Tuesday* (1921) and according to David Garnett inspired by a ghost at Asheham, the house itself is a felt presence much as it is in the novels of Elizabeth Bowen. In fact, with its strange atmosphere calling up unearthly but not unfriendly visitants from another age, the ancient place, thus haunted, becomes a link between the present and the distant past. Moreover, as Bernard Blackstone observes, a similar notion of something in a house "living on from one set of occupants to another and imposing its spirit" informs such later works as *To the Lighthouse, Orlando,* and *Between the Acts.*[35]

In *To the Lighthouse,* the summer home of the Ramsays on the Isle of Skye is, with the lighthouse itself, one of the impor-tant components of the novel. Simply in terms of structure, it integrates the rather plotless narrative by vividly establishing unity of place, so that, despite the long time span of the book's action, we are allowed to preserve a sense of continuity and re-latedness which otherwise might be missing. More important, in relation to theme, we come to feel, as Blackstone notes, that the dwelling has a soul of its own which exists through the three major sections of the novel.[36] Indeed, in the middle section, the house itself really becomes a character.

Furthermore, the "soul" of the house seems an extension of Mrs. Ramsay herself, one of Virginia Woolf's great unifiers. In the opening section, "The Window," it is this quiet but intuitive and maternal woman who creates community within the house. It is she who presides over the almost sacramental dinner which forms the climax to this first part—the dinner which, as Forster remarks, "exhales affection and poetry and loveliness, so that all the characters see the best in one another at last and for a moment." [37] Again, it is Mrs. Ramsay who cherishes the old house as a medium of communion between people, between herself and the past, between herself and the future, between one generation and another. Though she is almost too painfully sensitive to the flux of things and the precariousness of human relationships, the house, nonetheless, speaks to her of possible survivals and restorations. Her thoughts at the end of the day in the close of the first section bring this out movingly. After the union around the dinner, after sensing that her young guests, Minta Doyle and Paul Rayley, have become engaged during their visit, Mrs. Ramsay contemplates the part the house will play in the future. It will be a kind of magnetic field through which currents of feeling may pass even between the living and the dead:

> They would, she thought . . . however long they lived, come back to this night; this moon, this wind; this house: and to her too. It flattered her, where she was most susceptible of flattery, to think how, wound about in their hearts, however long they lived she would be woven; and this, and this, and this, she thought, going upstairs, laughing but affectionately, at the sofa on the landing (her mother's); at the rocking-chair (her father's); at the map of the Hebrides. All that would be revived again in the lives of Paul and Minta; "the Rayleys"— she tried the new name over; and she felt, with her hand on the nursery door, that community of feeling with other people which emotion gives as if the walls of partition had become so thin that practically (the feeling was one of relief and happi-

ness) it was all one stream, and chairs, tables, maps, were hers, were theirs, it did not matter whose, and Paul and Minta would carry it on when she was dead.[38]

The novelist herself, of course, avoids the sentimentality that this speculation of Mrs. Ramsay might seem to be leading to. In what follows, there is no working out of facile continuities, no mechanically fulfilled promises, no blinking reality. The poetically modulated but still impersonal "Time Passes" sequence, concentrating on the deserted, empty house, tells largely of decay and death. Ironically, as we learn in the final section, the marriage of Paul and Minta has not been a great success. Even Lily Briscoe, upon return to the house after ten years, feels a stranger, without attachment to the place she once enjoyed. Nevertheless, in the closing pages of the novel, it is the house that gives the reader the sense of coming back full circle to the opening; it is the house that restores Mrs. Ramsay to Lily Briscoe. Painting outside the house, Lily becomes aware of a presence at the window; it throws a shadow and assists her composition; and suddenly, it seems to be Mrs. Ramsay:

> Some wave of white went over the window pane. The air must have stirred some flounce in the room. Lily's heart leapt at her and tortured her.
> "Mrs. Ramsay! Mrs. Ramsay!" she cried, feeling the old horror come back—to want and want and not to have. . . . And then, quietly, as if she refrained, that too became part of ordinary experience, was on a level with the chair, with the table. Mrs. Ramsay—it was part of her perfect goodness—sat there quite simply, in the chair, flicked her needle to and fro, knitted her reddish-brown stocking, cast her shadow on the step. There she sat.[39]

The apparition in a familiar setting concretizes a moment of insight, as it does in the fiction of James. Through the medium of her house and her window, Mrs. Ramsay appears to return and prepares Lily for the final vision recorded on the last page of the novel.

In *Orlando,* Virginia Woolf's next work, the more typical

great house of tradition provides an image of historical as well as psychological continuity and anticipates the function of Pointz Hall in *Between the Acts*. While the delightful fantasy allows its protagonist, the androgynous Orlando, to survive through centuries and experience the great eras of English history as well as the sexual transformation from man to woman, the ancient mansion remains an anchor in reality, a still point in a constantly changing world. Early in the book, it is established for the reader as an unmistakable, almost living presence through the eyes of Orlando himself:

> There it lay in the early sunshine of spring. It looked a town rather than a house. . . . Courts and buildings, grey, red, plum colour, lay orderly and symmetrical; the courts were some of them oblong and some square; in this was a fountain, in that a statue . . . here was a chapel, there a belfry; spaces of the greenest grass lay in between and clumps of cedar trees and beds of bright flowers; all were clasped—yet so well set out was it that it seemed that every part had room to spread itself fittingly—by the roll of massive wall; while smoke from innumerable chimneys curled perpetually into the air.[40]

It offers Orlando a sense of transcendence and purpose. "Never had the house looked more noble and humane," he reflects to himself:

> Here have lived for more centuries than I can count, the obscure generations of my own obscure family. Not one of these Richards, Johns, Annes, Elizabeths has left a token of himself behind, yet all working together with their spades and their needles, their love-making and their child-bearing have left this. . . .
>
> Why, then, had he wished to raise himself above them? For it seemed vain and arrogant in the extreme to try to better that anonymous work of creation; the labours of those vanished hands. Better it was to go unknown and leave behind you an arch, a potting shed, a wall where peaches ripen, than to burn like a meteor and leave no dust. For after all, he said, kindling as he looked at the great house on the greensward below, the

unknown lords and ladies who lived there never forgot to set aside something for those who come after.⁴¹

For all the bizarre events that follow, the great house gives coherence to the book's good-humored romp with time and history. Epochs cinematically fade in and fade out; Orlando comes and goes; but his relation to his family seat remains unbroken—indeed, his arrivals and departures, his visits and revisits, create the rhythm of the narrative. Quite suitably, at the close, almost four centuries after the time of the opening, Orlando—now a woman living in 1928—is back at the ancestral home once again. And responsive to "the frail indomitable heart of the immense building" (p. 318), she there experiences a vision in which her own past and the past of England become one.

Between the Acts, though written over a decade after *Orlando,* returns to the theme of English history and to the emblematic country house. In fact, as her diary reveals, the house provided Virginia Woolf with the *donnée* of the novel, the last novel she was to write. Sketching out the work in 1938, she immediately came up with the title and setting:

> Why not *Poyntzet Hall:* a centre . . . English country; and a scenic old house—and a terrace where nursemaids walk and people passing—and a perpetual variety and change from intensity to prose.⁴²

And from its genesis through its execution, she continued to refer to the work in progress by the name of the house, later modified to Pointz Hall. Significantly, moreover, she envisioned the mood of the book as one of self-transcendence; it was to create the impression of a communal, not an isolated, sensibility:

> All literature discussed with real little incongruous living humor: and anything that comes into my head; but "I" rejected: "We" substituted: to whom at the end there shall be an invocation? "We" . . . the composed of many different things . . . we all life, all art, all waifs and strays—a rambling capricious but somehow unified whole—the present state of my mind?⁴³

And, as with the many other novelists already discussed, this impulse toward community suggested the English country-house setting.

Even without these jottings from Virginia Woolf's diary, there is no mistaking the symbolic import of Pointz Hall in *Between the Acts*. Along with the village pageant of English history designed by Miss LaTrobe—a burlesque of all such endeavors, to be sure—the Elizabethan manor house where it takes place contributes to the "capricious but somehow unified whole." Like the other dwellings in Virginia Woolf's fiction, it first of all provides unity of place, which is supported in this instance by both unity of time and unity of action. In a manner reminiscent of *To the Lighthouse,* the novel opens within Pointz Hall on the eve of the anticipated village pageant. Through the early chapters we are introduced to the occupants of the house and representatives of three generations: old Mr. Oliver and his widowed sister, Mrs. Swithin, his son Giles and his daughter-in-law Ida, and their small children. The pageant itself—bringing together family, neighbors, and villagers—temporarily at least—is performed on the grounds of the house. The pageant over and the visitors dispersed, the novel ends with the family returning to the house and going to bed. The cycle of a single day, the pageant, and Pointz Hall establish the classic unities with almost Racinian meticulousness.

As in Virginia Woolf's earlier novels, there are of course discordant notes within this harmony. At the very beginning, Mrs. Swithin prays for good weather for the coming event, while her brother skeptically recommends providing umbrellas. Ida Oliver, at odds with her husband Giles, thinks she is falling in love with a local gentleman farmer; Giles, in turn, is susceptible to the flirtatious Mrs. Manresa, one of the guests for the day. Even the pageant, in the eyes of Miss LaTrobe herself, is a failure, "another damned failure!" (*BA,* p. 98). Yet to overstress these disharmonies is to miss the special quality of the novel. As Elizabeth Bowen has remarked, *Between the Acts* moves toward reconciliation: "The thickets of mystery between person and person have been thinned, though in no place levelled down . . . the characters behold each other and the scene around them more calmly, and are beheld by Virginia Woolf more calmly, than in the other books."⁴⁴ And what helps to elicit and sustain this feeling of possible reconciliation is Pointz Hall and its spiritual curator Mrs. Swithin, though both are, oddly enough, left unmentioned by Elizabeth Bowen.

From this point of view *Between the Acts* resembles not only *To the Lighthouse* but even *Howards End*. Like the dwelling on the Isle of Skye and the one in Forster's novel, Pointz Hall is not described as an exceptional place. Middle-sized and unpretentious, it does not "rank among the houses mentioned in guide books." Perversely built in a hollow, facing north, it even seems to reflect human error and incapacity. Nevertheless, Pointz Hall remains "a desirable place to live in" (*BA*, p. 6). Certainly old Mrs. Swithin is at home there; and she, like Mrs. Ramsay and Mrs. Wilcox, belongs with the reconcilers, the healers, the "unifiers," as even her rationalist brother, who classifies himself among the "separatists," recognizes (*BA*, p. 118). Moreover, preoccupied with Wells's *Outline of History*, Mrs. Swithin is "given to increasing the bounds of the moment by flights into past and future" (*BA*, p. 9); and she reveals in the manner of these other women a near mystical feeling for the continuity of human life. Pointz Hall itself becomes a manifestation of this feeling of hers. The first third of the novel, in fact, provides a rather systematic tour of the place, displaying the dining room, the library, the nursery, the kitchen, the garden, and the barn, largely as viewed through her eyes and colored by her attachments. This is particularly evident when Mrs. Swithin tries to put at ease William Dodge, the homosexual, by taking him through the house and showing him the room and the very bed where she was born. "We have other lives, I think, I hope," she tells him. "We live in others . . . We live in things" (*BA*, p. 70).

It is not surprising, therefore, that E. M. Forster himself finds *Between the Acts* an "exquisite final tribute" to "something more solid than patriotic history and something better worth dying for." His words remind us of the circumstances attending its composition: Virginia Woolf finished *Between the Acts* during the Battle of Britain and ended her own life shortly after. For all its lightness, the novel therefore becomes something of a

testament, as Cyril Connolly has recognized. *"Between the Acts*
—what is the significance of the title?" he asks. "The pageant is
the false drama; the true one is enacted in the family relationship. . . . Her book is about the eternal England, the beautiful
threatened civilisation which she has always loved and which is
symbolized by Pointz Hall, the old but not illustrious manor,
the ancient garden, and the rather ordinary family who live in
it." [45] With such a theme, the novel also provides another suggestive coda for the country-house fiction written during the
tragic years *entre deux guerres.*

To turn from Virginia Woolf to Joyce Cary is almost to turn
back to the Galsworthian mode whose prosaic literalness she at-
tacked from the theoretical point of view in "Modern Fiction"
and countered in practice with her own symbolist novels. Two
such novelists, it would seem at first glance, might be coupled
only to be contrasted; yet, allowing for basic and obvious differences between Virginia Woolf's sophisticated imagination and
Cary's seeming matter-of-factness, there are, for our purposes,
several resemblances to be found between at least two of their
novels—namely, *Between the Acts* (1941) and *To Be a Pilgrim*
(1942). Written during the outbreak and first years of World
War II, both novels naturally reflect the apprehensions of what
was for England the most ominous stage of hostilities. What is
more important, Cary's novel, like Virginia Woolf's, goes beyond the inevitable anxieties of wartime to dwell on the pro-
founder mood of retrospection and reevaluation created by the
threat to English life and traditions. *To Be a Pilgrim* is the
product of much the same need for historical reorientation, of
the same impulse to relate the fragmented present to a possibly
more ordered past, and both to a reasonably humane future.
Most significant of all, Cary also turns for his major symbol to
an old country house: throughout his novel, Tolbrook Manor
corresponds in function to Pointz Hall.

Furthermore, Tolbrook occupies about the same place in the
body of Cary's fiction as Pointz Hall in Virginia Woolf's: it
brings to a climax a line of symbolic houses stretching through
previous works, such as *Castle Corner* (1938) and *A House of*

Children (1941). Indeed, for all his air of being an unambiguous, old-fashioned chronicler with easy affirmations, Cary on closer view turns out to be in his own way another modern novelist who is preoccupied with the problem of human isolation and who, therefore, looks upon the country house nostalgically, if realistically, as a remnant of lost community. "We are alone in our own worlds," he declares in the preface to his first trilogy. "We can sympathize with each other, be fond of each other, but we can never completely understand each other." [46] And in the trilogy itself he attempts to give formal extension to this theme by the technique of presenting individual books as three separate first-person narratives in the distinctive styles of Sara Monday, Gulley Jimpson, and Tom Wilcher, respectively. Yet at the same time Cary makes important counter-assumptions: "Each individual is separate," he remarks, "but we know directly that the world is full of things that unify it also." [47] For this reason he recognizes the need and validity of a communal symbolism: and it is noteworthy that, in his discursive pages as well as his fiction, Cary turns more than once to the symbol that draws its strength from familiar associations, and repeatedly cites the ancient house as his prime example. With almost Jamesian tones, he observes in one passage:

> All our love of the old is based on such associations or on sympathetic associations as created by the art of the time. Old buildings, antique furniture, have about them the associations of history, of period, as given to us by historians and novelists. They are enriched symbols of the past, suggesting to us all the various stories connected with them, the idea of men and women who have suffered with them.[48]

When Cary alludes to "old houses," he is speaking, rather like Elizabeth Bowen, from an Anglo-Irish background with its highly dramatic, almost claustrophobic sense of menace and disaster; and he obviously has in mind the places, familiar to him from boyhood, that were forced to live through an atmosphere of permanent crisis because of the land wars and local discontent. Castle Cary, his father's home in the North of Ireland, was lost through foreclosure just three years before Joyce

Cary was born; consequently he went to live in England and was educated there. His early years—again like Elizabeth Bowen's—were then divided between the two countries, specifically between Cromwell House, his aunt's property near London, and Whitecastle, an Ulster dwelling, rented rather than owned, where his grandmother entertained him during the holidays. For young Cary, however, these houses were precious because they were precarious. "Cromwell House and the Irish households of my various relations," he writes, "had a sense of life, both older and more modern than that of my English cousins. . . . We were more eager in our attachments. We knew, more consciously than other children, what family affection meant, as the one trustworthy thing among so many treacheries." And while supposing that Cromwell House might be described as a "feudal relic," he dwells on its intense solidarity and calls it "a place of civilized order":

> It was hierarchic . . . everyone had his place in it. . . . There were enormous pressures, as in every human society, but in Cromwell House at that time they were in balance. And the result was a society highly satisfactory to everyone's needs of body and soul—imagination, affection, humor, and pride—a house unforgetable to those who knew it.[49]

His affection for these households and their traditions, furthermore, gave Cary a historic sense of community extending beyond his personal and very Irish experience. It is revealing that when he attempts to define the geographic and historic "heart of England," he turns to the ancient Cotswolds, a comparatively unchanging "feudal" locality, and finds in the peaceful, domestic land and the proximity of church, cottage, and manor house the survival of a "living community." [50] Indeed, Cary's fiction is informed by both the Irish and the English sense of things, which become manifest—respectively, it might almost be said—in his constant preoccupation with change and continuity. We may even add that both the strengths and the weaknesses of his novels have their sources in ambivalence, in the tension between his deep appreciation of the conservative need for permanence and his radical awareness of the revolutionary dynamics of history.

The presentation of Tolbrook in *To Be a Pilgrim* not only reflects these preoccupations and tensions but it is also, as already noted, the culmination of Cary's earlier attempts to give them symbolic projection through the image of the house. The houses referred to in the very titles of *Castle Corner* and *A House of Children* are stages on the way to Tolbrook, though the novels themselves differ in scope and quality. *Castle Corner,* the more ambitious of the two, is really a failure. Taking his cue from Thomas Mann's *Buddenbrooks,* Cary ostensibly intended to chronicle the decline of an Anglo-Irish family through several generations and to employ the "castle," really a Georgian house in northern Ireland, as the major setting in the style of the German novelist's burgher mansion in Lübeck.[51] And indeed, when the very opening chapter presents the eighty-three-year-old master leading the traditional family prayers in the patrician dining room while his evicted tenants hurl passionate curses upon him and his house, a major conflict is dramatically stated and the possibilities of Castle Corner as a metaphorical index of revolutionary social change appear quite promising. Yet such potentialities are eventually lost in prolixities of plotting, an unmanageable number of characters, and geographical diffusion of setting beyond Ireland to England and even Africa. In the end, as Andrew Wright observes, Castle Corner does not constitute a symbol of sufficient strength to dominate the whole.[52]

A House of Children, though slighter, is actually an advance over *Castle Corner* in conveying a more unified impression of its house. The subject is still family life in an Anglo-Irish setting, but Cary leaves his larger historical concerns in the background, offering instead a kind of Proustian memoir in a minor key. Shifting from the vaguely omniscient and uncontrolled point of view of *Castle Corner* to the intimacy of the first person, he looks back upon the idyllic life of boyhood summers at Dunamara, an old house by a sea lough in Ireland. Through the dreamlike modulations of memory, the place is at once real and mystical. The sensitive narrator, recalling the classical dignity of its fine proportions, dwells also on the way the approaching tide seemed to turn the house into an ark or mermaid's tavern, full of waves, full of the sea. He summons up the smoky community of the kitchen and servants' gossip; he enjoys again the sense of regularity imparted by Dunamara's comfortable routine. In the end, memory's recapture of the world of Dunamara and the sensations of the past results in a much more poetic evocation of the house as setting and symbol than what is found in *Castle Corner*.

With *A House of Children*, therefore, Cary moved a stage closer to the complexities and successes of *To Be a Pilgrim*. In fact, it might be said that in *To Be a Pilgrim* the public perspective attempted in *Castle Corner* and the private one achieved in *A House of Children* meet and blend; the historical and the subjective planes of experience become one. Like the earlier novel, *To Be a Pilgrim* is a story of generations and revolutionary changes, but it is saved from becoming simply another diffuse chronicle by the distinct voice of its first-person narrator, the conservative Wilcher, and by the dominance of its setting, Tolbrook Manor, his family home. Opening with the return of Wilcher to Tolbrook, the novel records his memories of the house and its past, his reactions to the changes of the present, and his vacillating dispositions about its future. Seen through Wilcher's eyes, it thus becomes, as Charles G. Hoffman observes, a structural symbol resembling the lighthouse in Virginia Woolf's novel: "Like the lighthouse, it is the central focus of the novel, enclosing its formal structure and infusing its internal structure . . . a complex symbol illuminating theme." Even more suggestive in our present context are the resemblances to Pointz Hall in *Between the Acts;* for like the last of Virginia Woolf's symbolic houses, Tolbrook goes beyond the novelist's private frame of reference to display deep associations with English history and English traditions. Indeed, Walter Allen, looking back to Forster's Howards End for his comparison, finds in Tolbrook a symbol of England itself.[53]

Moreover, like the country houses of Virginia Woolf, Elizabeth Bowen, and Henry James, Tolbrook expands in meaning as the novel progresses and so assiduously repeats already familiar motifs that it might seem an intended summation, even climax, almost apotheosis, of the archetype. The beginning of *To Be a Pilgrim* discloses that Tolbrook, like so many other houses in modern fiction, has been neglected and rented out for years to strangers. When Wilcher—old, ill, distracted in mind—first hears his niece Ann's suggestion to return, the only question about Tolbrook that he entertains is "whether to sell it for the price of the materials or to find another tenant stupid enough to take the place in such bad repair" (*TBP*, p. 3). Refreshed by his return, however, Wilcher is soon excited by the thought of exploring the old house after his long absence and begins to identify himself with the place: "I opened all doors to these memories, from which in my late anxiety, I had fled, and at once my whole body like Tolbrook itself was full of strange quick sensations" (*TBP*, p. 6).

As Wilcher explores, everything about Tolbrook—its natural landscape, its rooms, its furniture, its total ambience—evokes not only memories but reflections; and throughout the novel, these keep shifting kaleidoscopically into configurations at once personal, social, historical, even religious. Inevitably, Tolbrook recalls to Wilcher his own past and the recent generations of his family—his Victorian parents, his sister Lucy and her dedicated religious career, his brother Edward and his abortive political one; and this family history, as Hoffman points out, also involves the history of England from the 1880s to 1939.[54] But Tolbrook reflects more than the immediate past in the simple way of saga: it is in itself a kind of palimpsest revealing the imprints of the great epochs and the great changes of English history as a whole. Originally, Tolbrook was a medieval priory. Relics from its ruins, the arched windows of his own room, remind Wilcher of both the ancient monk secure in an age of faith and the "new vigorous generation who snatched his peace away" (*TBP*, p. 103). Like Pointz Hall, Tolbrook is not and has never been a stately mansion; yet it preserves something of value from England's great times. The old topiary garden survives from Jacobean days; good rooms by the Adams brothers and an Angelica Kaufman ceiling retain their eighteenth-century graciousness; and the surrounding landscape—with the beauty and majesty of oak, elm, and ash in the magnificence of their age—speaks to Wilcher of an immemorial England.

Gradually, moreover, the exploration of Tolbrook by Wilcher and his revived sense of community with the house and the past take on religious overtones. Revisiting his mother's room, he recalls that as a family refuge it always possessed a quality that could only be described as "blessed." And now the room and its furnishings acquire an almost sacramental value: "I believe my tenants showed it off as a Victorian relic," he comments. "But to me it is a holy place. . . . I look at its faded hangings, its worn carpet, with the sense which only the old can know, of a debt that was never acknowledged and can never be paid, not only to my mother, but to the whole generation. Of storied richness which can return to the spirit only in the form of things it touched and loved" (*TBP*, pp. 23–24). Again, when caught in his own fear, anger, and doubt, Wilcher rebukes himself in the name of Tolbrook and what it religiously affirms: "You old fool," he tells himself, "you know there is love, there is hope, there is faith. Does not everything in this house say to you 'God is'?" (*TBP*, p. 100). Elsewhere, the great lime tree outside the house—like the marvelous wych elm in *Howards End*—becomes a religious object, affording a near mystic vision. "Within that burning tree," Wilcher declares, "I felt God's presence. And there I bathed in an essence of eternity" (*TBP*, p. 218).

From the beginning of his exploration of Tolbrook, Wilcher also recognizes, like some protagonist of Henry James, that "an old house like this is charged with history, which reveals to man his own soul" (*TBP*, p. 18). It is no wonder, then, that the very intensity of his involvement begets a sharp ambivalence. He comes to believe that he is too fond of Tolbrook ever to find peace and comfort there. What is more, his admiration goes out to those who have refused to root themselves in any place, who have been instead wanderers, free spirits, pilgrims—his sister Lucy, who left Tolbrook to join an evangelical preacher; his servant Sara, who can make a home anywhere; even his father, who could say of Tolbrook, which he loved, "Not a bad billet" or "Not a bad camp" (*TBP*, p. 8). Tempted by their freedom, Wilcher is ready to conclude: "The secret of happiness is to forget the past, to look forward, to move on. The sooner I can leave Tolbrook the better, even for an asylum" (*TBP*, p. 27). But the deepest and finest grain in Wilcher is a conservative one. His appreciation of the wanderers and the pilgrims is a saving act of the sympathetic imagination, a grace note lending piquancy to his genuine attachments. But Wilcher the pilgrim would be an imitation; Wilcher the conservative is authentic. "Even as a child," he confesses in a lucid moment of self-recognition, "I had a passionate love of home, of peace, of that grace and order which alone can give beauty to the lives of men living together. . . . I hated a break of that order. I feared all violence" (*TBP*, pp. 71–72).

For Wilcher, Tolbrook has remained an embodiment of that order—"a magic island preserved among the storms of the world by a succession of miracles" (*TBP*, p. 155). After his return, however, he is forced to face the breakage and violence done to Tolbrook itself. Exploring the past, he must also encounter the present, and the changes that he finds inevitably sting his soul. The present is represented in human form by the two unavoidable members of the younger generation who attend him at Tolbrook: his niece Ann, an irritatingly modern, cheerless doctor of medicine, and his nephew Robert, an unpolished, practical-minded farmer. The changes are glaringly embodied in what is physically happening to Tolbrook itself. The modern world of the machine has come and conquered in the guise of Robert's great noisy tractor; old trees are uprooted and familiar acres are cleared of friendly landmarks to make way for more efficient farming. In his zeal for modernization, Robert turns the beautiful eighteenth-century saloon into a storeroom for his reaper, and finally does his threshing there as well. With the whole house shaking around him, Wilcher can only remark ironically: "It is lucky that the Adams brothers used the classical proportion of the double cube. There's no other drawing room in the county would take a threshing machine" (*TBP*, p. 326).

Cary himself considered *To Be a Pilgrim* the tragedy of the conservative in a changing world. Wilcher, he explained, "loves his old home, his old friends, and the old ways. . . . He loves things as well as people, and cannot bear to lose them." [55] The observation defines Wilcher's plight but not its resolution in the novel itself nor the import of the final pages. From another point of view, the basic theme of *To Be a Pilgrim* is really the education of a conservative: paradoxically, despite Cary's declared in-

tention, the novel is also a comedy—a comedy of new understanding, of resignation and reconciliation. And this also finds
expression in Wilcher's changing relations with Ann, with Robert, with Tolbrook itself.

As he explores the house Wilcher is not only revisiting the
past, he is—like old Mrs. Swithin in *Between the Acts*—specu-
lating on the meaning of history and of change. He is struck
both by the fluidity of the historical process and by the diversity
of its currents. "We write of an age," he observes. "But there is
no complete age" (*TBP*, p. 133). The past, Tolbrook itself, he
recognizes, suffered changes no less revolutionary than those of
the present. In contrast to his cousin Blanche—one of the right-
ful claimants to Tolbrook—Wilcher does not remain a "blind
worshipper of exploded systems" (*TBP*, p. 128) and past forms.
"My grandfather," he is willing to concede to Ann, "actually
pulled down the ruins of the old chapel to build a byre" (*TBP*,
p. 131). For all the personal anguish his own losses inflict, Wilcher finally learns to accept even Robert's unsettling innovations
at Tolbrook and to understand them within a broadened historical purview:

> It is but a new life which flows through the old house. . . .
> Robert, I suspect, is . . . a peasant in the grain. But he
> does not destroy Tolbrook, he takes it back into history,
> which changed it once before from priory into farm, from
> farm into manor, from manor, the workshop and court of a
> feudal dictator, into a country house where young ladies
> danced and hunting men played billiards; where, at last,
> new-rich gentlemen spent his week ends from his office. And
> after that I suppose it was to have been a country hotel, where
> typists on holidays gaze at the trees, the crops, and the farmer's
> men with mutual astonishment and dislike. Robert has
> brought it back into the English stream and he himself has
> come with it; to the soft corn, good for homemade bread; the
> mixed farm so good for men; the old church religion which is
> so twined with English life that the very prayers seem to
> breathe of fields after rain and skies whose light is falling be-
> tween clouds. [*TBP*, p. 328] [56]

Surrendering Tolbrook to history and to the future, Wilcher affirms its continuance with at least some confidence. And his gesture and the final mood of the novel remind us, as I have said, of old Mrs. Swithin in *Between the Acts* and her imaginative attempt to view Pointz Hall against the background of human evolution supplied by Wells's history. Indeed, it might be concluded that Joyce Cary is trying to say very much the same thing as Virginia Woolf, though with less subtlety and greater risk of sentimentality. Both *To Be a Pilgrim* and *Between the Acts* end rather inconclusively on the eve of war; but in each the surviving house gives some promise, however tenuous, of the chance of future community.

Between the Acts and *To Be a Pilgrim* close just before World War II. *Brideshead Revisited* (1945), one of the most familiar and most disputed of country-house novels, opens sometime after the outbreak of hostilities. Like the earlier two, moreover, Waugh's novel makes the national crisis a moment for wistfully taking stock of the English past. Waugh himself, in fact, later called *Brideshead Revisited* "a souvenir of the Second World War rather than of the twenties or of the thirties with which it ostensibly deals." And he even placed the blame for the lushness and rhetoric others have criticized on his impulse to compensate for the bleak circumstances of its composition in the spring of 1944. "It seemed then," he later recalled, "that the ancestral seats which were our chief national artistic achievement were doomed to decay and spoliation like the monasteries in the sixteenth century. So I piled it on rather with passionate sincerity." [57]

Furthermore, as if following the grooves made by *Between the Acts* and *To Be a Pilgrim*, *Brideshead Revisited* also moves from a personal and immediate sense of the house to a broad historical one occasioned by the war. Indeed, like Cary's novel, Waugh's also employs a first-person point of view and a flashback technique allowing the reader to see the house in the present and also during revealing moments of the past. In the prologue the narrator, Charles Ryder, a middle-aged officer, finds himself stationed at an army camp in the vicinity of Brideshead Castle, the family seat of the Marchmains, an old Catholic family. This coincidence unlocks a flood of memories that form the substance of the plot: Ryder's friendship with Sebastian Flyte, the younger son of Lord Marchmain, at Oxford during the twenties; his first and later visits to the enchanting house; and his associations with its aristocratic occupants whose personal crises, including Marchmain's infidelity and eventual return to Brideshead, he chronicles along with his own. But what makes the novel memorable to most readers—despite questionable aspects of plotting and characterization—is the presentation of the house itself. Beginning with his nostalgic recollections of Brideshead, Charles Ryder closes with still another attempt, in the epilogue, to place the great house in the large changing context of England's social and religious history.

To be sure, Waugh as a convert to Roman Catholicism postulates an interpretation of English history radically different from Cary's or Virginia Woolf's. For him, the authentic religious and social traditions of England are to be derived from the distant past of the Old Faith. "England," he declares in a brief apologia, "was Catholic for nine hundred years, then Protestant for three hundred years, then agnostic for a century. The Catholic structure still lies buried beneath every phase of English life; history, topography, law, archeology everywhere reveal Catholic origins." In fact, *Brideshead Revisited* has been criticized even by its admirers for developing its Catholic theme with almost tractarian explicitness and a sentimentality unqualified by the author's earlier irony.[58] However, it seems more relevant in our present context to stress the point that even the differences to be found in *Brideshead Revisited, To Be a Pilgrim,* and *Between the Acts* are, after all, revealingly parallel: their creators obviously do not share the same interpretation of English history, but their individual perspectives serve just about the same thematic function in each of the three novels. What humanism is to Virginia Woolf, what Protestantism is to Joyce Cary, Roman Catholicism is to Waugh. Embodying and sustaining these respective traditions, their three houses—Pointz Hall, Tolbrook Manor, Brideshead Castle—symbolically affirm some kind of communality and order against the anarchy of a world at war, and even in the face of threatened disaster they give promise of a human and historical continuum.

In Waugh's novel the great house attains the highest symbolic status because, as Frank Kermode points out, it seems to become the emblem of the Augustinian City of God, upholding against the barbaric City of the World the tradition of beauty, peace, and grace. From this point of view, Brideshead is Waugh's own answer to Hetton Abbey in his earlier novel *A Handful of Dust,* considered in the preceding chapter. If Tony Last's pseudo-Gothic dwelling is, in Frederick Stopp's words, "the sign and potent cause of disintegration," Brideshead becomes—despite its own tragedies and griefs—"an agent of integration." [59] Restoring the balance, *Brideshead Revisited*—even more perhaps than *To Be a Pilgrim* and *Between the Acts*—gives us the sense of coming back full circle beyond the twenties, when the country house signified a decadent order meriting only the satire of Huxley and the jeremiads of Lawrence, to an earlier day when it was still celebrated as the "great good place" by Henry James, E. M. Forster, and Ford Madox Ford.

At times, *Brideshead Revisited,* like *To Be a Pilgrim,* might be thought to echo the meanings and motifs of others who have responded to the attractions of the country house. In its evocation of Brideshead, there are moments when the novel catches the mellower accents of James himself. Speaking of the great classical mansion as an "enchanted palace" (*BR,* p. 92), the narrator, Charles Ryder, lovingly conjures up its baroque rooms, terraced garden, and Italianate fountain to establish an Arcadian ambience resembling that of Gardencourt in *The Portrait of a Lady.* Moreover, not unlike Isabel Archer and Hyacinth Robinson, Ryder also comes to understand that it is an "aesthetic education" to live within its walls, and that this initiation in turn seems to be leading him on to higher spiritual mysteries. Nor is James the only one who comes to mind. The splendid fountain dominating the garden and the garden itself recall the symbolic landscape of Yeats and Eliot. Almost repeating the magnificent opening imagery of "Ancestral Houses," Ryder dwells on the hours he spent before the great carved fountain: "I felt a whole new system of nerves alive within me, as though the water that spurted and bubbled among its stones, was indeed a life-giving spring" (*BR,* p. 94). And the fountain recurs throughout the novel as a place of rendezvous and reconciliation until, in the epilogue, its basin stands empty and littered like the drained pool in "Burnt Norton": "Dry the pool, dry concrete, brown-edged"—lifeless, but suggesting the opportunity of renewal.[60]

Again, very much in the manner of the first part of "Burnt Norton," Ryder associates his youthful days at Brideshead with the Beatific Vision itself (*BR,* p. 91), and continues to look back upon the lovely, ancient place as a lost paradise: "It opened a prospect; the prospect one gained at the turn of the avenue, as I had first seen it . . . the old house in the foreground, the rest of the world abandoned and forgotten; a world of its own of peace and love and beauty . . . such a prospect perhaps as a high pinnacle of the temple afforded after the hungry days in the desert and the jackal-haunted nights" (*BR,* pp. 353–54). Even the closing pages offer suggestive correspondences with two more of Eliot's *Quartets.* Echoing Ecclesiastes but transforming its imagery, "East Coker" opens with meditation on the cycle of the generations:

> Old stone to new building, old timber to new fires . . .
> Houses live and die: there is a time for building
> And a time for living and for generation
> And a time for the wind to break the loosened pane
> And to shake the wainscot where the fieldmouse trots
> And to shake the tattered arras woven with a silent motto.[61]

In an identical mood, Ryder speculates on Brideshead, now tenantless and occupied by the army:

> The builders did not know the uses to which their work would descend; they made a new house with the stones of the old castle; year by year, generation after generation, they enriched and extended it; year by year the great harvest of timber in the park grew to ripeness; until . . . the place was desolate and the work brought to nothing; *Quomodo sedet sola civitas.* Vanity of vanities, all is vanity. [*BR,* p. 380]

But, as with Eliot, this is not the last word. Though Ryder is middle-aged, homeless, childless, and, by his own admission, loveless, he discovers a reason for passing beyond resigned pessimism to affirmation. Returning to the chapel at Brideshead, he finds the lamp before the tabernacle relit:

> Something quite remote from anything the builders intended has come out of their work, and out of the fierce little human tragedy in which I played . . . a small red flame . . . the flame the old knights saw from their tombs, which they saw put out; that flame burns again for other soldiers, far from home, farther in heart, than Acre or Jerusalem. [*BR*, pp. 380–81]

And by recognizing that the lamp could not be relit but for "the builders and the tragedians" of the house, he seems to supply the gloss for the lines of "Little Gidding":

> A people without a history
> Is not redeemed from time, for history is a pattern
> Of timeless moments. So, while the light fails
> On a winter's evening in a secluded chapel
> History is now and England.[62]

Above all, *Brideshead Revisited* brings to mind its immediate contemporaries in fiction: *Between the Acts* and *To Be a Pilgrim*. Like these two novels, it also recognizes the fluctuations and limitations of history and yet preserves a sense of continuity and hope through the shared image of community, the country house. For all its differences, Brideshead still belongs in the company of Pointz Hall and Tolbrook Manor. *Brideshead Revisited* is not, to be sure, Waugh's last word on the country house; but like the other two novels, it provides a kind of dénouement to the years between the wars. Waugh apparently felt so as he wrote, and, allowing his narrator to reflect on the country house and the changing reactions to it, he was obviously catching the tone of a time and perhaps declaring, *sotto voce,* his own intention in the novel:

> More even than the work of the great architects, I loved buildings that had grown silently with the centuries, catching the best of each generation, while time curbed the artist's pride and the Philistine's vulgarity, and repaired the clumsi-

ness of the dull workman. In such buildings England abounded, and in the last decades of their grandeur, Englishmen seemed for the first time to become conscious of what before was taken for granted, and to salute their achievements at the moment of extinction. [*BR*, pp. 251–52]

The salute, if belated, defines the mood of one generation of novelists; but the emphasis on extinction was, of course, premature, as Waugh himself admitted later when he called his book a "panegyric preached over an empty coffin." [63]

In any case, it is *Sword of Honour* (1965), the trilogy depicting Guy Crouchback's disillusioning misadventures in World War II, that provides Waugh's later and considerably subdued testament on the world of the country house and brings the thematic trajectory begun in *Decline and Fall* and *A Handful of Dust* to an end few readers of *Brideshead Revisited* would have predicted.[64] Indeed, if Waugh's most admiring critics usually expressed reservations about *Brideshead Revisited*, *Sword of Honour* unexpectedly reveals the novelist's own repudiation of its literary style as well as his embittered reconsideration of many of its social postulates. In its last book, for example, a passage commenting on the novel *The Death Wish* by the fictional author Ludovic (who is not of course to be confused with his creator) covertly discloses to the alert reader Waugh's retrospective uneasiness with Charles Ryder's rhetorical brocade and facile idealizations: "It was a very gorgeous, almost gaudy tale of romance and high drama," observes Waugh.

> But it was not an old-fashioned book. Had he known it, half a dozen other English writers, averting themselves sickly from privations of war and apprehensions of the social consequences of the peace, were even then severally and secretly and unknown to one another . . . composing books which would turn from the drab alleys of the thirties into the odorous gardens of a recent past transformed and illuminated by disordered memory and imagination." [*SH*, p. 737]

Elsewhere in the trilogy, moreover, Waugh is obviously countering the familiar charge that *Brideshead Revisited* snobbishly identifies the fate of Catholicism with the fate of the recusant aristocracy represented by the Marchmains. Listening to Mr. Goodall, a devout convert to the Roman church, who finds in the genealogies of the old recusant families the workings of divine Providence, Guy, himself a pious Catholic, cannot resist putting an ironic question: "Do you seriously believe that God's Providence concerns itself with the perpetuation of the English Catholic aristocracy?" "But of course," Mr. Goodall confidently replies, adding a marvelously double-edged remark: "And with sparrows too, we are taught to believe" (*SH*, p. 136).

As if in self-laceration for previously extolling upper-class conduct, Waugh, again quite unexpectedly but with evident calculation, allows the war career of the wellborn Captain Ivor Claire to bring to the surface unsuspected moral weaknesses that deflate Guy's romantic idolization of the English gentleman as a social type embodying unquestionable integrity and dependability. Before they enter combat, Claire, a masterful horseman and exemplary clubman, is for Guy the "fine flower" of his fellow officers: "He was quintessential England, the man Hitler had not taken into account" (*SH*, p. 386). But after the military debacle of Crete, Guy discovers that Claire deserted his men and conveniently arranged his personal evacuation from the island. To aggravate this disillusionment, higher authorities cover up the breach of honor by assigning Claire to India before available witnesses, including Guy himself, can offer testimony about the desertion. In contrast to Claire, moreover, the lower-class officer, Sarum-Smith, whom Guy is not at ease with socially, proves himself worthy enough. "He was not a particularly attractive man," reflects Guy, "but man he was" (*SH*, p. 492).

None of this, it is true, signifies anything like an about-face in Waugh's fundamental position. He remains a Roman Catholic in religion and a social conservative in the tradition of Edmund Burke. Despite the reservations just discussed, *Sword of Honor* also includes a wholly sympathetic portrait of another pious recusant and landed gentleman, Guy's father; and its positive references to another ancestral estate, Broome, the family seat of the Crouchbacks, once again serve to remind the reader of the possibility of order and continuity amid the general break-up and myriad dislocations of the war. *Sword of Honour* represents, rather, a subtle modification in Waugh's outlook—one of degree, perhaps, rather than kind, but an important one nonetheless. Somewhere between *Brideshead Revisited* and the trilogy, Waugh, one surmises, examined his conscience and faced up to his wishful thinking about the role of the church as an institution in the modern world and his tendency to convert the manners and accoutrements of the aristocracy into sacramental signs of an exclusive spirituality.[65] At least, something of this sort can be inferred from Waugh's less familiar but revealingly "transitional" work, *Helena* (1950), a historical novel about the age of Constantine, whose sainted but highly realistic protagonist rejects as false the Roman leader's identification of the Christian church with his secular empire. Indeed, Helena's stand is most relevant to a proper interpretation of *Sword of Honour*. Put simply, it might be said that where the Waugh of *Brideshead Revisited* would, like Constantine, wall out the barbarian hordes in the name of order and stability, the Waugh of the trilogy accepts —with, to be sure, a good deal of sardonic hedging—the more catholic and therefore eclectic ideal of Helena, who strives for a church without a wall, open to all mankind. Or, to state the point more pungently, if *Brideshead Revisited* assumes the Augustinian notion of the City of God, as Frank Kermode suggests, the trilogy moves toward the darker and more radical Augustinian insight about the City of the World: that not only modern society but every society—any historical order of things—is characterized by evil and contradictions. The English social hierarchy, accordingly, would be no exception.[66]

This realistic modification allows Waugh not only to return to the mode of his earlier fiction—with its essentially mock-epic point of view—but to give it free play with the very themes sentimentally sealed off from satirical scrutiny in *Brideshead Revisited*. But this return does not mean that Waugh simply repeats himself: whatever is mock-epic in the trilogy now at least assumes the possibility of epic seriousness, however distant this quality may appear to be from the absurdity of events as chronicled. This is evident in Waugh's complex handling of Guy himself. Guy, as many readers have noted, often brings to mind

Tony Last in *A Handful of Dust*. Like Tony, he is first presented as a *naïf*, a sympathetic but credulous idealist, ill-
equipped to cope with a world of self-interest and calculation.
Indeed, his ideals are also boyish fantasies of heroic action, with
the remembered storybook adventures of Captain Truslove and
the family legends of the Crouchback ancestor, the crusader-
knight Sir Roger de Waybroke, having the same distorting effect on his imagination as the Arthurian romances had on
Tony's. Like Tony, Guy also loses his wife to a man outside his
own social class, to the boorish Trimmer, the hairdresser
groomed as a war hero by the cynical peer-turned-propagandist,
Ian Kilbannock. And, again like the heir and master of Hetton
Abbey, Guy would compensate for his marital disaster and the
ensuing loneliness and emptiness by embarking on what promises to be an ennobling pilgrimage, his quest taking the form of
service with the gentlemanly regiment, the Halberdiers.

All the same, there are considerable differences between the
two protagonists. Guy's unsentimental education as an officer
witnessing the farcical disorder and tragic misery of a continent
at war is, unlike Tony's ridiculously abortive quest, not without
a measure of dignity and moments of genuine self-recognition.
Waugh allows Guy to perform certain acts that lend him a stature denied to the absurdly pathetic Tony. Significantly, these are
acts of charity. Influenced by his father's sincere belief that the
true Christian "accepts suffering and injustice" and is also
"ready to forgive at the first sign of compunction" (*SH*, p. 546),
Guy remarries his unfaithful wife, Virginia, knowing by her own
candid admission that she is pregnant by Trimmer, and, after
she is killed in an air raid, brings up the child as his own son
and heir. While serving in Yugoslavia, moreover, Guy makes it
his personal mission to assist the Jewish displaced persons whose
plight is ignored by the Partisan and Allied authorities. Comparatively small gestures in the panorama of destruction, they
are nonetheless, to paraphrase *The Waste Land,* moral fragments
shored against the ruins. In fact, it is revealing that it is his last
conversation with the woman leader of the Jewish refugees that
brings Guy's quest to a soul-scorching epiphany unforeseen at
the start. "Is there any place that is free from evil?" she asks him.

And adding that, in her experience, not only Nazis but many other people wanted war, that even good men wanted war to satisfy their honor, assert their manhood, or justify their privilege through danger, she confronts Guy with an overwhelming question: "Were there none in England?" And his reply, for all its brevity, becomes a tragic summation: "God forgive me," said Guy. "I was one of them" (*SH*, p. 788).

Finally, to come to the aspect of *Sword of Honour* most directly concerned with the country-house theme, the Crouchback seat of Broome, like the other elements just discussed, both resembles its counterparts in Waugh's previous novels and notably differs from them at the same time. Not so obviously central to the main action as Hetton Abbey and Brideshead are in their respective novels, Broome, through frequent allusion—it is mentioned on the first page and on the last—remains nonetheless a point of symbolic reference through the long and varied narrative of the war years. Like Brideshead, Broome is a repository of chivalric traditions and Catholic faith; in fact, it is almost unique in contemporary England, the reader is told, in that it has been held in uninterrupted succession by the male heir since the reign of Henry I and has never lacked a priest for its chapel. Yet Broome is not at all romanticized nor invested with the enchantments that the nostalgic Charles Ryder associated with Brideshead; on the contrary, it possesses an everyday solidity missing from the other's dreamlike ambience. Rather than seeming secret and aloof from the world of the commonplace, Broome is physically close to its village—the approaching drive being a continuation of the village street—and so to Guy's father recalls an age when the proximity of a great house to its neighbors made for easy and expected community. "Every good house stands on a road or a river or a rock," the old man observes, adding in support of Waugh's Catholic thesis: "Only hunting lodges belong in a park. It was after the Reformation that new rich men began hiding away from their people" (*SH*, p. 280).

Broome's recent fate has also been quite different from Brideshead's. In what appears to be an allusion to Ryder's closing words about the light burning in the chapel of the Marchmains, the novelist observes that "the sanctuary lamp still burned at

Broome as of old" (*SH*, p. 22). But this is not a sign that the house has been left untouched by the changing world outside. In fact, Guy's father has rented the estate to a convent school for girls, and it is in their chapel—converted from one of the long, paneled galleries—that the lamp now burns. Had such alterations been made at Brideshead, they might have seemed desecrations of the wonderland Ryder wished to remember; but to Broome they bring a sense of continuity and restored vigor much like that which old Wilcher perceives in his nephew's farming at Tolbrook. Waugh, indeed, describes the activities of the schoolgirls—the old great hall is now their recreation room—rather matter-of-factly, with only friendly irony and no trace of sentimentality. Guy's father, "for whom family pride was a schoolboy hobby compared with his religious faith," never mourns the loss of Broome but simply remains fortified by its memory: "He still inhabited it as he had known it in bright boyhood and in early, requited love" (*SH*, pp. 40–41). Furthermore, because Broome has survived, retaining its religious affiliations, it serves as a kind of spiritual lodestone through Guy's unsettling peregrinations, and, with its traditions of chivalry and charity, adds a communal import to his seemingly quixotic personal choices.

Finally, Guy's return to Broome after the war, his settling down—significantly in the "Lesser House" and not the main hall—with his second wife, the practical Domenica, and the son of Virginia and Trimmer, furnishes the needed coda for Waugh's unpredictable modulations of the country-house motif. In keeping with the theme and tone of the rest of the trilogy, it is an ambiguous coda, ironic and Christian at once. For who is the heir to Broome after all but young Trimmer, the offspring of the man who personifies for Waugh the intolerable vulgarity and deracination of the modern world. Such a conclusion, leaving many questions unanswered, prompting speculation rather than assurance, will recall other country-house novels—*Parade's End, The Heat of the Day,* and *To Be a Pilgrim*—that likewise feature inheritance to symbolize a transmission of values and point to an open, indeterminate future rather than to the fixities of the past. To one critic, Waugh's final ambiguity brings to mind *Howards*

End. "As at the end of *Howards End,*" comments Malcolm Bradbury, "the son who is to inherit mixes the classes. In this sense
he may be a symbol of Guy's failure, but the very continuance of
the line, for which Guy as heir is responsible, is ensured by the
same fact. The young Trimmer is one of Waugh's deepest ironies." Yet there is more than irony. What Waugh obviously intended to be read as his own "unconditional surrender" to
modern circumstance does not necessarily preclude other and
quite hopeful inferences. Broome is not Brideshead, but neither
is it Hetton Abbey, the manor transformed into a breeding
ground for silver foxes. Broome is not demeaned by Trimmer's
son; it raises him up. To quote Bernard Bergonzi, "As old Mr.
Crouchback would surely have observed, even a Trimmer has a
soul to be saved, and his child is being brought up in the Faith;
has become an inhabitant of the City in Helena's sense rather
than the Marchmains'." The emphasis must fall, in sum, not
simply on the heir, but on what his heritage may be.[67]

Though discussed last here, *Sword of Honour* is not by any
means the last treatment of the country house in English fiction.
Postwar novels that take up the theme again, if only in a minor
key, include L. P. Hartley's *Eustace and Hilda* (1947) and *The
Go-Between* (1953), Eric Linklater's *Laxdale Hall* (1951), Ivy
Compton-Burnett's *A Heritage and Its History* (1959), Rumer
Godden's *China Court* (1960), and Richard Hughes's *The Fox
in the Attic* (1961). Nonetheless Waugh's trilogy, obviously because of its wartime setting but also because of its ironic incon-
clusiveness coupled with measured hope, conveniently and fittingly serves to mark the completion of a social and cultural
cycle. Today the future of the country house simply as an emblem, let alone an actuality, is obscure, as are indeed the futures
of most other social institutions and forms, whether older or
more recent. Still, it is not likely to lose its imaginative appeal
and wholly disappear from view. Facing the problems of contemporary society, many are tempted to indulge in blind, unpro-
ductive criticism, even to surrender to an apocalyptic cynicism,
rather than to forward genuine reconstruction. Yet at the edge
of the mind of the most bitterly embattled social critic of what-

ever persuasion, there surely stands some benign image of human community. Without some such image, the sense of possible renewal remains hopelessly abstract and all effort barren. In light of this, what will help to give the country house lasting interest and value for many readers is its unmistakable tangibility and its attractive representation of many of the qualities essential for civilized community, whatever the social order or historical era. If only in retrospect, the country house will continue to embody "that perfect idea of living that, in actual living, cannot realize itself." [68]

The Poetry of Property

THE COUNTRY HOUSE IN

EARLIER ENGLISH LITERATURE

'Tis not, what once it was, the World;
But a rude heap together hurl'd;
All negligently overthrown,
Gulfes, Deserts, Precipices, Stone.
Your lesser World contains the same.
But in more decent Order tame;
You Heaven's Center, Nature's Lap.
And Paradice's only Map.

> Andrew Marvell,
> "Upon Appleton House"

In his engaging essay "Castles and Culture" Harry Levin explains the ambiguous appeal that the storied mansions of Europe have held for the American imagination by noting, in particular, the prominent role played by ancient houses in English fiction. "The English novel, from *Waverley* to *Brideshead Revisited*," he specifically observes, "resolves around great houses and conjures with the perquisites of a settled order." [1] Certainly the English novel has made this whole milieu and its traditions familiar; still, for the sake of inclusiveness, it should be added that the novel was not the first literary genre to feature the great households as a symbolic setting. Actually, the earliest celebrations of the country house as such are to be found not in narrative or drama but in the poetry of the seventeenth century. Poets like Michael Drayton and Ben Jonson, personally intimate with one historic house or another through aristocratic patronage, gladly sing praises to its beauty, graciousness, and hospitality. In *Poly-Olbion* (1622), Drayton's long poem about the typography and antiquities of England, he commends Sir Henry Rainsford's home at Clifford Chambers:

> . . . dear Cliffords seat (the place of health and sport)
> Which many a time hath been the Muses quiet port.

And in what appears to be the first poetic inventory of a stately mansion, he finds in the lofty rooms, galleries, gardens, and antique statues the properties of a "thousand paradises." [2]

But it is Jonson's "To Penshurst" of course that formally initiates, as G. R. Hibbard has lucidly demonstrated, the kind of panegyric to the country house that will recur through English poetry from Carew and Marvell to Pope. For in paying homage to the ancestral home of the Sidneys, Jonson does much more than describe the house; he transforms its whole style of life into a symbol of humane order and true community. [3] Indeed, "To Penshurst" manages to orchestrate so many of the motifs later developed by novelists as well as poets that it almost seems designed to serve as an overture to any discussion of the country house in English literature. Running through the poem is a basic contrast between traditional values—custom, continuity, taste, liberality—and decadent values based purely on wealth

and displayed in conspicuous extravagance. As Jonson's opening
lines declare, riches do not account for the essential greatness of
Penshurst:

> Thou are not, Penshurst, built to envious show,
> Of touch, or marble, nor canst boast a row
> Of polish'd pillars, or a roofe of gold:
> Thou hast no lantherne, whereof tales are told;
> Or stayre, or courts; but stand'st an ancient pile
> And these grudg'd at, art reverenc'd the while.
>
> [ll. 1–6] [4]

On the contrary, the mention of such expensive and apparently
imported materials as basalt, marble, and gold rather than local
stonework reveals that Jonson would rebuke the ostentation of
the *nouveaux riches* who have risen to power through the Tudor
revolution. Indeed, as Jeffrey Hart has remarked, in the emphasis
on the word "built," there is implied an almost Burkean distinction between the "organic" community of the old order and the
more "mechanical" one newly emerging; Penshurst has not been
"built" according to specification, but as "an ancient pile"—long
associated with the basic natural elements of earth, air, wood,
and water emphasized in lines 7 and 8—almost appears to be an
organic feature of the landscape.[5]

The rest of the poem, in fact, develops the analogy between
the natural order of the landscape and the human order of the
life inside the house. Images of outdoor fertility and indoor
feasting nicely correspond. The luxuriant description of the
estate grounds—well-stocked with sheep and kine and fish,
flourishing with ripe fruit—prepares the way for praise of the
master's abundant table and unstinting hospitality. Moreover
the same kind of harmony existing within the little world of
Penshurst is evident in Penshurst's relations with the larger
world outside its walls. Justice and generosity characterize its
dealings with all levels of society:

> And though thy walls be of the countrey stone,
> They are reared with no mans ruine, no mans grone,
> There's none, that dwell about them, wish them downe;
> But all come in, the farmer, and the clowne;

And no one empty-handed, to salute
Thy lord and lady, though they have no sute.
[ll. 45–50]

And in the closing lines Jonson, like subsequent celebrants of the great house, indirectly criticizes the materialism and vulgarity of a society departing from traditional virtues by complementing Penshurst as an ideal abode quite superior to buildings obviously newer but unbearably pretentious:

Now, Penshurst, they that will proportion thee
With other edifices, when they see
Those proud, ambitious heaps, and nothing else,
May say, their lords have built, but thy lord dwells.
[ll. 99–102]

Furthermore, by modeling "To Penshurst" on certain Latin poems—particularly Martial's Epigram 3.58 and Horace's Epodes 2 and 16—Jonson also introduces the association of the English country house, its garden and landscape, with the classical theme of the *beatus vir*, "the happy man," who finds true contentment by retiring from the anxious and decadent life of the city to a quiet rural abode where he may practice not simply a mild epicureanism, but the more stoic virtues of simplicity, independence, and magnanimity. The genealogy of this theme and its poetic metamorphoses have been copiously documented by Maren-Sofie Røstvig, so that it now becomes clear that the ideal occupant of the country house may be taken as still another variation of the *beatus vir*, recurring not only through English topographical poetry but in the fiction of the eighteenth and nineteenth centuries as well, including the novels of Sir Walter Scott and Jane Austen, who probably absorbed the Horatian notion through her reading of Cowper's poetry, *The Task* in particular. In fact, without implying any definite line of influence, it might be said that the *beatus vir* reappears still later in the guise of James's Mr. Longdon in *The Awkward Age*, just as the compelling need for retirement of at least a momentary kind motivates the protagonists of "The Great Good Place" and "Flickerbridge." [6]

Following Jonson, other poets laud other historic houses—indeed, a host of works seem to derive directly from "To Penshurst." The outstanding examples in the seventeenth century include Thomas Carew's "To Saxham" and "To My Friend, G. N., from Wrest," Robert Herrick's "A Panegyrick to Sir Lewis Pemberton," and of course "Upon Appleton House," Andrew Marvell's witty encomium to the country seat of Lord Fairfax. But the century also produced Charles Cotton's lines on Pooley in "A Journey into the Peak," and Edmund Waller's own poem to the Sidneys, "At Penshurst." The underlying thematic assumptions of these poems are continuous with Jonson's. Indeed, their renewed emphasis on the traditional country house during this era of remarkable social change—a change visually reflected in the new style of domestic architecture—was another attempt, as G. R. Hibbard observes, to voice and define "the values of a society conscious of its own achievement of a civilized way of living, and conscious also of the forces that threatened to undermine and overthrow that achievement." [7] In fact, Donne's "Second Satire," though not a country-house poem as such, specifically criticizes the new masters of great houses as status seekers who sumptuously entertain to impress others while ignoring their responsibilities to the needy. Rebuking their "fulsome Bachanalls," he cries: "Where's th'old landlords troops, and almes? . . . we allow good workes as good, but out of fashion now." [8] And Marvell, to dramatize his appreciation of the Fairfax home, employs a double irony: first contrasting the tasteful moderation of Appleton House with the conspicuous splendor of its countertype; and then contrasting the showy magnificence of the latter with the insignificance of its owner—two contrapuntal motifs that anticipate, if they do not influence, the ironic tactics of Pope [9] and Yeats and a line of novelists from Smollett to James.

In the eighteenth century even Pope appears to echo Jonson's poem, particularly at the end of *Epistle IV* (*To Richard Boyle, Earl of Burlington, Of the Use of Riches*):

> His Father's Acres who enjoys in peace,
> Or makes his Neighbours glad, if he increase
> Whose chearful Tenants bless their yearly toil,
> Yet to their Lord owe more than to the soil . . .

And in his tribute to Lord Bathurst of Cirencester, Pope, like Jonson, entertains the notion of an admirable house, though this is characteristically suggested by a satirical portrait of its antitype:

> Like some lone Chartreux stands the good old hall,
> Silence without, and Fasts within the wall,
> No rafter'd roofs with dance and tabor sound,
> Nor noontide-bell invites the country round;
> Tenants with sighs the smoakless tow'rs survey
> And turn th' unwilling steeds another way:
> Benighted wanderers, the forest o'er;
> Curse the sav'd candle, and unop'ning door;
> While the gaunt mastiff growling at the gate
> Affrights the beggar whom he longs to eat.[10]

Pope was all the more conscious of the social implications and literary potentialities of the country house because of his purchase and occupation of the modest villa at Twickenham, up the Thames from London. His years there suggestively correspond to those Henry James spent at Lamb House in Rye and Yeats at Thoor Ballylee. As Maynard Mack displays in his magnificently alusive and beautifully illustrated book on the important symbolic role Twickenham came to play in the poet's life and thought, this semirural estate, "with all its emblems of philosophical and poetic 'retreat,' afforded a clarifying and defining focus" for Pope's own "sense of himself as a spokesman for an idealized community, a way of life, a point of view." "Here," as Mack elaborates,

> he could live at his sweet will . . . and could set against the world beyond the thicket which hedged his property (the world of stratagem and compromise and money-grubbing and self-interest—into which he often entered because he had to and because it answered to the vein of stratagem and compromise and self-interest in his nature), an imagined ideal of patriarchal virtues and heroic friends: a community of the garden and the "grot." [11]

Throughout the eighteenth century other poets—most notably William Cowper in "Retirement" and *The Task*—pursued a

number of the themes of the country-house poetry derived from
Jonson, stressing, in particular, the now-familiar Horatian contrast between the rural world of stability and peace and the commercial plutocracy and questionable sophistications of London.
By mid-century, moreover, the novelists were taking up many of
the same themes. Satirically responding to the disruptions that a
London-based or London-oriented gentry were causing in the
country-house milieu, the novelists also deplored the decline of
noblesse oblige, the rackrenting of absentee landlords, the mania
for erecting pretentious mansions, and the competitive impulse
to carry through grandiose "improvements" of old estates.[12] Indeed, the rise of realistic fiction, with its emphasis on localized
setting and its reflection of the growing interest of readers in
buildings and architecture, gave the country house a place of
primary importance in narrative, so that it acquired the dramatic
"presence" and immediacy that would allow its transformation
into the kind of emblem associated with the line of novelists
from Jane Austen to Evelyn Waugh.

The generation of Richardson, Fielding, and Smollett led the
way. To be sure, Richardson's epistolary style might seem to in-
hibit full description of background, even by his indefatigable
penwomen; nonetheless, the country houses in *Pamela* (1741),
Clarissa (1748), and *Sir Charles Grandison* (1754) are quite
vividly rendered, with considerable attention paid to their in-
teriors. "Pamela's residence in Lincolnshire and Bedfordshire,"
as Ian Watt observes, "are real enough . . . and some of the
descriptions in *Clarissa* anticipate Balzac's skill in making the
setting of the novel a pervasive operating force—the Harlowe
mansion becomes a terrifyingly real physical and moral environment." [13] Grandison Hall, moreover, is not only described in
great detail but the ample rooms and seemingly boundless lawns
are obviously meant to symbolize the free and bounteous nature
of its master, who, while reflecting the fashion for improvement,
would combine the best of the old and the new:

> This large and convenient house is situated in a spacious
> park; which has several fine avenues leading into it. . . .
> The park is remarkable for its prospects, lawns and rich-

appearing clumps of trees of large growth, which must have been planted by the ancestors of the excellent owner; who, contenting himself to open and enlarge many fine prospects, delights to preserve, as much as possible, the plantations of his ancestors, and particularly thinks it a kind of impiety to fell a tree that was planted by his father.

On the south side of the river, on natural and easy ascent, is a but plain villa, in the rustic taste, erected by Sir Thomas; the flat roof of which presents a noble prospect. This villa has convenient lodging-rooms, and one large room in which he used sometimes to entertain his friends.[14]

Indeed, as Edward Malins has pointed out, the Grandison estate represents all the best features of a "Capability" Brown renovation without any evidence of that great landscapist's regrettable excesses: "As Richardson paints his hero in idyllic colours, unmixed with the muddy tones of vice and folly, so it is clear that he intended this description to epitomize the perfect setting, even though it is seen through the rose-coloured glasses of a sentimental woman." [15]

And though Fielding usually places more emphasis on narrative action than its setting (the estate of Lady Booby, so important to *Joseph Andrews,* is, for example, never really visualized), he does go a good step beyond literal reference in his description of Squire Allworthy's home in *Tom Jones* (1749); for here, as D. S. Bland observes, the novelist not only describes the place in full, but stresses those details that help to characterize its owner as an orderly, quiet-living man of taste, in contrast to the bullying Squire Western, of whose estate no such picture is given:

> The Gothic style of building could produce nothing nobler than Mr. Allworthy's house. There was an air of grandeur in it that struck you with awe . . . and it was as commodious within as venerable without.
>
> It stood on the south-east side of the hill, but nearer the bottom than the top of it, so as to be sheltered from the northeast by a grove of old oaks . . . and yet high enough to enjoy a most charming prospect of the valley beneath. . . .

The left-hand side presented the view of a very fine park, composed of very unequal ground, and agreeably varied with all the diversity that hills, lawns, wood, and water, laid out with admirable taste, but owing less to art than to nature could give.[16]

As is the case of other ideal houses and their ideal residents still to come, the correspondence between such a harmonious setting and Squire Allworthy's decency and felicity appears eminently fitting. Indeed, though Fielding later in the novel writes with warmth of Esher, Stowe, Wilton, Eastbury, and Prior Park, Tom Jones himself, as Edward Malins has noted, never meets another man as magnanimous as Allworthy, nor does he visit an estate as gracious as his.[17]

Not long after Fielding, Smollett manipulated his settings to achieve a variety of effects. In *Peregrine Pickle* (1751), Commodore Trunion decorates his house as a battleship and lives there as though he were still at sea—a piece of comic expressionism that may have influenced Captain Shotover's equally nautical dwelling in *Heartbreak House* or Wemmick's fantastic duplication of a medieval castle in *Great Expectations*. In *Ferdinand Count Fathom* (1753) Smollett accentuates an atmosphere of terror in several scenes, foreshadowing Gothic thrills to come. And the emphasis on the cultural implications of houses in Smollett's acknowledged masterpiece, *Humphry Clinker* (1771), may be said to anticipate a similar technique of Scott, just as his satirical questioning of the fashion for extravagant improvements looks forward to the caustic elaboration of this theme by Jane Austen. Brambleton Hall, the home of the protagonist, Matthew Bramble, is, for example, presented as an idyllic retreat, conforming to the ancient Horatian ideal. "Shall I state the difference between my town grievances, and my country comforts?" the seasoned old Bramble writes to a friend. "At Brambleton-hall, I have elbow-room within doors, and breathe clear, elastic salutary air." And he continues with a veritable catalog of the many satisfactions to be had on his modest estate—including the satisfactions of responsibilities fulfilled and neighborly relations with those around him:

Without doors, I superintend my farm, and execute plans of improvements, the effects of which I enjoy with unspeakable delight—Nor do I take less pleasure in seeing my tenants thrive under my auspices, and the poor live comfortably by the employment which I provide—You know I have one or two sensible friends, to whom I can open all my heart; a blessing which, perhaps, I might have sought in vain among the crowded streets of life.[18]

Later in the same novel, Bramble's visits to three other squires —namely, Burdock, Baynard, and Dennison—further dramatize this social ideal by contrasting their respective houses. Burdock's house, as befits this ill-mannered brute mated with an arrogant shrew, looks like a great disorderly inn, neither elegant nor comfortable despite its size, seemingly crowded with insolent servants. And the clearly-intended antithesis to be found in Bramble's detailed accounts of Baynard's and Dennison's estates provides what Smollett obviously considered an object lesson on the wrong way and the right way to execute improvements. Visiting his friend Baynard, Bramble can only bemoan costly and ridiculous changes wrought by the man's deluded wife:

The tall oaks that shaded the avenue, had been cut down. . . . The house itself, which was formerly a convent of Cistercian monks, had a venerable appearance: and along the front that looked into a garden, was a stone gallery, which afforded the most agreeable walk, when I was disposed to be contemplative —Now the old front is covered with a screen of modern architecture; so that all without is Grecian, and all within Gothic. As for the garden, which was well stocked with the best fruit which England could produce, there is not now the least vestige remaining of trees, walls, or hedges—Nothing appears but a naked circus of loose sand, with a dry basin and a leaden triton in the middle.[19]

At Dennison's, in contrast, Bramble listens approvingly to the encouraging story of how moderation and good management transformed a ruined, uninhabitable house, with fields lying in waste, into a model estate that sets the standard for rural felicity.

Before the close of the eighteenth century, furthermore, the symbolic possibilities of buildings as setting were significantly augmented by the development of the Gothic romance in the hands of Horace Walpole and Ann Radcliffe. The complex and sometimes dialectical interrelationships of the realistic and Gothic modes in fiction are, of course, too subtle and manifold to be unraveled here.[20] Put briefly, it may be said that from the point of view of formal technique, the often denigrated Gothic school made both writers and readers more fully aware of setting as an integral element of narration, even exercising a long-range influence on such novelists as Henry James and Elizabeth Bowen; while at the same time, from a thematic point of view, its sensationalism, violence, and generally sinister import represented a challenge to the structured, rational expectations of those novelists who found in the country house the ideal, if not the actuality, of a social order.[21] Within the context of this Appendix, consequently, it is more advisable to consider a series of works as nodal points of development rather than emphasize debatable lines of influence.

Walpole, it is now commonly agreed, helped to establish architectural setting as a functional part of fiction. His *Castle of Otranto* (1765), for all its sensationalism and absurdities, was an epoch-making book. Because of Walpole's innovation, as Montagu Summers observes, the true protagonist of the Gothic romance is not the persecuted heroine, nor the murderous villain, but "the remote and ruined castle with its antique courts, deserted chambers, pictured windows . . . the ancient manor, hidden away in the heart of a pathless forest, a home of memories of days long gone before."[22] As Summers points out, after Walpale, trappings of terror aside, buildings in fiction seem to acquire a personality and energy of their own. The houses in Jane Austen, the Brontës, Dickens, and Henry James frequently find an ancestor in shabby Otranto—a castle which, for all the Italianate melodrama occurring there, is largely modeled after the English manor houses of the Tudor period.

Along with his portentous castle, moreover, Walpole bequeathed to later writers of fiction a number of serviceable "props" and motifs that in time were to become conventions in works far more ambitious than his. The ancestral portrait, hauntingly lifelike to the beholder, is one obvious but important example, repeatedly taken up not only by died-in-the-wool Gothicists but writers like Hawthorne and James as well. Even the fantastic destruction of Otranto in the closing chapter of the romance introduced a motif with great potentialities. For, although Walpole resorted to the highly ridiculous supernatural machinery of a statue incredibly expanding in size to bring the walls down in ruin, he did make the fate of the house the kind of symbolic climax others could subtly appropriate for thematic ends of their own. The clap of thunder shaking Otranto's ancient foundations finds a counterpart in the sound of the axe felling Chekhov's cherry orchard or the bombs landing on Shaw's Heartbreak House, just as its outlandish debris prefigures the ashes of Thornfield in *Jane Eyre* and James's lovely Poynton.

Mrs. Radcliffe, influenced by Walpole, went beyond him. Despite its function, Otranto is still described in the lucid, open-air style of the eighteenth century. Walpole, while providing the properties of horror, generates little of its atmosphere. To effect the consummate shudder, Mrs. Radcliffe added devices of her own. Aiming at what she considered "sublimity," she at least brought a needed style to Walpole's structure. Particularly in *The Mysteries of Udolpho* (1794) her descriptions contrast light and shade in a painterly way and emphasize the lofty aspects of tall arched windows and high towers. Her buildings, therefore, have a new capacity for arousing emotion—indeed, we may agree with Warren Hunting Smith that Mrs. Radcliffe's castle of Udolpho remains the most interesting edifice the Gothic romance has to offer.[23] For all its theatricalism, Udolpho, as first seen through the eyes of the heroine, has the kind of authority few earlier buildings in fiction possess:

"There," said Montoni, speaking for the first time in several hours, "is Udolpho."
Emily gazed with melancholy awe upon the castle, which she understood to be Montoni's; for though it was now lighted up by the setting sun, the Gothic greatness of its features, and its mouldering walls of dark grey stone, rendered it a gloomy

and sublime object. As she gazed, the light died away on its walls, leaving a melancholy purple tint, which spread deeper and deeper as the thin vapour crept up the mountain, while the battlements were still tipped with splendour. From those, too, the rays soon faded, and the whole edifice was invested with the solemn darkness of evening. Silent, lonely, and sublime, it seemed to stand the sovereign of the scene, and to frown defiance on all who dared to invade its solitary reign.[24]

The effects of such a structure as Udolpho may be only horror and a meretricious awe; nevertheless, it did suggest new possibilities for architectural setting in fiction. In the novels of her more respectable descendants, the techniques that Mrs. Radcliffe exploited for sensational ends assisted in the creation of a genuine symbolism. In fact, the serious symbolic fiction of the nineteenth and twentieth centuries finds one of its origins in the cross-fertilization of the devices of the Gothic romance and the socio-psychological motifs of the more realistic tradition. Henry James, for one, was obviously quite familiar with Gothic fiction and exploited its conventions for his own artistic purposes not only in his "ghostly" tales but in such serious novels as *The Portrait of a Lady*.[25] Indeed, against this literary background, the plights of such Jamesian heroines as the governess in *The Turn of the Screw,* Isabel Archer, and even Milly Theale and Maggie Verver—all of whom are forced to discover the darker moral realities behind the engaging appearances of Old World mansions—remind us that the American novelist was often presenting his own seemingly disguised variation on one of the staple plots of English fiction: namely, the situation of an innocent young girl, with a certain kind of sensibility and awareness, coming as an outsider of some sort, whether servant or orphan, into a strange, imposing house whose inhabitants and style of life will be unfamiliar and possibly threatening. First adumbrated by Richardson, particularly in *Sir Charles Grandison,* the situation was given a fresh lacquering, so to speak, with Mrs. Radcliffe's portrayal of Emily in *Udolpho,* from whom may be traced a lineage including Jane Austen's young ladies Catherine Morland in *Northanger Abbey* and Fanny Price in *Mansfield*

Park; Jane Eyre; and Maud Ruthyn in Le Fanu's *Uncle Silas,* a novel admired, interestingly enough, by James himself and by Elizabeth Bowen.

To be sure, Mrs. Radcliffe was not alone in her endeavors. Several novels of the late eighteenth century domesticate the Gothic mode for serious literary purposes. The fact that fiction was at the time a feminine preoccupation undoubtedly helped: women novelists from Mrs. Radcliffe herself down to Elizabeth Bowen and Virginia Woolf have usually showed special concern with the homes of their characters.[26] In any case, two important mutations are Charlotte Smith's *Old Manor House* (1793) and Maria Edgeworth's *Castle Rackrent* (1800). Both novels offer variants on the kind of house inaugurated by Walpole, but they locate their dwellings not in the mysterious Apennines but in contemporary England and Ireland. Ragland Hall, the decaying mansion of Mrs. Smith, certainly has features of the Gothic castle —hidden passageways, turrets, strange nocturnal noises—but these are not the essence of the novel; indeed, the supposed ghosts turn out to be smugglers. What the novelist obviously intends to represent in the old manor house is the decline of the aristocracy in a world of rising tradesmen and parvenus. Moreover, like the poets, she anticipates the much-used nineteenth-century technique of contrasting houses—balancing Ragland Hall and the loyalty of its inhabitants to immemorial custom against the once-splendid neighboring castle purchased, remodeled, and abused by rich merchants. Therefore despite lapses into melodrama *The Old Manor House* not only prefigures the social themes of later novelists like Wells, Galsworthy, and Waugh but their literary strategies as well.

Castle Rackrent discovered still another possibility for the country-house novel and so became an important influence in English, Irish, and even continental fiction. Concentrating on the old castle in Ireland as a family seat, Miss Edgeworth chronicles the history of four generations of its owners as they appear to their old servant Thady Quirk. The tale is largely one of ruin through misalliance and mismanagement, drink and debt. Yet at the same time, because of the perspective offered by the old Irish narrator with his vitality and humor, there emerges a certain appreciation of the old order of pride and liberality—an order which the calculating and the unscrupulous constantly menace and finally supplant. In consequence, the passing of the house from one high-living and inadequate heir to another, until the son of the servant becomes its master, affords a clear correlative for the ambiguous social theme. As one of the first family chronicles and regional novels, *Castle Rackrent* was as much as an innovation and influence as *The Castle of Otranto*. It served as a model for Sir Walter Scott and even Turgenev; and, as Cyril Connolly points out, it helped to create the Anglo-Irish literature of the "big house" that descends to Somerville and Ross, Elizabeth Bowen, and Joyce Cary.[27]

In English literature, the most important disciple of Maria Edgeworth was, of course, Scott. As the novelist himself revealed in the general preface to the Waverly series, his first piece of fiction was an attempt to do for his own country what Miss Edgeworth had achieved for Ireland. Indeed, with what he learned from her and from Walpole—whose romance he complimented in an introduction to the 1821 edition—Scott more than any other transformed the spectral castle of the Gothicists into a solid edifice rising out of the soil of a given historic place and time and weathering genuine cultural conflicts.[28] Already in *Waverley* (1814), the two major houses—Waverley-Honour and Tully-Veolan—reflect the social and political actualities of a definite era. The very chapter titles—"Waverley-Honour—A Retrospect" and "A Scottish Manor-House Sixty Years Since"—precisely delimit period; and as young Edward Waverley travels from the sober English estate with its prudent ease and complacent pride in ancient lineage to the warm-blooded, romantic household of the Baron of Bradwardine in the Scottish Highlands, his passage evokes something of the challenging ambivalence Henry James himself made the *sine qua non* for his own dramas of comparative culture. Waverley, in fact, reaches its climax with an account of the Jacobite Rebellion—a historic conflict which, as Donald Davie points out, should be viewed not simply as a conflict between the Highlanders and the English but between the old order and the new, the past and the future, even the "heroic" and the "unheroic." Scott himself takes a complicated and balanced attitude toward the defeat of Baron Bradwardine's forces, both recognizing its inevitability and at the same time expressing an elegiac feeling toward what has been lost in consequence. And once again, at the end of the novel as in the earlier sequences, contrasting codes of value are presented in association with the two houses.

Upon returning to Tully-Veolan after the suppression of the Highlanders, young Waverley surveys the havoc, here recorded with photographic precision that recalls and at the same time transcends the description of the ruins of Otranto:

> Upon entering the courtyard, Edward saw the fears realized which these circumstances had excited. The place had been sacked by the king's troops, who, in wanton mischief, had even attempted to burn it. . . . The towers and pinnacles of the main building were scorched and blackened; the pavement of the courtyard was shattered; the doors torn down entirely, or hanging by a single hinge; the windows dashed in and demolished, and the court strewed with articles of furniture broken to fragments. The accessories of ancient distinction, to which the baron, in the pride of his heart, had attached so much importance and veneration were treated with peculiar contumely. The fountain was demolished, and the spring, which had supplied it, now flooded the courtyard. The stone basin seemed to be destined for a drinking trough for cattle from the manner in which it was arranged upon the ground . . . and one or two of the family pictures, which seemed to have served as targets for the soldiers, lay on the ground in tatters. With an aching heart, as may well be imagined, Edward viewed the wreck of a mansion so respected.
>
> [*W*, 2 : 281–82]

The poignancy of such destruction is accentuated by the nobility of Baron Bradwardine's own response to the loss of his house and home:

> "I did what I thought my duty," said the good old man, "and questionless they are doing what they think theirs. It grieves me sometimes to look upon these blackened walls of

the house of my ancestors; but doubtless officers cannot always keep soldiers' hands from depridation and spullize. . . . Indeed I have myself seen as sad sights as Tully-Veolan now is, when I served with Marechal Duke of Berwick. To be sure we may say with Virgilius Maro, *Fuimus Troes*—and there's the end of an auld sang. But houses and families and men have a' stood lang eneuch when they have stood till they fall with honour; and now I hae gotten a house that is not unlike a *domus ultima.* [*W, 2 : 295–96*]

But, as Davie points out, the old Highlander's feudal sense of honor is very much in danger of becoming a barbaric impulse, and in a new era it must be supplanted by reasonableness and the civilizing if tamer virtues of taste and feeling.[29] Significantly, it is the Horatian image of the *beatus vir* that Scott finally alludes to when he has the high-spirited Flora MacIvor ironically predict Edward's life as master of Waverley-Honour:

"I will tell you where he will be at home, my dear, and in his place—in the quiet circle of domestic happiness, lettered indolence, and elegant enjoyments of Waverley-Honour. And he will refit the old library in the most exquisite Gothic taste, and garnish its shelves with the rarest and most valuable volumes;—and he will draw plans and landscapes, and write verses, and rear temples, and dig grottoes;—and he will stand in a clear summer night in the collonade before the hall, and gaze on the deer as they stray in the moonlight or lie shadowed by the boughs of the huge old fantastic oaks:—and he will repeat verses to his beautiful wife, who will hang upon his arm;—and he will be a happy man." [*W, 2 : 190*]

The prediction comes true with the marriage of Edward and the Baron's daughter, Rose; and the restoration of the Bradwardine property allows the novel to come to a conventional close with a happy final reference to the two estates in the Baron's grateful toast—"The Prosperity of the United Houses of Waverley-Honour and Bradwardine" (*W, 2 : 362*).

Following the success of *Waverley*, Scott poured forth new settings in such profusion—including lawless Osbáldistone Hall in *Rob Roy* (1817), the forlorn estate of Ravenswood in *The Bride of Lammermoor* (1819), and, needless to say, the ubiquitous castles of *Ivanhoe* (1820) and *Kenilworth* (1821)—that he brought the ancient household with the rich texture of its historic life and manners into the mainstream of English fiction. With his deep-seated awareness of history as a truly extra dimension, Scott embodied in his novels a sense of the past that obviously helped to shape the consciousness of writers who would employ the house in a more sophisticated way. Young Henry James himself, in declaring his liking for Scott's novels, found special charm in their "poetic reverence" toward history.[30] Indeed this reverence is clearly evident in *Old Mortality* (1816), where Scott sets his conservative characters against his revolutionary characters in terms of contrasting settings: the Bellendens existing, at least initially, in the traditionally structured estate of Tillietudlem, the diabolic Burley being the rootless inhabitant of various Gothic dens.

To be sure, the many country houses that recur in English fiction throughout the nineteenth century do not always derive directly or solely from Scott. Some, in fact, stem from the Gothic tradition by way of reaction and parody. The novels of Jane Austen offer the best example. Until recently little attention had been given to her description of background because there seemed to be little enough to begin with. However, as Lord David Cecil, Lionel Trilling, and others have shown, the settings and particularly the houses Jane Austen does choose to describe usually have a definite symbolic function. It is not without significance, therefore, that her early work *Northanger Abbey* (finished in 1803, though published in 1813) is a burlesque of Mrs. Radcliffe and the Gothicists in general. To deflate their conventions, she established with authority and charm the old medieval abbey where Catherine Morland expects to undergo the terrors read about in novels like *Udolpho*.[31] In her later fiction, moreover, Jane Austen turned this manipulation of the house to more straightforward purposes of revealing character and extending theme. In *Pride and Prejudice* (1813), for example, the good taste manifest at Pemberley deepens Elizabeth Bennet's appreciation of Darcy's qualities: "Elizabeth was delighted. She had never seen a place for which nature had done more, or where natural beauty had been so little counteracted by an awkward taste." [32] In *Emma* (1816), likewise, Donwell Abbey—an appellation anticipating those of Trollope and James—is admired by the heroine as a reflection of its occupants, the Knightleys: "It was just what it ought to be, and it looked what it was— and Emma felt an increasing respect for it, as the residence of a family of such true gentility, untainted in blood and understanding." [33]

Mansfield Park, of course, stands out as the country-house novel par excellence of its time, the true prototype of the modern line represented by *The Portrait of a Lady, To Be a Pilgrim,* and *Brideshead Revisited.* No prior work of fiction outside the Gothic tradition itself makes so many references to buildings, rooms, furnishings, gardens, and landscapes not as documentary details of setting, but as indispensable symbolic components perfectly integrated with story and theme. As recent critics have come to perceive, from the moment the heroine, Fanny Price, enters the splendid estate of her uncle, Sir Thomas Bertram, until she marries Edmund, the son of the house, and settles down within its domain, Mansfield Park is unmistakably the center of gravity for interpreting the novel's meaning and system of values. "For the author as well as the heroine," Lionel Trilling remarks, almost inevitably employing a Jamesian allusion, "Mansfield Park is the good place—it is The Great Good Place." And noting how, upon Fanny's final return to the Park, summer has changed the lawns and trees to freshest green, Avrom Fleishman discerns implications of an earthly paradise regained: "This Eden, it is suggested, is the only heaven we are likely to know— at least the only heaven Jane Austen can imagine.[34]

Throughout the novel individual characters are portrayed in terms of their contrasting and changing relationships with Mansfield Park and its mode of life. Tony Tanner, who has perhaps given the closest reading yet of the book's house symbolism, groups the characters as guardians, interlopers, and inheritors. As Tanner observes, Sir Thomas himself, though not without faults, is the major guardian: "He believes in 'duty' and is just, benevolent and responsible. In his absence Mansfield Park falls into confusion: after his return, order is restored."[35] The Crawfords, while attractive and energetic, are really interlopers, Londoners, motivated by self-seeking ambition rather than the principles Mansfield Park represents. Fanny, who comes to appreciate the property and repose of Mansfield, therefore emerges the true heir. As Sir Thomas recognizes in blessing her marriage to Edmund, "Fanny was indeed the daughter he wanted" (*MP*, p. 382).

Furthermore, perhaps taking a cue from Charlotte Smith's *Old Manor House*, Jane Austen here brings to perfection the contrapuntal device of employing houses as morally symbolic foils. There is the ideal house, Mansfield Park, and, to use the title of James's novel, "the other house," in this case Sotherton, the residence of the Rushworths. Measured against Mansfield, Sotherton is found seriously wanting: its extreme ways illustrate the excess and defect of Mansfield's golden mean: the house itself is oppressive to its visitors and is even referred to as a prison, while the untamed wilderness outside seems to promise not liberty but sinister license.[36] And though Mr. Rushworth is only too willing to expose Sotherton to the new and chic "improvements" recommended by Mr. Crawford, its old customs like family chapel have, to Fanny's regret, been allowed to lapse. Moreover, if Sotherton shows the corruption of good manners, the anarchy of the Price household in Portsmouth displays the absence of any manners whatsoever. Fanny's return visit to her home and her contrasting of life there with the life she has come to know at Mansfield Park really provides the climactic epiphany of the whole novel. She now sees the Portsmouth house as a kind of anticommunity: "It was the abode of noise, disorder, and impropriety. Nobody was in their right place, nothing was done as it ought to be" (*MP*, p. 317). In sharp antithesis, Mansfield Park takes on the qualities of true community:

—she could think of nothing but Mansfield, its beloved inmates, its happy ways. Everything where she now was was in full contrast to it. The elegance, propriety, regularity, harmony, and perhaps above all, the peace and tranquility of Mansfield, were brought to her remembrance every hour of the day, by the prevalence of everything opposite *here*.

. . . At Mansfield, no sounds of contention, no raised voice, no abrupt bursts, no tread of violence, was ever heard; all proceeded in a regular course of cheerful orderliness; everybody had their due importance; everybody's feelings were consulted. [*MP*, p. 320]

Thus transforming the country house into a symbol of what constitutes true community, *Mansfield Park* has significantly led its recent critics to compare it with some of the twentieth-century works discussed in the main text. Avrom Fleishman notes its resemblance to Forster's *Howards End:* "Both novels take their titles from the names of country places . . . both have as their theme an attitude expressed in the epigraph of *Howards End:* 'Only connect.' " Tony Tanner mentions its affinity with Ford's *Parade's End:* "Like Jane Austen, Ford portrays a world of traditional values being infiltrated and undermined by modern types—unscrupulous, ambitious, cruel, selfish, and false." Lionel Trilling recognizes that Mansfield Park itself is continuous with the kind of great house celebrated by Yeats: "It is the house 'where all's accounted, ceremonious,' of Yeats's 'Prayer for My Daughter.' "

> How but in custom and ceremony
> Are innocence and beauty born? [37]

While Jane Austen made the mode of Mrs. Radcliffe a stepping-stone in her own fictional development, Thomas Peacock turned parody of Gothic to new and delightfully malicious uses, particularly in *Nightmare Abbey* (1818). In his first novel, *Headlong Hall* (1816), Peacock had already introduced his own mutation, the country-house party given over to comic symposium that allows talk rather than action to expose the intellectual monomanias of the guests. But in *Nightmare Abbey*, his satire of the excesses of Romanticism, the venerable pile "in a highly picturesque state of semi-dilapidation" is an integral part of the burlesque.[38] Its ruined tower, unweeded garden, spooky halls, and inevitable owls, deflating gloom through travesty of Gothic, provide the perfect *mise en scène* for the melancholia of his loquacious romantics. Peacock, moreover, learned to vary and adapt setting to other ends, so that even though his *Crotchet Castle* (1831) and *Gryll Grange* (1861) offer the expected assembly, there are, as one critic notes, subtle variations in the social atmosphere of his different country houses.[39] Indeed, Peacock's success with his own convention probably encouraged its revival in Mallock's *New Republic* (1877), Shaw's *Heartbreak House*, and Huxley's *Crome Yellow*.

The Gothic mode, despite parody and deflation, survived nonetheless, and its leading Victorian heirs—the Brontës, Dickens, Le Fanu, Collins—managed to exploit anew the overworked stage properties of Walpole and Mrs. Radcliffe by transforming them into symbols that often anticipate the poetic fiction of our time.[40] Masters of the Gothic *frisson*, these novelists also mount their dramas in "haunted houses," only their Otrantos are plagued not by specters from another world, but by the immediate horrors and evils of nineteenth-century society. In *Jane Eyre* (1847), for example, Thornfield Hall is still another haunted dwelling with a macabre secret; but what shocks its young governess even more than the mysterious screams from a sealed room is the revelation of her adored master's intended bigamy. Again, in *A Woman in White* (1860), Blackwater Park, one of Collins's most sinister houses, with its uninhabited wing, stagnant lake, and stifling overgrowth of trees, seems to transcend the theatrical villainy of Sir Perceval, its owner, to insinuate the decadence of a class. Dickens, of course, repeatedly adapted the gloomy decor of the Gothic romance to metaphorical ends and in *Great Expectations* (1861), to take one instance, designed Miss Havisham's barred house as a symbolic prison, whose famous cobwebby room and stopped clock offer images of a general social paralysis.[41]

Moreover, to counterbalance the figuratively haunted house, these Victorians also created its symbolic opposite, the house of life and order and community. Their novels often employ houses dialectically as foils to contrast modes of social life or realms of moral being. *Jane Eyre*, in fact, as Barbara Hardy demonstrates, has for its major symbolic action the orphaned heroine's search for a home: the progress of Jane—from loveless Gateshead to Lowood and Thornfield (a house with a "haunted" room), and from these to the final serenity of Ferndean Manor—follows a pattern of moral development resembling a religious parable; and the destruction of Thornfield by fire transmutes the Gothic motif of ruin into a symbol of the moral purgation necessary before Jane and Rochester may be reunited.[42] Emily Brontë's *Wuthering Heights* (1847) revolves about the antithesis of Wuthering Heights itself and Thrushcross Grange—with the stormy vitality of the one apparently irreconcilable with the gracious but effete order of the other until their representative offspring, Hareton and the second Cathy, are joined together in what may be taken as a Blakean marriage of heaven and hell. Similarly, *Bleak House* (1853)—whose every locality, from the foggy Thames-side to Krook's warehouse, functions as an emblem —counterpoints Chesney Wold, the cheerless mansion of Lady Dedlock, with the house ironically named in the title, the once desolate structure restored to brightness and comfort by charitable Mr. Jarndyce and eventually cared for by Esther Summerson as its happy mistress. Even *Uncle Silas* (1864), Le Fanu's psychological thriller, uses its two houses to create a tension. Elizabeth Bowen notes that when Maud, the young heroine, leaves Knowl, the comfortable, well-tended home of her childhood, for Bartram-Haugh, her uncle's somber house, it is the drama of the girl's suspension between two worlds rather than the melodrama of her possible fate that heightens interest.[43]

Dickens, the Brontës, Collins, and Le Fanu bear out the contention of one historian of the English novel that the Victorians did not divorce sensation fiction from a genuine criticism of life, and that it was possible for a "thriller" to be taken seriously.[44] For these novelists, the Gothic house was, therefore, a readymade symbolic vehicle for a serious criticism of life and society. However, the preoccupation with the house as symbol was not confined to those who unashamedly took up the conventions of Walpole and Mrs. Radcliffe. The more conventionally "serious" Victorians—Thackeray, Disraeli, George Eliot, Trollope—impatient with the nocturnal and the grotesque, inspecting England under the light of common day—also recognized the possibilities of the country house as a social and literary symbol.

Disraeli, indeed, displays the great houses of his fiction with such operatic lavishness that Henry James himself smiled at this obsession with the trappings of the nobility. "Jewels, castles, horses, riches of every kind," James complained of *Lothair*, "are poured into the story, without measure, without mercy." Yet behind this lavishness there was, in fact, what James did not mention—a political motive. A Tory Radical, Disraeli meant to challenge the anarchy of a laissez faire society. "There is no community in England," his spokesman declares in *Sybil* (1845); "there is aggregation . . . men may be drawn into contiguity, but they still continue virtually isolated." Community, for Disraeli, was based on the traditionally conservative concept of society as an organism, with the nation as a family, the land as a legacy, and the nobleman as a paternal public servant. An obvious embodiment of this communal tradition was, to be sure, the great old houses of England. "The moral influence of residence," Disraeli explicitly observes in *Coningsby* (1844), "furnishes some of the most interesting traits of our national manners. . . . The ancient feudal feeling that lingers in these sequestered haunts, is an instrument which, when skillfully wielded, may be productive of vast social benefit." And John Holloway has shown in an extensive analysis how the great houses recurring in Disraeli's novels—Montacute in *Tancred* (1847), Château Désir in *Vivian Grey* (1827), Hellingsley and Beaumanoir in *Coningsby*—are represented as "the focus of a vigorous patriarchal society." Moreover, since the aristocracy admired by Disraeli is really one of quality, not lineage, and since failures like Lord Marney in *Sybil* are also portrayed, the honest ambivalence of the novelist, as Holloway adds, helps to qualify his extravagance: "When his work cannot be accepted as describing the world as it is, one accepts it as having shifted to describing the world as it should be." [45] Holloway's comment is not without relevance to the interpretation of later celebrants of the country house like Henry James, Ford Madox Ford, and Evelyn Waugh.

Thackeray, praised for his realism and censured for his moralism, has only recently received attention for his occasional but pointed symbolism. Yet as satirist of the fashionable world Disraeli idealizes, Thackeray not only depicts the country house as a representative social milieu, he can at times extend his description with an image, allusion, or overtone beyond the demands of simple scene-setting. This is perhaps only too obvious in *Vanity Fair* (1848), where Thackeray sums up the parasitism of the gentry in the name of Queens Crawley, the estate of Sir Pitt, and then allows the disillusioned Becky Sharpe to find its old hall "as glum as the great hall in the dear castle of Udolpho." But in *Henry Esmond* (1852), Castlewood Hall—at once beautiful, strange, and ambiguous—is a subtle and authentic symbol. It is not simply a setting in the ordinary sense, as Karina Williamson has shown. With its image "formed from fragmentary and fleeting impressions, of sunlight reflected from windows or rocks glimpsed in flight" Castlewood takes on an indefinite quality, "transient and static, as if it were caught always at a moment of arrested motion." Indeed, as an immutable image and "focus of emotion" for the characters and their changing relationships, Castlewood produces something of the same effect as the resonant dwellings of Henry James and Elizabeth Bowen.[46]

Of all the mid-Victorians, Thackeray's discipline Trollope might seem the country-house novelist par excellence, if only because his fiction exhibits the greatest number of houses. Symbolically, however, he did the least with them. Ullathorne Court in *Barchester Towers* (1857), Greshambury House in *Doctor Thorne* (1858), and Ongar Park in *The Claverings* (1867), to mention a few, are placed before the reader in a workmanlike way; but they are not dramatically rendered in relation to their inhabitants, nor symbolically expressive of their condition and fate. As Lord David Cecil has noted in comparing a description of a country house by Trollope and one by James, the English novelist is merely accurate, while the American reveals in every line the transforming touch of the imagination. Still, the old emphasis on the utilitarian methods of Trollope can be overdone. Michael Sadleir, while regretting the perfunctory and unpictorial settings in many of the novels, has also demonstrated that Trollope could make architecture genuinely expressive when he wished. If supposedly elegant Ongar Park in *The Claverings* is barely realized, Clavering itself, as he notes, is "cold, square and hard as the bitter man who owns it." And the description of the Humbletwaite Hall in *Sir Harry Hotspur of Humbletwaite* (1871)—"the longest and most arresting description of a big country house in the whole of Trollope's works"— makes the essential dignity of Hotspur "vivid and unmistakable." And it was James himself, an old admirer of Trollope's "heavy shovelfuls of testimony to constituted English matters," who relished his names of places and houses for being "full of colour," and who, in arguing that the "Duke of Omnium and Gatherum Castle" really ministered to illusion rather than destroying it, may have been admitting a literary influence on his own taste for the figurative and even fantastic appellation.[47]

Between the houses of George Eliot and Henry James there is of course a deeper affinity. In her early work "Mr. Gilfil's Love-Story" (1857), the idyllic evocation of Cheverel Manor—itself modeled on Arbury Hall, the seat of the Newdigates—corresponds with Milly Theale's perception of Matcham. Mood, lighting, even the artistic allusion are the same:

> And a charming picture Cheverel Manor would have made that evening, if some English Watteau had been there to paint it: the castellated house of grey-tinted stone, with the flickering sunbeams sending dashes of golden light across the many-shaped panes in the mullioned windows.[48]

> The great historic house had, for Milly, beyond terrace and garden, as the centre of an almost extravagantly grand Watteau composition, a tone as of old gold kept "down" by the quality of the air, summer full-flushed but attuned to the general perfect taste.[49]

Moreover, in *Middlemarch* (1872), Lowick Manor, the home of Mr. Casaubon, has much the same function as the forbidding residence of Gilbert Osmond in *The Portrait of a Lady*. The account of Dorothea Brooke's first visit to Lowick—like that of Isabel Archer to Osmond's villa—portends much of what is to come. The house is described, as D. S. Bland notes, as having two sides, one "happy," the other "melancholy": one looks toward corn and pastures; the other, toward untended flower beds and somber yew trees. But since the visit takes place in November the air of autumnal decline prevails, giving import of Casaubon's condition and the fate of Dorothea's coming marriage to him.[50] Like James, whom she may have influenced in this, George Eliot recognized the symbolic value of the true house and "the other house."

To sum up, from Jane Austen to George Eliot and the middle Trollope, the country house appeared in fiction as a symbolic paradise or symbolic prison. And here, literary symbolism largely reflected social reality.[51] Mid-Victorian stability made the great house—depending on the novelist's point of observation—attractive in its prosperity and prestige or intimidating in its power. Later Victorians, however, responding to change and stress, rehearsed a theme to which the novelists of the twentieth century would give complete orchestration—namely, the decline of the country house. Some novels, indeed, spell out its doom with images of destruction and decay. Meredith and Hardy play still another variation on the old Gothic motif of the house's final apocalyptic ruin; the last chapter of Meredith's *Harry Richmond* (1871), showing Riversley Grange, the house of the novel's opening, consumed by fire, is matched by the last chapter of Hardy's *A Laodicean* (1881), where the castle of the De Stacys—whose ancient aura has aroused Paula Power's latent predilection for aristocracy—perishes in another blaze.[52] And in *Esther Waters* (1894), George Moore—whose family hall in County Mayo knew desolation and was itself later burned down during the Irish Troubles—brings his protagonist back to Woodview, the fine bustling house she knew in her youth, to show the lodge gate empty, the windows shattered, the park leased, the garden neglected. The circularity of Moore's novel, as E. K. Brown says, is obvious. Esther and Woodview mirror each other: "both have declined in the same way: both are in the last phase." [53] Observing the decline of the country house other novelists of course expressed quite a different attitude—an attitude of elegy and nostalgia—which brings us back to the substance of the main text.

Tradition and an Individual Talent

THE LITERARY BACKGROUND OF THE COUNTRY HOUSE IN JAMES'S FICTION

To be at all critically, or as we have been fond of calling it, analytically, minded—over and beyond an inherent love of the general many-coloured picture of things—is to be subject to the superstition that objects and places, coherently grouped, disposed for human use and addressed to it, must have a sense of their own, a mystic meaning proper to themselves to give out: to give out, that is, to the participant at once so interested and so detached as to be moved to a report of the matter. That perverse person is obliged to take it for a working theory that the essence of almost any settled aspect of anything may be extracted by the chemistry of criticism and may give us its right name, its formula, for convenient use.

Henry James, *The American Scene*

If James knew the English country house as a tourist and guest, his reading obviously made him aware of its literary and symbolic potentialities. A few words should, therefore, be said about possible literary influences. These include not only the English novelists discussed in Appendix A but American and French novelists as well. Hawthorne, of course, comes to mind, since it seems but a short step from the ancestral dwelling in *The House of the Seven Gables* to the symbolic residences of James. To assume, however, that Hawthorne is the only influence, as one critic apparently does, involves a rather shortsighted view of James's development as a novelist. No single author, no single tradition of the novel, it is safe to say, determined his literary course. From boyhood, James was an omnivorous reader, and what is baffling to the student of his models and sources, as Oscar Cargill has noted, is the "whole question of how much of his enormous reading remained in his subconscious mind to influence his creative imagination." [1] In his treatment of the country house, the influence of several novelists and fictional schools may coalesce. Along with Hawthorne should be included Balzac, the English novelists of the nineteenth century, and even the denigrated Gothic tradition.

Of them all, Hawthorne is undoubtedly a primary influence. Since James shared with Hawthorne an analogous historic role as an American novelist, he undoubtedly saw him as an ancestor, a model, and perhaps a warning. Several critics—T. S. Eliot, F. O. Matthiessen, and Marius Bewley, for example—have concerned themselves with this relationship. If we ask in our present context what influence Hawthorne had upon James, we naturally think in specific terms of their fictional houses. It should be noted first, however, that in rereading Hawthorne as an apprentice novelist James discovered among other things a general notion of symbolism that he could adapt to his own fictional purposes. In his discussion of *The Scarlet Letter,* for example, James analyzes the symbolism of the novel in some detail; and though he actually finds much of it "mechanical" and "overdone," he shows in his summation of Hawthorne's practice that he has gone beyond the specific symbols to grasp the theory behind them. "Hawthorne is perpetually looking for images," he

observes, "which shall place themselves in picturesque correspondence with the spiritual facts with which he is concerned,
and of course the search is the very essence of poetry." [2] In employing such terms as *image* and *correspondence,* now so basic
to our literary vocabulary, James was undoubtedly recording
his own discovery of a symbolic method he would practice in the
future, and he thus established, with a modest fanfare, his own
place in the symbolist tradition of the nineteenth and twentieth
centuries.

Finding in Hawthorne's symbolism the rationale for his own
treatment of the country house as an image that "corresponded"
with the spiritual and social facts that engaged him, James must
also have taken the old mansion in *The House of the Seven
Gables* as one of his models, if only unconsciously. Robert W.
Stallman has noted that the houses in *The Portrait of a Lady,*
like the Pyncheon house, serve to interpret their inhabitants
metaphorically and has attributed the similarity to the fact that
James completed his study of Hawthorne shortly before writing
the novel.[3]

Hawthorne, however, was not the only influence. James also
learned from Balzac, as his criticism testifies. Shortly before
writing his study of Hawthorne, James published an essay on the
French novelist; and, like the other, it may be taken as a literary
ave atque vale of the departing apprentice to his master, in
which he acknowledges his artistic debts at the very moment of
assuming his own independent path. As the essay reveals, one
lesson that James obviously learned from Balzac was the importance of physical setting in a work of fiction. "The place in
which an event occurred," James writes, "was in his view of
equal moment with the event itself; it was part of the action
. . . it had a part to play; it needed to be made as definite as
anything else." In fact, James gives even more attention to
Balzac's way of employing buildings and houses and rooms than
he does to Hawthorne's, declaring that he has always found
them "extremely interesting": "He was a profound connoisseur
in these matters; he had a passion for bric-a-brac, and his tables
and chairs are always in character." No longer a novice himself,
James can also admit that Balzacian detail can be excessive and

exhausting; nevertheless, he maintains that in the Frenchman's greatest passages there is nothing superfluous and singles out the description of the Maison Vauquer as "one of the most portentous settings of the scene in all literature." [4]

Furthermore, the conservative vision of society that James shared with Balzac may be more than a matter of affinity. One is struck by the relevance of James's remarks on Balzac's presentation of the French social hierarchy to his own portrayal of the world of the English country house. In a late essay on the French novelist, for example, James takes note of what he regards as a pronounced motif in Balzac's fiction—the obsession with the aristocracy, above all with its "old families" and "great ladies." Curiously, upon broaching the topic James makes a charge against Balzac that unfriendly critics have often leveled against him. "Balzac," he observes, "frankly revelled in his conception of an aristocracy—a conception that never succeeded in becoming his happiest." [5] All the same, James suggests, nothing would be more interesting than to attempt a general measure of the part played by the "old families" in *La Comédie humaine*. Balzac's "delectable class," he then proposes, is not to be taken as a result of realistic observation: it represents rather the author's "free and amused creation." And if Balzac is betrayed by his own spontaneity, there is still, for James, good argument for allowing the novelist to indulge this free play of his imagination. Balzac, after all, James went on, labored in the "complicated but dreadfully definite French world" of the postrevolutionary nineteenth century. What he sought—and what his readers needed—was some perspective on the present; and he found it, James contends, in his own glamorized sense of the ancient and patriarchal France that had passed away:

Half our interest in him springs still from our own sense that, for all the convulsions, the revolutions and experiments that have come and gone, the order he describes is the old order that our sense of the past perversely recurs to us as something happy that we have irretrievably missed. His pages bristle with the revelation of the lingering earlier world. . . . His conservatism, the most entire, consistent and convinced that ever

was—yet even at that much inclined to whistling in the dark
as if to the tune of "Oh how mediaeval I *am!*"—was doubtless
the best point of view from which he could rake his field." [6]

And so, too, with James himself, a certain kind of conservatism
was "doubtless the best point of view from which he could rake
his field." Certainly, his country houses, like the old families and
great ladies of Balzac, must be partly understood as the outcome
of his "free and amused creation."

It seems unlikely, at first glance, that the Gothic romance,
with its haunted castles and lugubrious mansions, could be
another direct influence on James. Hawthorne and Balzac exploited the conventions of the Gothicists and so would have
transmitted them to James; but it is evident that James had his
own intimacy with the school of horrors. As a matter of fact, no
major novelist makes as many specific allusions to sensationalists
like Walpole, Mrs. Radcliffe, Poe, Collins, and Le Fanu as does
James. To be sure, he is not preoccupied with the "haunted
house" as such; even his "ghost stories," as Leon Edel points out,
dispense with the elaborate props of the Gothic novel.[7] Nevertheless, James does adapt some of the Gothic devices to his own
fictional purposes. Ghosts or at least allusions to ghosts function
symbolically in a remarkable number of works, including the
realistic *Portrait of a Lady*. The destruction of the beautiful
house in *The Spoils of Poynton* provides an apocalyptic climax
not unlike the ruin of Walpole's Otranto and Poe's house of
Usher. Moreover the Gothic novel, with its sharpened sense of
place, may have shown James still another way of making the
country house—the compelling authority of the edifice itself, its
great staircases, old corridors, pictured galleries, and expressive
rooms—reverberate with symbolic overtones.

Finally, there is the unquestionable influence of the English
novel. It is true of course that, from an aesthetic point of view,
James found little to admire in earlier English fiction. Educated
to French standards of form, he looked upon Richardson and
Fielding as preachers; charmed though he was by Scott, he could
relegate his work to *l'enfance de l'art*.[8] Nevertheless, what the
English did offer was the very social and historic stuff that

kindled his imagination. Ever since his boyhood delight in *Cornhill* magazine, with its periodic supply of Victorian fiction, James immersed himself in Dickens, Thackeray, Trollope, George Eliot, and their "great heavy shovelfuls of testimony to constituted English matters." Behind James's country houses runs a long line of fictional English domiciles, from Addison's Coverley Hall to the manors of *Waverley,* from Thackeray's Castlewood to the estates of Jane Austen and George Eliot. In this company, the Jamesian country house is no longer the isolated, quixotic phenomenon some critics assume, nor can James's preoccupation be dismissed as small-minded or wistful or snobbish. Rather, James here provides an instance of the relation between a convention and an individual talent.

❧ Notes ❧

INTRODUCTION

1. "The Country House," *England's Heritage* (London, 1935), p. 102.
2. *English Country Houses* (London, 1944), p. 7.
3. Richard Rush, quoted by E. W. Bovil, *English Country Life, 1780–1830* (London, 1962), p. 55.
4. *English Hours,* ed. and introduction by Alma Louis Lowe (London, 1960), p. 55.
5. *Dodsworth* (New York, 1929), p. 77.
6. *Personal History* (New York, 1937), pp. 317–18.
7. A parallel development can be traced in American literature, from Cooper's *Pioneers,* Hawthorne's *House of the Seven Gables,* and Poe's "Fall of the House of Usher" down to Cather's *Professor's House,* Faulkner's *Absalom, Absalom!* and Tate's *Fathers.* For the discussion of the American novelist's preoccupation with the house as a social emblem, see Harry Levin, "Castles and Culture," appendix to *The Power of Blackness* (New York, 1958), pp. 239–48; and Allen Guttmann, "Images of Value and the Sense of the Past," *New England Quarterly* 25, no. 1 (March 1961) : 3–26. Frank Kermode considers the function of the house in Allen Tate's *Fathers* in "Old Orders Changing," *Puzzles and Epiphanies* (New York, 1962). Willa Cather's *Professor's House* has been the subject of both formal and psychoanalytic criticism in, respectively, E. K. Brown's *Rhythm in the Novel* (Toronto, 1950) and Leon Edel's *Literary Biography* (Toronto, 1957).
8. For discussion of the country house in earlier English literature, see Appendix A, "The Poetry of Property."
9. *The Descent into Hell* (New York, 1949), pp. 241–47.
10. Ishmael's epithet in Melville's *Moby-Dick* reminds us of the nineteenth-century ancestry of the theme of isolation, a theme which had of course been sounded generations before Melville by the Romantic poets. In realistic fiction one of its first expressions is Stendhal's presentation of Julien Sorel in *Le Rouge et le Noir.* "*Vivre isolé . . . Quel torment,*" cries the condemned young man in his prison cell, thus formulating in a phrase a condition that would be endlessly explored by others.
11. T. S. Eliot, *The Complete Poems and Plays: 1909–1950* (New York, 1952), p. 49.
12. The phenomenon of isolation and its causes have, of course, been studied from various points of view—sociological, psychological, and philosophical as well as literary. On isolation in contemporary literature, see William York Tindall, "Exile," *Forces in Modern British Literature: 1885–1956* (New York, 1956); Frank Kermode, "The Artist in Isolation," *Romantic Image* (London, 1957); Stanley Romaine Hopper, "The Problem of Moral Isolation in Contemporary Literature," *Spiritual Problems in Modern Literature* (New York, 1957); David Daiches, *The Novel and the Modern World,* rev. ed. (Chicago, 1960); Colin Wilson, *The Outsider* (Boston, 1956). Perceptive comments on isolation in nineteenth-century culture are to be found in Wylie Sypher's *Loss of the Self in Modern Literature and Art* (New York, 1962) and Morse Peckham's *Beyond the Tragic Vision* (New York, 1962). Isolation in American fiction is the theme of Edwin T. Bowden's *Dungeon of the Heart* (New York, 1961).

The problem of isolation has been ascribed to a great variety of causes. Some, tracing its origins as far back as the Renaissance and the Reformation, note the great psychological burdens placed upon the individual by the collapse of medieval hierarchies and the Protestant emphasis on the private conscience. Others note more recent factors such as the decay of religious belief, the scientific neutralization of nature, the atomization of society by laissez faire capitalism, and the anonymity of urban life, as well as the obvious threats of war and revolution. See, for example, Erich Fromm, *Escape from Freedom* (New York, 1941); Fritz Pappenheim, *The Alienation of Modern Man* (New York, 1959); Eric Kahler, *The Tower and the Abyss* (New York, 1957); Eric and Mary Josephson, eds., *Man Alone: Alienation in Modern Society* (New York, 1962).

13. *Point Counter Point* (New York, 1928), p. 90.

14. C. P. Snow, *The Masters* (New York, 1951), p. 146. This theme evidently means much to Snow personally, for in his much-discussed essay on the "two cultures" he makes himself quite explicit, even repeating the words of his character: "The individual condition of each of us is tragic," he observes. "Each one of us is alone: sometimes we escape from solitariness, through love or affection or perhaps creative moments, but those triumphs are pools of light we make for ourselves while the edge of the road is black: each of us dies alone" (*The Two Cultures and the Scientific Revolution* [New York, 1959], p. 6). His concern also indicates that the title for his series of novels—*Strangers and Brothers*—was not casually chosen.

15. "Paysage Moralisé," *The Collected Poetry of W. H. Auden* (New York, 1945), p. 48.

16. For an excellent analysis of Lawrence's symbolism here, see Frederick R. Karl's "Lawrence's 'The Man Who Loved Islands': The Crusoe Who Failed" in *A D. H. Lawrence Miscellany*, ed. Harry T. Moore (Carbondale, Ill., 1959), pp. 265–79.

17. Lawrence Durrell, *Cleo* (New York, 1960), p. 276. I am indebted for some of these observations on islands to William York Tindall, *The Literary Symbol* (New York, 1955), pp. 134–35, though I have added examples of my own. Islands are also discussed in W. H. Auden, *The Enchafèd Flood* (New York, 1950). Classification of and commentary on island imagery in the poetry of Auden's generation is included in Joseph Warren Beach, *Obsessive Images: Symbolism in the Poetry of the 1930s and 1940s* (Minneapolis, 1960), pp. 119–31.

18. *Escape from Freedom*, p. 19. The passage from which the quotation is taken should be considered for its literary as well as its psychological implications: "The physiologically conditioned needs are not the only imperative part of man's nature. There is another part just as compelling, one which is not rooted in bodily processes but in the very essence of the human mode and practice of life: the need to be related to the world outside oneself, the need to avoid aloneness. To feel completely alone and isolated leads to mental disintegration just as physical starvation leads to death. This relatedness to others is not identical with physical contact. An individual may be alone in a physical sense for many years and yet be related to ideas, values, or at least social patterns that give him a feeling of communion and 'belonging.' . . . This lack of relatedness to values, symbols, patterns, we may call moral aloneness."

For suggestive discussions of community from political and sociological viewpoints, see Robert A. Nisbet, *Community and Power* (formerly *The Quest for Community*) (New York, 1962); and Raymond Williams, *The Long Revolution* (New York, 1961). Nisbet, in his own words, chooses to deal with the "*political* causes of the manifold alienation that lie behind the contemporary quest for community" (p. xix); nevertheless, his early chapters provide an illuminating survey of intellectual and literary trends, though making only brief references to Kafka, Joyce, and Eliot, and examining none of them in depth. Like other recent thinkers, Williams finds the word *community* the most appropriate for his emphasis: "We preserve from the early Liberalism, the absolutes of 'individual' and 'society,' but we add to these, as mediating terms, 'community' and 'association,' to describe local and face-to-face relationships through which the great abstractions of Individual and Society operate in detail" (p. 204).

Of course, in any consideration of the contemporary concern with community, the name of the philosopher Martin Buber must be given a prominent place. It is evident that Buber's analysis of the I-and-thou relationship—particularly in *Between Man and Man* (New York, 1959)—has influenced, both directly and indirectly, many other treatments of the theme.

19. *The Letters of D. H. Lawrence*, ed. Aldous Huxley (New York, 1932), p. 65; "Nottingham and the Mining Countryside," *Phoenix: The Posthumous Papers of D. H. Lawrence* (London, 1936), p. 139.

20. T. S. Eliot, "Choruses from 'The Rock,'" *Complete Poems and Plays*, p. 101,

21. *Notes on Life and Letters* (London, 1931), p. 254. For suggestive remarks on the ship as community symbol, see also W. H. Auden, *The Enchafèd Flood*, pp. 8–9, 66–67.

22. Detailed illustration of this point requires more space than my present purpose allows. *The Masters* alone would yield a number of examples; in fact, a good many of its chapter titles indicate the motif: "A Small Party in the Combination Room," "Negotiations After a Feast," "'A Nice Little Party,'" "Two Cigars in the Combination Room." These should be compared with contrasting titles of isolation and conflict: "Success and Envy," "Quarrel with a Friend," "We're All Alone," "Argument in the Summer Twilight," "Each is Alone."

23. Arnold Kettle has associated Mrs. Moore with Mrs. Wilcox and Mrs. Ramsay in *An Introduction to the English Novel*, 2 vols. (New York, 1960), 2 : 162. Frederick Karl and Marvin Magalaner have included Mrs. Gould in their company in *A Reader's Guide to Great Twentieth-Century English Novels* (New York, 1959), p. 61. Such comparisons have usually been made in passing and, therefore, superficially; it is hoped that some of the aspects of the "vital woman" discussed in more detail here may indicate more clearly and emphatically the importance of the type.

24. *Nostromo* (New York, 1951), pp. 50, 582.

25. Technically, my approach may seem to be "archetypal," but it is more properly designated as "iconographic," using the term in the same sense that W. H. Auden apparently intended when he gave his essay *The Enchafèd Flood* the subtitle "The Romantic Iconograph of the Sea." In other words, I take Auden to be alluding in a rather precise way to the method of classification and interpretation of image types employed by students of the fine arts. Even if he is not, other critics have considered the usefulness of this method. Harry Levin, for example, comments that "some of us have been collecting images, but not interpreting them very

satisfactorily; others have been tracing the history of ideas, without paying much attention to formal context." He goes on to recommend as models for literary students the researches undertaken in the plastic arts by iconology. "Could we hope," Levin asks, "for a discipline which would bring the tools of critical analysis to bear upon the thematic relationship between the idea and the image?" (see his essay "Symbolism and Fiction," *The Contexts of Criticism* [New York, 1963], pp. 204–05).

M. H. Abrams has also expressed his own preference for the term *icon* over the much-used *archetype*. Noting that archetypal criticism can be charged "with blurring, if it does not destroy, the individual properties of the literary products it undertakes to explicate," he prefers to call the image distinctive to a period or school an "icon"—indicating, for example, that in nineteenth-century literature guilt-haunted wanderers, Satanic rebels, and metaphorical winds and breezes are peculiarly Romantic images or "icons" (see "The Correspondent Breeze: A Romantic Metaphor," *English Romantic Poets*, ed. M. H. Abrams [New York, 1960], pp. 49–52).

Neither Levin nor Abrams refers to specific iconological studies, but they probably have in mind works such as Erwin Panofsky's. Panofsky provides an illuminating discussion of his own methodology in "Iconography and Iconology: An Introduction to the Study of Renaissance Art," in *Studies in Iconology* (New York, 1939). I had undertaken this examination of isolation and community symbols in general and the English country house in particular before reading Panofsky; but I find his approach suggestive, since he propounds very clearly a method and purpose that analogous literary studies sometimes seem to lack.

26. *Philosophy in a New Key* (New York, 1948), p. 285.
27. Walter Pater, "The Child in the House," *Miscellaneous Studies* (London, 1928), p. 153; Langer, *Philosophy in a New Key*, p. 237. Ferdinand Tönnies, the nineteenth-century German sociologist, also presents a suggestive discussion of the traditional household to illustrate his distinction between *Gemeinschaft* and *Gesellschaft*, in his *Community and Society*, trans. and ed. Charles P. Loomis (East Lansing, Mich., 1957), pp. 42–43, 50–59.

Like the vital woman and the ship, the house may be psychologically associated with Jung's mother archetype. Symbols of the mother, as Jung points out, appear in ideal places representing the goal of our redemption, such as Paradise and the Heavenly Jerusalem; institutions arousing devotion or feelings of awe, such as the church or the university; places suggesting fertility, like a garden; or hollow objects offering protection. Obviously, the house resembles a good many of these, and may appeal for many of the same reasons (see C. G. Jung, "Psychological Aspects of the Mother Archetype," *The Archetypes and the Collective Unconscious* [New York, 1959], p. 81).

28. C. E. Montague, "Country Houses," *The Right Place* (London, 1926), pp. 167, 158, 179.
29. *The Present Age in British Literature* (Bloomington, Ind., 1958), p. 19. Actually, the country house was already popular with tourists in the eighteenth century, though for other reasons (see the amusing account of B. Sprague Allen, *Tides in English Taste, 1619–1800*, 2 vols. [New York, 1958], 1 : 77).

30. "The Big House at Coole," *A Weekend in the Middle of the Week* (New York, 1958), p. 143.
31. *The Seven Lamps of Architecture* (London, 1907), pp. 182, 183.

CHAPTER 1

1. "A Small Boy and Others," *Henry James: Autobiography*, ed. Frederick W. Dupee (New York, 1956), p. 13. Nash's work consisted of four folio volumes of lithographs published between 1839 and 1849. See also John Steegman, *The Artist and the Country House* (New York, 1949), p. 14.
2. Vernon Louis Parrington, *Maincurrents in American Thought*, 3 vols. (New York, 1927), 3 : 239; Van Wyck Brooks, *The Pilgrimage of Henry James* (London, 1928), pp. 75–77; Rebecca West, *Henry James* (London, 1916), p. 106; Ezra Pound, "Henry James," *The Literary Essays of Ezra Pound*, ed. T. S. Eliot (New York, 1954), p. 300.
3. L. C. Knights, "Henry James and the Trapped Spectator," *Explorations* (New York, 1947), pp. 162, 169.
4. "The Portrait of a Lady," *The Lost Childhood and Other Essays* (London, 1951), p. 44.
5. This is not to deny, of course, the place of James in that tradition. Lionel Trilling has written illuminatingly of the relation of at least *The Princess Casamassima* to what he calls the theme of "the Young Man from the Provinces" in nineteenth century fiction (see "The Princess Casamassima," *The Liberal Imagination* [New York, 1951], pp. 61–68). And it might be argued that the Jamesian "international novel" really transfers the social and cultural drama inherent in this theme from the national stage to the transatlantic arena. Moreover, James's criticism of society from the 1880s on really continues a line of attack that began with Stendhal and Balzac. Yet, saying all this, we are aware that James is also interested in something else as well; nineteenth century society per se is not his basic subject, as it is Balzac's or Dickens's or Zola's.
6. "A Prediction," *Henry James: A Collection of Critical Essays*, ed. Leon Edel (Englewood Cliffs, N.J., 1963), p. 55. The article originally appeared in 1924.
7. The phrase occurs in the preface to "The Altar of the Dead," *The Art of the Novel: Critical Prefaces by Henry James*, with an introduction by Richard P. Blackmur (New York, 1934), p. 242.
8. For the quotation from Eliot I am indebted to Alan Holder's "T. S. Eliot on Henry James," *PMLA* 79 (September, 1964) : 494; Joseph Warren Beach, *The Method of Henry James* (Philadelphia, 1954), pp. 122–23; F. R. Leavis, "Henry James and the Function of Criticism," *The Common Pursuit* (London, 1952), p. 231; Ezra Pound, "Henry James," p. 324 (the italics are Pound's).
9. In the copious material on James now available, there are of course any number of comments on his settings. A résumé of the most important works of criticism relevant to our purpose should perhaps be presented here, though more detailed references will be made at necessary points below. Elizabeth Cary in *The Novels of Henry James* (New York, 1906), the first full-length study of his fiction, includes a chapter on "James and the Genius of Place," which provides suggestive observations on his

English country houses; today, however, in a period of close textual analysis, her treatment seems sketchy and undeveloped. Another early work, *Pictures and Passages from Henry James* (New York, 1916), a pleasant anthology edited by Ruth Head, assembles a few of his descriptions under the heading "Country Houses, Gardens, and Parks," and thus emphasizes—quite unintentionally, it would appear—the recurrence of the motif; but no critical commentary or annotation supplements the selections.

More recent critics are inevitably concerned with James's symbolism and give their attention to his symbolic use of setting. William Troy, perhaps the first of these, speculates somewhat tentatively on the function of the garden in such works as *The Portrait of a Lady* and *The Turn of the Screw;* but he makes no mention of James's houses; see Troy, "The Altar of Henry James," in *The Question of Henry James,* ed. F. W. Dupee (New York, 1945). In "Henry James and the Garden of Death," *University of Kansas City Review* 19 (Winter 1952) : 137–43, Louise Dauner extends Troy's insight with further illustration, but she also neglects to consider the function of the house itself. Quentin Anderson in *The American Henry James* (New Brunswick, N.J., 1957) considers James's figurative use of various kinds of houses. His observation concerning James's frequent use of contrasting houses for symbolic and thematic reasons (pp. 236–37) is of particular relevance and I shall return to this below. However, Anderson analyzes only the houses of *The Wings of the Dove* and *The Golden Bowl* in detail, and he is not concerned with the special qualities of the English country house that James found so rich in meaning. Edwin T. Bowden in *The Themes of Henry James* (New Haven, 1956) offers excellent comments on the houses he has reason to discuss, namely those in *The Portrait of a Lady, The Spoils of Poynton,* and *The Awkward Age.* Both J. A. Ward, *The Imagination of Disaster: Evil in the Fiction of Henry James* (Lincoln, Neb., 1961), and D. W. Jefferson, *Henry James* (New York, 1961), though not interested in the house per se, do examine its function in the more satirical works of the middle period. Allen Guttman discusses the significance of the house as home for such American writers as Cooper, Thoreau, Hawthorne, Twain, and Faulkner, and includes James among them with a brief account of the houses in *The Portrait of a Lady* and *The Sense of the Past;* but Guttman does not explain why James finds his symbolic homes in England rather than America (see his "Images of Value and the Sense of the Past," *New England Quarterly* 35, no. 1 (March 1962) : 3–26.

The best analyses, as I have said above, are to be found in studies of James's individual novels: for Medley of *The Princess Casamassima,* there is Lionel Trilling, "The Princess Casamassima"; for Gardencourt, there are Richard Chase's discussion in *The American Novel and Its Tradition* (New York, 1957), pp. 117–37, and Robert W. Stallman, "The Houses that James Built—*The Portrait of a Lady,*" *The Houses that James Built and Other Essays* (East Lansing, Mich., 1961).

For a discussion of possible literary influences on James see Appendix B, "The Literary Background of James's Country Houses."

10. *The Power of Blackness* (New York, 1958), p. 243.

11. *The American, The Novels and Tales of Henry James,* New York Edition, 26 vols. (New York: Charles Scribner's Sons, 1907–09), 2 : 406.

12. Quoted by Van Wyck Brooks, *The Dream of Arcadia: American Writers and Artists in Italy, 1760–1915* (New York, 1958), p. 171.

13. "This *is* the Temple," Mrs. Gracedew says of the mansion of Summersoft (*The High Bid, The Complete Plays of Henry James*, ed. Leon Edel [New York and Philadelphia, 1941], p. 582). For this specific point, I am indebted to Quentin Anderson, *American Henry James*, p. 170. Anderson also discusses the figurative use of the house in the religious writings of Henry James, Senior, and argues that his father's practice influenced the novelist. "Every house that deserves the name," James Senior wrote, "stands forth to the beholder a pure form of heavenly Art, beckoning onward and upward the soul" (quoted by Anderson, p. 171).

14. Rebecca West, *The Court and the Castle* (New Haven, 1957), pp. 204–05.

15. *Autobiography*, p. 50.

16. "Abbeys and Castles," *EH*, pp. 143–46.

17. "North Devon," *EH*, p. 62; "Warwick," *EH*, p. 53; "North Devon," *EH*, p. 63.

18. "Abbeys and Castles," *EH*, p. 147; "In Warwickshire," *EH*, p. 139.

19. Troy, "The Altar of Henry James," p. 268.

20. "Abbeys and Castles," *EH*, pp. 143, 144.

21. "In Warwickshire," *EH*, p. 131.

22. "Old Suffolk," *EH*, pp. 200–01.

23. "English Vignettes," *EH*, p. 153.

24. "Chester," *EH*, pp. 44, 45.

25. *The Letters of Henry James*, ed. Percy Lubbock, 2 vols. (New York, 1920), 1 : 125.

26. James himself declared: "Nothing is my *last word* about anything—I am interminably super-subtle and analytic—and with the blessings of heaven, I shall live to make all sorts of representations of all sorts of things" (*The Selected Letters of Henry James*, ed. Leon Edel [New York, 1955], p. 76). The italics are James's.

27. *The Notebooks of Henry James*, ed. F. O. Matthiessen and Kenneth B. Murdock (New York, 1955), p. 23.

28. *Ibid.*, pp. 34–35.

29. In the original version, Lackley Park was called Lockley Park; Giorgio Melchiori finds in this a possible influence of Tennyson and "Locksley Hall" (see his "Locksley Hall Revisited," *Review of English Literature* 6, no. 4 (October 1965) : 9–25.

30. "James, like the disinherited Searle," writes Van Wyck Brooks, "had come to [England] to regain his birthright" (*The Pilgrimage of Henry James*, pp. 72–73). Brooks's basic thesis is that Searle's fate is really James's own. Rebecca West in her early study of the novelist maintains in a similar fashion that in "A Passionate Pilgrim" James made "the first statement of the persistent illusion, to which he was helped by his odd lack of the historic sense and which confused his estimate of modern life, that the past would have been a happier time for those who like himself loved fastidious living" (*Henry James*, p. 27). In fairness to West, one must also note—as I have done in the text—that her later remarks on James in *The Court and the Castle* reveal a more sympathetic understanding of his preoccupation with English aristocratic life.

31. Christof Wegelin argues, on the other hand, that James's own point of view is that of the narrator (*The Image of Europe in Henry James* [Dallas,

1958], p. 34); and, as a student of James's travels, Robert Charles LeClair also maintains that James is represented by the narrator (*Three American Travellers in England: James Russell Lowell, Henry Adams, Henry James* [Philadelphia, 1945], p. 193). Both thus correct the facile identification of James with Searle, but in doing so they lessen the fascinating ambiguity involved.

32. "Chester," *EH*, p. 45.
33. LeClair, *Three American Travellers*, p. 196.
34. Ford, *Henry James: A Critical Study* (New York, 1916), p. 110.
35. From this point on, the discussion will follow the general chronology of James's works, but not strictly so; a thematic arrangement is also employed in order to clarify the relationships existing among works sometimes separate in time.
36. See William Troy, "The Altar of Henry James," pp. 268–69; and Dorothy Van Ghent, *The English Novel: Form and Function* (New York, 1953), pp. 214–15.
37. Arnold Kettle, *An Introduction to the English Novel*, 2 vols. (New York, 1960), 2 : 19.
38. Chase, *The American Novel*, p. 121; but this pivotal aspect even Chase and Stallman ignore.
39. Stallman, "The Houses That James Built," p. 26.
40. The physical details here, particularly of color, suggest that James may have had Compton Wynyates in mind as a model for Gardencourt. He described the ancient dwelling in *EH*, pp. 138–39.
41. *The Ivory Tower* (New York, 1917), p. 287.
42. Ralph later employs the same image. "You want to drain the cup of experience," he tells Isabel (*PL*, 1 : 213).
43. Van Ghent, *The English Novel*, p. 432.
44. Stallman, "The Houses That James Built," pp. 19, 23, 32, 9.
45. Ibid., pp. 25, 27.
46. It might even be argued that in writing *The Portrait of a Lady* James was influenced, perhaps quite unconsciously, by the archetypal situation of the Pure Maiden and the Seducer which Leslie Fiedler derives from the sentimental fiction of Richardson and the Gothic tales of terror (see *Love and Death in the American Novel* [New York, 1960], Part I, pp. 3–149). In any case, Madame Merle's phrase "castle in the Apennines" seems a definite allusion to Mrs. Radcliffe's Udolpho.
47. The sinister implications of the name of the house are discussed by Oscar Cargill, who suggests that "The Black Rock Palace," its literal meaning, may be taken as "dark fortress or citadel" (*The Novels of Henry James*, pp. 88, 144).
48. Edwin T. Bowden, *The Dungeon of the Heart: Human Isolation and the American Novel* (New York, 1961), pp. 100–01.
49. *The Art of the Novel*, pp. 60–61.
50. Detailed analysis of this theme is, of course, not possible in the present context. It has been discussed at length and from various points of view: see Lionel Trilling, "The Princess Casamassima"; Irving Howe, "Henry James: The Political Vocation," *Politics and the Novel* (New York, 1957); John Roland Dove, "The Alienated Hero in *Le Rouge et Le Noir* and *The Princess Casamassima*," *Studies in Comparative Literature*, ed. Waldo F. McNeir (Baton Rouge, 1961).

51. Trilling, "The Princess Casamassima," pp. 84–85. Trilling also notes that the whole of Yeats's "Ancestral Houses" might be read as a "most illuminating companion-piece to *The Princess Casamassima*"; this seems to apply as well to much of James's fiction in which the country house recurs.
52. In a letter to Charles Eliot Norton, written at about the time of *The Princess Casamassima*, James spoke of the English upper class as "very much the same rotten and *collapsible* one as that of the French aristocracy before the revolution" or "more like the heavy, congested and depraved Roman world upon which the barbarians came down" (*Letters*, ed. Lubbock, 1 : 124).
53. Trilling, "The Princess Casamassima," p. 85.
54. "Henry James: The Political Vocation," p. 153.
55. Introduction, *The Aspern Papers and The Spoils of Poynton*, Dell Laurel Henry James (New York, 1959), p. 12.
56. Ibid.
57. Stevenson, *The Crooked Corridor: A Study of Henry James* (New York, 1949), pp. 140–41.
58. (The italics throughout are James's.) The notion apparently meant much to James personally. In the preface to "The Aspern Papers," he also speaks of the "poetry of the thing outlived and lost and gone" (see *The Art of the Novel*, p. 164).
59. The name of Poynton suggests at first "point" or apex, some high aesthetic standard; its later fate may imply "poignancy" as well.
60. The social criticism of James has usually been swept out of view by his detractors; more recent commentators, however, have done justice to its pungency and seriousness. For a discussion of James and the English scene, see, particularly, chap. 3, "Evil in London," in J. A. Ward's *Imagination of Disaster;* and chap. 4, "English Themes," in D. W. Jefferson's *Henry James*. I am partially indebted to them for a general sense of James's preoccupations in his "middle" period.
61. "The Turn of the Screw," New York Ed., 12 : 158, 174.
62. "The Turn of the Screw as Poem," *Forms of Modern Fiction*, ed. William Van O'Connor (Minneapolis, 1948), p. 219.
63. *Notebooks*, pp. 192, 196. *Notes sur Londres* was, according to the editors of the *Notebooks* (p. 196), written by Henriette Consuelo (Sansom), Contesse di Puliga, who used the pen name "Brada." It is instructive to compare the views James expresses here with the recollections of Beatrice Webb in *My Apprenticeship* (New York, 1926), pp. 41–51. Although she does not mention James, her account of the fashionable life in London and the country house during the late nineteenth century corroborates James's insights.
64. "Broken Wings," New York Ed., 16 : 149–50.
65. *Henry James*, p. 50. Jefferson mentions a few but not all of the stories I have referred to, though he probably has some of them in mind.
66. "The Two Faces," New York Ed., 12 : 411–12.
67. The word is James's—see *Notebooks*, p. 196.
68. "The Real Thing," New York Ed., 18 : 320, 316.
69. "The Death of the Lion," New York Ed., 15 : 123.
70. "Broken Wings," p. 123.
71. *The Sacred Fount* (New York, 1901), pp. 199–200.

72. "The Three Voices of Poetry," On Poetry and Poets (New York, 1957), pp. 96, 109–10.
73. See also Notebooks, p. 128. The entry shows that "Covering End" is one story in which James had the theme uppermost in his mind.
74. Anderson, American Henry James, p. 236.
75. Bowden, Themes of Henry James, p. 80.
76. Anderson, American Henry James, p. 258; Ward, Imagination of Disaster, p. 133.
77. Ward, Imagination of Disaster, pp. 148–49.
78. Anderson, American Henry James, p. 337.
79. Autobiography, pp. 196–97; Anderson, American Henry James, pp. 174–77.
80. The Sense of the Past (New York, 1917), p. 65. This unfinished novel is usually considered James's last work; however it was conceived in the nineties and reflects James's preoccupations at the time, as Cargill makes clear in The Novels of Henry James, pp. 480–83.

CHAPTER 2

1. Ford, It Was the Nightingale (Philadelphia and London, 1933), p. 199. From a strictly chronological point of view, the term "Edwardian" admittedly lacks precision; but it is useful nonetheless. The historian G. P. Gooch proposes designating as Edwardian the era commencing with the death of Queen Victoria and closing with the outbreak of the Great War, arguing that, although Edward VII died in 1910, the England over which he reigned persisted without change until the opening of hostilities ("The Edwardian Decade," Edwardian England, ed. F. J. C. Hearnshaw [London, 1933], p. 9). For literary purposes, in any case, it is convenient to consider as Edwardian those authors like Wells, Galsworthy, and others who, in E. M. Forster's words, "did good work after 1920," but "got their impressions and formed their attitudes in an earlier period before the first of the two world wars" ("English Prose between 1918–1939," Two Cheers for Democracy [New York, 1951], pp. 283–84). Neither the completed Forsyte Saga nor the Tietjens cycle of novels appeared until the twenties, but in our present context they can be more intelligently discussed as culminations of themes that had already preoccupied their creators in the prewar years. For discussion of the literary aspects of the Edwardian period, see also Richard Ellmann's "Two Faces of Edward," and Gordon N. Ray's "H. G. Wells Tries to Be a Novelist," both in Edwardians and Late Victorians, ed. Richard Ellmann (New York, 1959). Since the writing of the present chapter, the preoccupations of the period have been explored by Samuel Hynes, The Edwardian Turn of Mind (Princeton, N.J., 1968).
2. Ellmann, "Two Faces of Edward," p. 200. An exception perhaps is Belchamber (1904) by Howard Sturgis. Rather old-fashioned in style, this minor country-house novel remains a charming reminder of Qu'Acre (Queens Acre), where Sturgis, its American owner, played host to Henry James and Edith Wharton (see Gerard Hopkins's introduction to Belchamber [London, 1935]).
3. E. M. Forster (Norfolk, Conn., 1943), p. 118.
4. The Condition of England (London, 1909), pp. 12, 11. Masterman, in fact, draws upon some of the fiction of Wells, Galsworthy, and even

James for documentation, though his purpose is sociological analysis, not literary criticism. It is possible that the novels of Ford and Forster that came after *The Condition of England* may have felt its influence.

5. Ibid., pp. 203–04.
6. *Experiment in Autobiography* (New York, 1934), p. 531.
7. Ray, "H. G. Wells Tries to Be a Novelist," p. 158.
8. For details, see J. R. Hammond, "The House Where the Time Machine Was Born," *Wellsian* 1, no. 5 (July 1961) : 8; and Quennell, "H. G. Wells," *The Singular Preference* (New York, 1953), p. 169.
9. Wells, *Experiment in Autobiography*, pp. 32–34, 81. Further details may be found in Margaret Meade-Fetherstonhaugh and Oliver Warner, *Up Park and Its People* (London, 1964).
10. Ray, "H. G. Wells Tries to Be a Novelist," p. 142; Gregory, "H. G. Wells: 'A Wreath for the Liberal Tradition,' " *The Dying Gladiator and Other Essays* (New York, 1961), p. 120; Quennell, "H. G. Wells," pp. 169, 173–74.
11. Since the present chapter was written, a detailed analysis of the thematic function of Wells's architectural and topographical description has been presented by David Lodge, *The Language of Fiction* (London, 1966), pp. 214–43.
12. *Condition of England*, pp. 234–35.
13. "The Structure of H. G. Wells' *Tono-Bungay*," *English Fiction in Transition* 4, no. 2 (1961) : 1–3. I am indebted to this article for the disease imagery mentioned here.
14. Schorer, "Technique as Discovery," *Critiques and Essays on Modern Fiction*, ed. John W. Aldridge (New York, 1952), p. 73.
   It might be noted, for example, that chronologically this last visit of George to Bladesover takes place some decades after his boyhood experiences there; but by placing it early in the novel rather than toward the close, where it seems to belong, Wells robbed George's reflections of their climactic position and thereby lessened their thematic value.
15. William York Tindall, *Forces in Modern British Literature: 1885 1956* (New York, 1956), p. 144.
16. The likelihood of this influence seems strengthened by the resemblances others have found between *Where Angels Fear to Tread* and *The Ambassadors* (see Trilling, *E. M. Forster*, pp. 56–57; and Frederick Crews, *E. M. Forster: The Perils of Humanism* [Princeton, N.J., 1962], p. 80). Though not suggesting an influence, Alwyn Berland discusses some interesting similarities between *The Princess Casamassima* and *Howards End* ("James and Forster: The Morality of Class," *Cambridge Journal* 1, no. 5 [February, 1953] : 259–80).
17. Lionel Trilling, "The Great Aunt of Mr. Forster," *A Gathering of Fugitives* (Boston, 1956), p. 4. Trilling's whole discussion of Forster's relation to a family tradition is highly suggestive. For a thoughtful analysis of Forster's sense of place, including houses, see also J. B. Beer, *The Achievement of E. M. Forster* (London, 1962), pp. 41–45 and chap. 5, passim.
18. Austin, "The Problem of Continuity in Three Novels of E. M. Forster," *Modern Fiction Studies* 7, no. 3 (Autumn 1961) : 222–25. I am indebted to this study for the references from Forster's works given in this paragraph: *A Room with a View* (New York, 1953), pp. 288, 211; and *The Longest Journey* (Norfolk, Conn., n.d.), p. 138.

19. Forster, *England's Pleasant Land, A Pageant Play* (London, 1940), pp. 17, 8; "The Abinger Pageant," *Abinger Harvest* (New York, 1952), pp. 162–63. Woolf, "The Novels of E. M. Forster," *The Death of the Moth and Other Essays* (New York, 1942), pp. 162–63.
20. Berland, "James and Forster," p. 261; Crews, *E. M. Forster*, p. 112. Needless to say, I have not attempted here to survey the manifold interpretations of *Howards End* but to suggest something of their variety and range.
21. "A Room without a View," *Observer*, July 27, 1958, p. 15.
22. Elsewhere, though middle-class and liberal, Forster observes that "the feudal ownership of land did bring dignity, whereas the modern ownership of movables is reducing us again to a nomadic horde" (*HE*, p. 171).
23. For this last specific point, I am indebted to Austin, "Problem of Continuity," p. 226.
24. It is significant that several of Margaret's disagreements with Henry are over houses. One of the first concerns the country house in Oniton. Determined to create "new sanctities" (*HE*, p. 254) there for herself and her husband after their marriage, Margaret is casually informed by Henry on their honeymoon that he has let the place out to a prep school without ever telling her his plans. "I loved the place extraordinarily," she tells him. "Don't you believe in having a permanent home, Henry?" (*HE*, p. 197). Elsewhere she disagrees with his objection to Helen's spending a night at Howards End.
25. Trilling, *E. M. Forster*, p. 135; Forster, in a letter quoted by Jonathan Spence in his "E. M. Forster at Eighty," *New Republic*, October 5, 1959, p. 21; J. B. Beer, *Achievement of E. M. Forster*, p. 199; see also p. 206.
26. There has been some comment on these resemblances. Tindall, while emphasizing the differences in value between *The Man of Property* and *Howards End*, has noted the similarity between Soames Forsyte and Henry Wilcox, their common philistinism and acquisitiveness (Tindall, *Forces*, p. 94). Robert Nichols once remarked upon but never explored the similarities between *Howards End* and *The Country House* ("John Galsworthy," *Nation and Athenaeum* 34, no. 25 (March 1924) : 284–85). Very recently David Garnett found the two novelists alike in their common hatred for the spirit of their age and the inhumanity of the British ruling classes ("E. M. Forster and John Galsworthy," *Review of English Literature* 5, no. 1 [January 1964] : 7, 11).
27. H. V. Marrott, *The Life and Letters of John Galsworthy* (New York, 1936), p. 316.
28. Ibid., p. 24.
29. Dudley Barker, *John Galsworthy: The Man of Principle* (New York, 1963), pp. 28, 30, 135–36, 122. The ornate details of Coombe Warren described by Barker, p. 28 (the mullion windows, gables, and a kind of spire) are replaced in *The Man of Property* by the designs of the fictional architect, Bosinney.
30. Marrott, *Life and Letters*, p. 204.
31. "John Galsworthy: Aspects of an Attitude," *Studies in Honor of John Wilcox*, ed. A. Dayle Wallace and Woodburn O. Ross (Detroit, 1958), p. 206.
32. A still earlier novel, *The Island Pharisees* (1904), questioning almost every aspect of the English social system, also concentrates on the country house.

33. "John Galsworthy," *Selected Literary Criticism*, ed. Anthony Beal (New York, 1956), p. 122.
34. Preface to *The Forsyte Saga* (London, 1950), p. ix.
35. Galsworthy has the same horror of London as Forster. Contrasting Robin Hill with the city, he comments elsewhere: "Who would have thought that behind them, within ten miles, London began—that London of the Forsytes with its wealth, its misery, its dirt, its noise; its jumbled stone isles of beauty, its gray sea of hideous brick and stone? That London which had seen Irene's early tragedy, and Jolyon's own hard days; that web; that princely workhouse of the possessive instinct!" *(MP*, p. 535).
36. Obviously a contrast is also intended between Robin Hill and Soames's new place, Mapledurham, which houses his collection of pictures and another wife, acquired this time in a marriage of convenience.
37. Joseph Warren Beach, *The Twentieth-Century Novel: Studies in Technique* (New York, 1932), p. 252; R. H. Mottram, *John Galsworthy* (London, 1953), p. 29.
38. Lawrence, "John Galsworthy," p. 130; Galsworthy, preface to *The Forsyte Saga*, p. ix. Galsworthy's remark, incidentally, was not a reply to Lawrence's study, for that did not appear until five years later.
39. *Ford Madox Ford: A Study of His Novels* (Baltimore, 1961), p. 212. For further comparison, see also pp. 210–11.
40. Ford Madox Ford, *Memories and Impressions* (New York, 1911), p. 216.
41. *Henry James: A Critical Study* (New York, 1916), pp. 103, 62.
42. *Return to Yesterday* (London, 1931), p. 217.
43. *It Was the Nightingale*, p. 93.
44. "A House (Modern Morality Play)," *Chapbook: A Monthly Miscellany*, no. 21 (March 1921) : 23.
45. *Henry James*, p. 110. John A. Meixner also finds the influence of James apparent in Ford's early novel *The Benefactors* (1905), particularly in the "great family house, which embodies the traditions and worth of its possessor, and which is gradually stripped and finally lost—the counterpart of the spiritual deprivation which is at the heart of the book" *(Ford Madox Ford's Novels: A Critical Study* [Minneapolis, 1962], p. 130).
46. Young, *Ford Madox Ford* (London, 1956), p. 27; Ambrose Gordon, Jr., "At the Edge of Silence: *The Good Soldier* as 'War Novel,'" *Modern Fiction Studies* 9, no. 1 (Spring 1963) : 67–68.
47. Meixner, *Ford's Novels*, pp. 184–85, 188; Cassell, *Ford Madox Ford*, p. 157.
48. James Hafley, "The Moral Structure of 'The Good Soldier,'" *Modern Fiction Studies* 5 (Summer 1959) : 123.
49. Like the other houses in the Edwardian novels already discussed, Groby has some basis in fact. As Ford revealed, his portrait of Tietjens was in good part inspired by his young friend Arthur Marwood, a Yorkshire squire, who died just before the war (see Ford, *It Was the Nightingale*, pp. 207–10, 221). Groby house is apparently modeled on Busby Hall, the property of the Marwood family since 1587. Adjacent to the village of Carlton-in-Cleveland, near Stokesley, Yorkshire, Busby occupies a prominent position at the foot of Cringle Moor. Rebuilt in 1764, it is but a Georgian shell of an earlier interior and owes its charm to its beautiful setting rather than its architectural merits. In the garden is a large horse-chestnut tree. Like many other houses, Busby has been converted into flats. (This information about Busby has been supplied in a letter to the

author from Miles Shepherd, F.L.A., Borough Librarian and Curator, Middlesbrough, Yorkshire, August 13, 1964). I have also learned from G. H. Marwood, who inherited Busby in 1935, that it is doubtful that Ford ever visited the estate, since the family was not in residence from 1905 to approximately 1925 (letter dated September 1, 1964).

50. W. H. Auden, "Il Faut Payer," *Mid-Century* 22 (February 1961) : 5.
51. Cassell, *Ford Madox Ford*, p. 214.
52. A *Treatise on the Novel* (London, 1947), p. 123.
53. Tietjens, in fact, sees his own plight as God's punishment for his sexual sins: before he married his wife, he had sexual relations with her in a railway carriage (*PE*, p. 121).
54. *It Was The Nightingale*, p. 199.
55. See Tietjens's remark, *PE*, pp. 306–07.
56. For details, see E. V. Walter, "The Political Sense of Ford Madox Ford," *New Republic*, March 26, 1956, p. 18. In Ford's work, the new motor car is even more ominous than in *Howards End*. As Paul L. Wiley observes, the collision of Tietjens's poor horse with General Campion's auto even prefigures the mechanical slaughter of the war itself (*Novelist of Three Worlds: Ford Madox Ford* [Syracuse, N.Y., 1962], pp. 228–29). Again, the mechanical-minded American tenants of Groby cut down the Great Tree with the latest form of tree-stump extractor—"the Wee Whizz Bang" (*PE*, p. 823) and mangle the great dovecote in erecting a new power station (p. 801). In contrast, even on the Western Front, Tietjens is sustained by his idyllic vision of a serene English hillside where a man might stand up.
57. Williams, "Parade's End," *Selected Essays* (New York, 1954), p. 323; Meixner, *Ford's Novels*, pp. 220, 221.

CHAPTER 3

1. C. F. G. Masterman, whose *Condition of England* was referred to in the last chapter, also comments on the fate of the country house in his *England After the War* (New York, 1923), pp. 48–50.
2. Consider, for example, Wemmick's fantastic home-made castle in *Great Expectations*. Webster, "Smollett and Shaw: A Note on a Source for *Heartbreak House*," *Shaw Review* 4, no. 3 (September 1961) : 16–17. Smollett's Commodore Trunnion, as Webster points out, is another retired seaman who turns his house into a ship. Julian Kaye also remarks that Shaw must have recalled the ship-as-society metaphor that was frequently employed by Carlyle (*Bernard Shaw and the Nineteenth-century Tradition* [Norman, Okla., 1955], pp. 13–16). The biographical background of Heartbreak House is explored by Stanley Weintraub, *Journey to Heartbreak: The Crucible Years of Bernard Shaw, 1914–1918* (New York, 1971), pp. 162–64.
3. *Shaw and the Nineteenth-Century Theatre* (Princeton, N.J., 1963), p. 321.
4. Wilson, "The House Party Novel" in "Aldous Huxley: A Symposium," *London Magazine* 2, no. 8 (August 1955) : 56; Alexander Henderson, *Aldous Huxley* (London, 1935), p. 131.
5. Quennell, *The Sign of the Fish* (New York, 1960), p. 120. The second volume of Lady Ottoline's own memoirs, which has not yet been published,

will probably contain a great deal about this period. The first volume, *Memoirs of Lady Ottoline Morrell: A Study in Friendship, 1873–1915* (New York, 1964), records the impression Garsington made upon her after her first view of it: "The vision of this house as we passed it one night touched some spot of desire, and I exclaimed, 'That is the only country house that I could live in'" (p. 227). Other visitors have described similar impressions. Siegfried Sassoon, visiting Garsington while on leave from the trenches in the summer of 1916, found it an "enchanting house"—"one of the few houses where I could feel unembarrassed and at liberty to do as I pleased" (*Siegfried's Journey* [New York, 1946], pp. 12, 29). The effect of the place on W. B. Yeats and D. H. Lawrence will be discussed below. Garsington is now the residence of the historian and biographer Sir John Wheeler-Bennett.

6. Information in a letter to the author from L. P. Hartley, September 2, 1964.

7. Quennell, *Sign of the Fish*, p. 122. See also *Victorian Country History of Oxfordshire*, ed. M. D. Lobel, vol. 5 (London, 1957), p. 58. Christopher Hussey has given a detailed description of Beckley Park in *Country Life*, March 23, 1929, pp. 400–08. Hussey makes no mention of Huxley or *Crome Yellow*, but his comments on the plumbing at Beckley suggest that Huxley may have been familiar with the interior. Observing that "among the books that await writing is a *chronicon cloacinium*, a history of sanitation," Hussey enjoys noting that "at Beckley . . . three *garde robe* flues are accommodated in the projected gables at the back. . . . They descend into the inner moat" (p. 404). Huxley's own preoccupation with privies, however, may derive from a reading of the Elizabethan Sir John Harington's *Metamorphosis of Ajax*, as William York Tindall suggests (*Forces in Modern British Literature: 1885–1956* [New York, 1956], p. 102).

8. Frederick R. Karl and Marvin Magalaner, *A Reader's Guide to Great Twentieth Century English Novels* (New York, 1959), p. 261.

9. Huxley's questioner would receive a rather grim answer if he had the opportunity to read the novels of Ivy Compton-Burnett. She, of course, has managed to people her late-Victorian mansions with civilized monsters and to reconstruct domestic terrors hitherto undisclosed. If my study seems to neglect her remarkable fiction, I might add by way of explanation that her method of employing stylized dialogue in place of narration and description has precluded her use of the house as a genuinely symbolic setting; and with the exception of *A Heritage and Its History* (1959) her novels do not make the country house itself a definite theme.

10. *Knole and the Sackvilles* (London, 1923), p. 2. Knole and its history inspired Virginia Woolf's *Orlando*, as I shall note in more detail below.

11. Ibid., p. 18.

12. V. Sackville-West, *English Country Houses* (London, 1941), pp. 7, 48.

13. Specific details indicate that Chevron is obviously modeled on Knole.

14. *The Letters of W. B. Yeats*, ed. Allan Wade (London, 1954), p. 849.

15. Raymond Williams has discussed the influence of *Anna Karenina* on Lawrence and reads *Lady Chatterley's Lover* as a rebuttal to it (see "Lawrence and Tolstoy," *Critical Quarterly* 2, no. 1 (Spring 1960) : 33–38). On the other hand, Harry T. Moore argues that Lawrence also had Galsworthy's *Man of Property* in mind in his depiction of Clifford Chatterley (see *Life and Works of D. H. Lawrence* [New York, 1951], p. 285). The point is of

interest because Galsworthy himself was probably influenced by Tolstoy's novel in composing *The Forsyte Saga* (see Gilbert Phelps, *The Russian Novel in English Fiction* [London, 1956], p. 123).

16. Harry T. Moore, *The Intelligent Heart: The Story of D. H. Lawrence* (New York, 1954), pp. 24–25.
17. *The Letters of D. H. Lawrence*, ed. Aldous Huxley (New York, 1932), p. 277.
18. Ibid., p. 243.
19. Ibid., p. 287.
20. "From *Study of Thomas Hardy*," *D. H. Lawrence: Selected Literary Criticism*, ed. Anthony Beal (New York, 1956), pp. 179–80. See also Lawrence's "Aristocracy," *Reflections on the Death of a Porcupine* (Philadelphia, 1925).
21. *Letters*, p. 284.
22. Ibid., pp. 285–86.
23. Moore, *The Intelligent Heart*, p. 201. See also Peter Quennell, *Sign of the Fish*, p. 120.
24. *Women in Love* (New York, 1920), p. 109.
25. *Sex, Literature and Censorship*, ed. Harry T. Moore (New York, 1953), p. 119.
26. Moynahan, *The Deed of Life: The Novels and Tales of D. H. Lawrence* (Princeton, N.J., 1963), pp. 145–46; Schorer, introduction, *Lady Chatterley's Lover* (New York, 1957), p. xxxv.
27. In this connection, Lawrence's comments on the decaying mansion of Poe's "Fall of the House of Usher" are worth noting. He found the trappings vulgar and overdone, but he paid close attention to their serious implications (see *Selected Literary Criticism*, pp. 341–43).
28. Note particularly Moynahan, *Deed of Life*, pp. 146–50.
29. The phrase "more window than wall" indicates that Lawrence had in mind the historic Hardwick Hall in Derbyshire.
30. *Letters*, p. 693.
31. *Vile Bodies* (London, 1947), p. 118.
32. Stopp, *Evelyn Waugh: Portrait of an Artist* (Boston, 1958), p. 204; Waugh, preface to *Brideshead Revisited*, rev. ed. (London, 1964), p. 10, and "Footlights and Chandeliers," *Spectator*, no. 6943 (July 1961): 96; Linklater, "Evelyn Waugh," *The Art of Adventure* (London, 1948), p. 56. For further discussion of Waugh and England's stately houses, see James F. Carens, *The Satiric Art of Evelyn Waugh* (Seattle, 1966), pp. 24–30.
33. Stopp, *Evelyn Waugh*, p. 204.
34. *The Modern Novel in Britain and the United States* (New York, 1964), p. 211.
35. Mr. Waugh informs me that no actual houses served as models for either Hetton or Brideshead (postcard to the author, August 9, 1964). There are, of course, many examples of houses built or redecorated under the influence of the Gothic revival—to mention a few of the better known, Belvoir Castle in Leicestershire, Lord Lytton's Knebworth in Hertfordshire, and Pugin's own Scarisbrick Hall in Lancashire.
36. "*A Handful of Dust*: Critique of Victorianism," *Modern Fiction Studies* 7, no. 4 (Winter 1961–62): 327.
37. Kermode, *Puzzles and Epiphanies* (New York, 1962), p. 171; Eliot, "Tradition and the Individual Talent," *Selected Essays* (New York, 1950), p. 4.

38. Isherwood, *Lions and Shadows: An Education in the Twenties* (Norfolk, Conn., 1947), pp. 296–97.
39. Ibid., p. 297.

CHAPTER 4

1. In recent years, particularly, the recollections and histories of actual country houses have made up a peculiarly English subgenre. Osbert Sitwell in his five-volume autobiography, generally entitled *Left Hand! Right Hand!* (London, 1944–50), describes life at Renishaw, his family home in Darbyshire and, by making the house central, provides the episodic memoirs with a coherent design. For accounts of other historic houses, see as follows — Blenheim: Consuela Vanderbilt Balsan, *The Glitter and the Gold* (London, 1953); Castle Howard and Haddon Hall: Diana Cooper, *The Rainbow Comes and Goes* (London, 1958); Charlecote: Alice Fairfax-Lucy, *Charlecote and the Lucys* (London, 1958); Chatsworth: Violet Marxham, *Paxton and the Bachelor Duke* (London, 1936); Longleat: The Marchioness of Bath, *Before the Sunset Fades* (Warminster, 1951); Woburn Abbey: John, Duke of Bedford, *A Silverplated Spoon* (London, 1959).
2. "The Princess Casamassima," *The Liberal Imagination* (New York, 1950), p. 85. That Yeats himself recognized an affinity between himself and the American novelist is evident in his comment associating Jane Austen's novels and James's: "These novels [Austen's] were simply a description, an elaboration, of good breeding—that is to say, a quality which only a few happily nurtured people ever found. Then he [Yeats] did not find that pursuit again until he got to the writings of Henry James" (quoted by Donald Torchiana, *W. B. Yeats and Georgian Ireland* [Evanston, Ill., 1966], p. 212).
3. "Ancestral Houses," *The Collected Poems of W. B. Yeats* (New York, 1959), p. 198. (Subsequent references to the poems of Yeats are quoted from this edition. Page numbers appear in brackets following the quotation.)
   Compare with these lines, for example, Laura Wing's remarks on the English in James's *A London Life*, discussed in chap. 1.
4. Henn, *The Lonely Tower: Studies of the Poetry of W. B. Yeats* (London, 1950), pp. 3–10. Henn, it should be added, gives the most detailed account of this Irish social background and serves as corrective to both Louis MacNiece's charge of "snob idyllicism" (in *The Poetry of W. B. Yeats* [New York, 1941], p. 86) and the laudatory exaggerations of C. Day Lewis in "Yeats and the Aristocratic Tradition" *(Scattering Branches*, ed. Stephen Gwynn [New York, 1940]). For another consideration of Yeats's use of the aristocracy as myth, see also L. C. Knights, "Poetry and Social Criticism: The Work of W. B. Yeats," *Explorations* (New York, 1947); and B. L. Reid, "The Houses of Yeats," *Hudson Review* 18, no. 3 (Autumn 1965): 331–50.
5. Yeats's childhood reminiscence is quoted by Norman Jeffares, *W. B. Yeats: Man and Poet* (London, 1949), p. 106; see also p. 227.
6. Oliver St. John Gogarty recalls Lady Ottoline and Yeats at Garsington— "a country house of music undisturbed"—in his poem "To a Lady" *(Collected Poems of Oliver St. John Gogarty* [New York, 1954], pp. 24–25).

The present occupant of Garsington Manor, Sir John Wheeler-Bennett, informs me that there were peacocks and a fountain in Lady Ottoline's time. The interior of the house, however, does not really provide for the long corridors of "Ancestral Houses." Yeats obviously made an amalgam of the houses he knew (see also Torchiana, *Yeats and Georgian Ireland*, p. 313).

7. Yeats, *Dramatis Personae* (New York, 1936), pp. 36, 77; Jeffares, *W. B. Yeats*, pp. 106, 170–71. Vivid impressions of Coole have been left by a number of writers, particularly Sean O'Casey in "Where Wild Swans Nest" (*Inishfallen, Fare Thee Well* [New York, 1949], pp. 182–99); and Oliver St. John Gogarty in "The Big House at Coole" (*A Weekend in the Middle of the Week* [New York, 1958]). For other information on Coole, see also Elizabeth Coxhead's *Lady Gregory: A Literary Portrait* (New York, 1961).

Since the above was written a full-length study of the influence of the Italian writer on Yeats has appeared: Corinna Salvadori, *Yeats and Castiglione: Poet and Courtier* (Dublin, 1965).

8. *The Letters of W. B. Yeats*, ed. Allan Wade (New York, 1955), p. 796.
9. *The Darkling Plain* (London, 1950), p. 205. See also Torchiana, *Yeats and Georgian Ireland*, pp. 357–65.
10. *The Collected Plays of W. B. Yeats* (New York, 1953), pp. 431–32.
11. Colum, *Castle Conquer* (New York, 1923), pp. 375–76; Edward Lord Dunsany, *The Curse of the Wise Woman* (New York, 1933), p. 3. The Anglo-Irish literary partnership of Somerville and Ross (Edith Somerville and her cousin Violet Martin) are best known for their portrayal of the Big House during prerevolutionary days, particularly in such works as *The Real Charlotte* (1894) and *Memories of an Irish R.M.* (1899). Edith Somerville lived to depict the impact of the Troubles in her milieu (for an admirable discussion see Thomas Flanagan, "The Big House of Ross-Drishane," *Kenyon Review* 28, no. 108 [January 1966] : 54–78).
12. Lennox Robinson, *The Big House* (London, 1928), pp. 109, 111.
13. "Midsummer Night Madness," *The Finest Stories of Sean O'Faolain* (Boston, 1957), pp. 7–8, 18, 41.
14. "A Broken World," *Finest Stories*, pp. 90, 94. I am indebted to Benedict Kiely's *Modern Irish Fiction: A Critique* (Dublin, 1950), p. xi, for drawing my attention to this particular story and its implications.

Of course, not all the Irish writers are elegiac about the great house. Sean O'Casey, for one, made the obsession with old houses and past ways the object of an engaging satire that has certain affinities with the early novels of Waugh. Indeed, the resemblances between his *Purple Dust* (1940) and *A Handful of Dust* go beyond their titles, for the play, like the novel, burlesques familiar country-house motifs by exposing antiquarian delusions.

15. No one has yet made a consistent study of the Big House in Elizabeth Bowen's work, though several critics have of course commented incidentally on its function in the novels (see William Heath, *Elizabeth Bowen: An Introduction to Her Novels* [Madison, Wis., 1961]; Frederick R. Karl, *The Contemporary English Novel* [New York, 1962]; and Barbara Seward, "Elizabeth Bowen's World of Impoverished Love," *College English* 18 [October 1956] : 30–37). A more detailed study by Sister M. Corona Sharp, O.S.U., "The House as Setting and Symbol in Three Novels by Elizabeth

Bowen," *Xavier University Studies* 2, no. 3 (December 1963), does not concentrate on the Big House as such and is univocal and misleading in its emphasis on the house as a symbol of isolation.

16. *Collected Impressions* (New York, 1950), pp. 198–99. The second edition of *Bowen's Court* (1965) reveals that the house was sold and, contrary to her expectations, demolished.

17. *Collected Impressions*, p. 161.

18. *Seven Winters and Afterthoughts: Memories of a Dublin Childhood and Pieces on Writing* (New York, 1962), pp. 120, 3; introduction to *Uncle Silas* (London, 1947), pp. 8, 19.

19. Introduction, *Uncle Silas*, p. 8.

20. *Seven Winters*, p. 204.

21. For calling my attention to this point, I am indebted to Sister Maria Corona Sharp, "House as Setting and Symbol," p. 95.

22. *Seven Winters*, p. 204.

23. Bowen, "Elizabeth Bowen's World," p. 34. Bowen, *The Hotel* (London, 1960), p. 247; and *To the North* (London, 1961), pp. 136–37. For a detailed analysis, see Heath, *Elizabeth Bowen*, pp. 66–67.

24. Sister Maria Corona Sharp, "House as Setting and Symbol," pp. 95–98. Sister Sharp presents an excellent analysis of the townhouse, but says nothing of the implied contrast to the country house and its values. Bowen, *The Death of the Heart* (New York, 1955), p. 82.

25. "The Big House," *Collected Impressions*, p. 199.

26. Heath, *Elizabeth Bowen*, pp. 111–12.

27. Seward, "Elizabeth Bowen's World," p. 36.

28. Tindall, *Forces in Modern British Literature: 1886–1956* (New York, 1956), p. 292; John Russell, *Henry Green: Nine Novels and an Unpacked Bag* (New Brunswick, N.J., 1960), p. 9.

29. *Pack My Bag: A Self-Portrait* (London, 1940), pp. 7, 68.

30. *The Literary Symbol* (New York, 1955), p. 96.

31. Stokes, *The Novels of Henry Green* (New York, 1959), p. 95.

32. Russell, *Henry Green*, pp. 131, 141.

33. Other significant works of the period for which the country house was setting or source of imagery should at least be mentioned. Consider, for example, Wishwood in Eliot's *Family Reunion* (1939) and the opening sections of both "Burnt Norton" (1936) and "East Coker" (1940). Auden's *Age of Anxiety* (1947) also employs a country house and Eliotic garden in one sequence.

34. Virginia Woolf, *A Writer's Diary*, ed. Leonard Woolf (New York, 1953), p. 313; E. M. Forster, "Virginia Woolf," *Two Cheers for Democracy* (New York, 1951), p. 248; V. Sackville-West, quoted by Dorothy Brewster, *Virginia Woolf* (New York, 1962), p. 121; Garnett, *The Flower of the Forest* (New York, 1956), pp. 102–03. It might be added that Mrs. Woolf was both generous and shrewd about the actual historic role of the great houses as cultural transmitters. Like H. G. Wells, she recognized that such houses as Lyme Park were "little fortresses of civilization" where culture was possible: "If these spaces won from the encroaching barbarity had not persisted till the foothold was firm and the swamp withheld, how would delicate spirits have fared—our writers, musicians, artists—without a wall to shelter under, or flowers upon which to sun themselves" (*The Captain's Deathbed and Other Essays* [New York, 1950], p. 156). At the

same time, as Dorothy Brewster observes, the novelist could also say that what are euphemistically called "the stately homes of England" were often "comfortably padded lunatic asylums" (*Virginia Woolf*, pp. 11–12). Brewster is quoting from Virginia Woolf's essay "Lady Dorothy Nevil."

35. Garnett, *The Flower of the Forest*, pp. 102–03. Blackstone, *Virginia Woolf: A Commentary* (New York, 1949), pp. 51–52.

36. Blackstone, *Virginia Woolf*, p. 101.

37. Forster, "Virginia Woolf," p. 252.

38. *To the Lighthouse* (New York, 1927), pp. 170–71.

39. Ibid., p. 300.

40. *Orlando* (New York, 1928), pp. 105–06. Virginia Woolf gave the manuscript of *Orlando* to V. Sackville-West, who in turn left it to Knole in her will. "I felt there was so much about Knole in it," she wrote, "that that was the right place for it" (see Aileen Pippet, *The Moth and the Star* [Boston, 1955], p. 272). The manuscript is now on exhibition in the great hall at Knole. For another consideration of the influence of Knole and the Sackvilles on *Orlando*, see Leon Edel, *Literary Biography* (Toronto, 1957), pp. 89–98.

41. *Orlando*, pp. 106–07.

42. *A Writer's Diary*, pp. 279–80. Poyntzet, the original name Virginia Woolf gave to the house, suggests poinsettia, the perennial plant, and may have been chosen for its connotation of the enduring. The final name, Pointz, may be a echo of Poynton in James's novel. One wonders, also, if more than a coincidence is at work in the fact that the first entry about Poyntzet Hall and the contemplated novel is made on the same day that Virginia Woolf recorded the death of Lady Ottoline and the account of her funeral. Mrs. Woolf was another of the visitors to Garsington (see *Diary*, p. 54).

43. Ibid., p. 280.

44. Bowen, "Virginia Woolf," *Collected Impressions*, p. 72.

45. Forster, *Two Cheers for Democracy*, p. 248; Cyril Connolly, ed., *Great English Short Novels* (New York, 1953), p. 756.

46. Cary, *First Trilogy: Herself Surprised, To Be a Pilgrim, The Horse's Mouth* (New York, 1958), p. ix.

47. From a BBC interview quoted by Robert Bloom, *The Indeterminate World: A Study of the Novels of Joyce Cary* (Philadelphia, 1962), p. 17.

48. Cary, *Art and Reality* (New York, 1958), p. 73. "Essentially we live in a symbolic world," Cary observes (p. 60). "All art uses a symbol. There is no other means by which one individual mind can express itself in material form and so communicate with another" (p. 57).

49. Cromwell House was, strictly speaking, a suburban rather than a country house (see Cary's "Cromwell House," *New Yorker*, November 3, 1956, pp. 45–51). For a detailed discussion of Cary's early background, see Lionel Stevenson "Joyce Cary and the Anglo-Irish Tradition," *Modern Fiction Studies* 9, no. 3 (Autumn 1963) : 210–16.

50. Cary, "The Heart of England," *Holiday* 17 (January 1955): 79. See also "The Meaning of England," *Holiday* 23 (April 1958): 117.

51. See Stanley Weintraub, "*Castle Corner:* Joyce Cary's *Buddenbrooks*," *Wisconsin Studies in Contemporary Literature* 5, no. 1 (Winter–Spring 1964): 54–63.

52. *Joyce Cary: A Preface to His Novels* (New York, 1959), p. 66. Charles G. Hoffmann makes much the same comment in *Joyce Cary: The Comedy of Freedom* (Pittsburgh, 1964), pp. 46–47.
53. Hoffmann, *Joyce Cary*, p. 83; Allen, *The Modern Novel in Britain and the United States* (New York, 1964), p. 247.
54. Hoffmann, *Joyce Cary*, p. 83.
55. Preface to *First Trilogy*, p. xi.
56. The reconciliation, moreover, is not one-sided. Throughout the novel not only Robert but Ann herself becomes more deeply involved with Tolbrook and its life. Attending Wilcher in the old family rooms, she finds contentment and a new sense of company. Though a skeptic, she is curious enough to go to the morning prayers Wilcher has revived to satisfy the nostalgic old housekeeper. Touched by the family history, she begins the biography of her Edwardian father. Significantly, even her literary opinion of Jane Austen reveals her changed attitude toward Tolbrook. "I used to think *Pride and Prejudice* best," she remarks to her uncle, "but now I like *Mansfield Park* better" (*TBP*, p. 87).
57. Evelyn Waugh, preface to *BR*, p. 10.
58. Waugh, "Come Inside," *The Road to Damascus*, ed. John O'Brien (Garden City, N.Y., 1949), p. 20. Frank Kermode's comments on the didacticism of *Brideshead Revisited* in "Mr. Waugh's Cities," *Puzzles and Epiphanies* (London, 1962), pp. 174–75.
59. Kermode, "Mr. Waugh's Cities," pp. 170–72; Frederick J. Stopp, *Evelyn Waugh: Portrait of an Artist* (Boston and Toronto, 1958), p. 107.
60. These similarities between Waugh's novel and Eliot's poems hardly seem coincidental. Not only does the narrator quote *The Waste Land* (*BR*, p. 41), he also echoes Eliot's Alice-in-Wonderland imagery from *The Family Reunion* and "Burnt Norton" when he speaks of "that low door in the wall" which might lead him to "an enclosed and enchanted garden" (*BR*, pp. 39–40).
61. T. S. Eliot, *Complete Poems and Plays*, p. 123.
62. Ibid., pp. 144–45.
63. Preface to *BR*, p. 10.
64. For consideration of the trilogy in relation to Waugh's earlier fiction, see Bernard Bergonzi, "Evelyn Waugh's Gentlemen," *Critical Quarterly* 5, no. 1 (Spring 1963): 23–36; and Herbert Howarth, "Quelling the Riot: Evelyn Waugh's Progress," *The Shapeless God: Essays on Modern Fiction*, ed. Harry J. Mooney and Thomas F. Staley (Pittsburgh, 1968).
65. Consider, in this light, Waugh's "confessional" novel, *The Ordeal of Gilbert Pinfold: A Conversation Piece* (Boston, 1957).
66. One wonders if Waugh was familiar with the analysis of the *City of God* presented by another English convert to Catholicism, the historian Christopher Dawson, who deliberately emphasizes Augustine's drastic realism about the injustice and evil inherent in all earthly kingdoms. (See Dawson's "Saint Augustine and His Age," *Saint Augustine*, ed. M. C. D'Arcy, S.J., [New York, 1957], pp. 61–64. The original edition was first published in 1930 and reissued in 1945 under the title *A Monument to Saint Augustine*.)
67. The similarities between Ford's Tietjens and Guy have been noted by Howarth, "Quelling the Riot," pp. 86–87, and by Walter Allen, *The*

Modern Novel, p. 212. Bradbury, *Evelyn Waugh* (London, 1964), p. 114; Bergonzi, "Evelyn Waugh's Gentlemen," p. 36.
68. Bowen, *Collected Impressions*, p. 161.

APPENDIX A

1. Levin, appendix, *The Power of Blackness* (New York, 1958), p. 246. While concerned with an American context, Levin's eloquent and allusive discussion is highly relevant to any consideration of architectural symbolism in literature.

The emergence of physical background, whether country house or any other, as a setting sufficiently particularized to offer symbolic possibilities, was a slow process in all literary genres, as Warren Hunting Smith showed in a painstaking review of architectural description in earlier English literature (*Architecture in English Literature* [New Haven, 1934], pp. 1–5). I should add that in preparing this Appendix I am more heavily indebted to Smith's whole study than my specific references may indicate. For further consideration of the treatment of physical background in fiction, see also Ian Watt, *The Rise of the Novel: Studies in Defoe, Richardson, and Fielding* (Berkeley and Los Angeles, 1957), pp. 26–27; and D. S. Bland, "Endangering the Reader's Neck: Background Description in the Novel," *Criticism* 3, no. 2 (Spring 1961) : 121–39.

Other sources that have bearing on the topics of this Appendix include B. Sprague Allen, *Tides in English Taste (1619–1800): A Background for the Study of English Literature*, 2 vols. (Cambridge, Mass., 1937); Elizabeth Wheeler Manwaring, *Italian Landscape in Eighteenth Century England* (New York, 1925); Christopher Hussey, *The Picturesque* (London, 1927); Edward Malins, *English Landscaping and Literature, 1660–1840* (Oxford, 1966).

Related points of interest may also be found in the following architectural studies: Ralph Dutton, *The English Country House* (London, 1936); Sacheverell Sitwell, *British Architects and Craftsmen* (London, 1945); Nicholas Pevsner, *The Buildings of England* (London, 1950 *et seq.*); and John Summerson, *Architecture in Britain, 1530–1830*. Summerson's book includes an extensive bibliography. For the development of the country house within a social and historical context, see G. M. Young, "The Country House," *England's Heritage* (London, 1935); and G. M. Trevelyan, *Illustrated Social History of England*, 4 vols. (London, 1949). Economic aspects of the country-house milieu are illuminatingly documented by G. E. Mingay, *English Landed Society in the Eighteenth Century* (Toronto, 1963); and F. M. L. Thompson, *English Landed Society in the Nineteenth Century* (Toronto, 1963).

2. *Poly-Olbion*, song 14, ll. 161–62, *Poems of Michael Drayton*, ed. John Buxton, 2 vols. (Cambridge, Mass., 1953), 2 : 609, 674.

3. G. R. Hibbard, "The Country House Poem of the Seventeenth Century," *Journal of the Warburg and Courtauld Institutes* 109 (1956) : 159–74. As Hibbard notes, Jonson is not the first to employ Penshurst in this way. Sir Philip Sidney himself was apparently using Penshurst as a model in his description of the house of Kalander in the *Arcadia* (see *The Countess of Pembroke's Arcadia*, ed. Albert Feuillerat [Cambridge, 1962], p. 14).

Allen in *Tides in English Taste* also suggests that the features of the building accentuated in the description—simplicity, convenience, durability—embody Sidney's own architectural ideal and imply something of a personal criticism of the age's increasing taste for aggrandizement. For a discussion of the *Arcadia* itself as an interpretation of the ethos of the great house, see also John F. Danby, *Poets on Fortune's Hill: Studies in Sidney, Shakespeare, Beaumont and Fletcher* (London, 1952), chap. 2.

4. *Poems of Ben Jonson*, ed. George Burke Johnston (Cambridge, Mass., 1951), pp. 76–79.

5. Summerson considers the relationship between Tudor patronage and the new fashions in domestic architecture (*Architecture in Britain*, chap. 2). Hibbard also notes that "houses like Holdenby and Wollaton Hall were not designed to meet the needs of household living . . . but for the reception of Elizabeth and her court, and as an expression of the owners' sense of their own importance" ("The Country House Poem," p. 160). Jeffrey Hart, "Ben Jonson's Good Society," *Modern Age* 7, no. 1 (Winter 1962–63) : 63; see also p. 64. Penshurst's relation to its natural setting is discussed at length by Paul M. Cubeta, "A Jonsonian Ideal: 'To Penshurst,' " *Philological Quarterly* 42, no. 1 (January 1963) : 15.

6. I am indebted to Professor Alistair M. Duckworth of the University of Virginia for calling my attention to this Horatian theme in English literature. See Horace, *Epodon Liber* 2. ll. 1–2: "Beatus ille qui procul negotiis, / ut prisca gens mortalium . . ." (*The Odes and Epodes*, with an English translation by C. E. Bennett [Cambridge, Mass., 1914], p. 364). For discussion of the classical influence on Jonson, see Hibbard, "The Country House Poem," pp. 159, 163. Røstvig, *The Happy Man: Studies in the Metamorphoses of a Classical Ideal*, 2 vols. (Oslo, 1954, 1958). For a critique and further application of Røstvig's theses, see also E. M. W. Tillyard, *Some Mythical Elements in English Literature* (London, 1961), chap. 5, "Retirement," pp. 72–107. The Roman background influencing the development of Horace's own thought and its parallels in English history are concisely examined by Leslie Gale Burgevin, "A Little Farm: The Horatian Concept of Rural Felicity in English Literature," *Horace: Three Phases of His Influence* (Chicago, 1936), pp. 49–75.
Quite possibly, the Horatian sense of felicity may have been transmitted to James by reading Tennyson, one of the English poets to whom he most often alludes.

7. Hibbard, "The Country House Poem," p. 159.

8. *The Complete Poetry and Selected Prose of John Donne*, ed. Charles M. Coffin (New York, 1952), p. 95. Similar criticism also recurs in Herrick's "A Panegyrick to Sir Lewis Pemberton."

9. I am indebted to Hibbard for calling my attention to this aspect of Marvell's poem ("The Country House Poem," p. 171). In "On Lord Holland's Seat near M———e, Kent," Gray does another turn on this ironic motif by finding in the bleak landscape and the simulated Gothic ruins of Henry Fox's estate eminently suitable surroundings for the last days of this despised politician.
Pope's variations on these motifs are more fully discussed by Maynard Mack, *The Garden and the City: Retirement and Politics in the Later Poetry of Pope, 1731–1743* (Toronto, 1969).

10. *The Poems of Alexander Pope*, ed. John Butt, 6 vols. (London, 1951), vol. 3, pt. 2 *Epistles to Several Persons (Moral Essays)*, ed. F. W. Bateson, pp. 149–50, 106.
11. Mack, *The Garden and the City*, pp. 8–9, 66. The Jonsonian and Horatian contexts of a number of Pope's poems are two of the important topics treated in Mack's study. As noted in my preface, *The Garden and the City* appeared too late for me to profit from it in the preparation of my main text; but its relevance to my total purpose cannot be overstressed.
12. For discussion of Cowper and the Horatian tradition, see Tillyard, *Mythical Elements*, p. 102. The influence of Cowper on Jane Austen is considered by Malins, *English Landscaping and Literature*, chaps. 6 and 7.
    The economic context of these changes is elaborated by Mingay, *English Landed Society*, chap. 1, especially pp. 12–13. The literary treatment of the squire has, of course, received considerable attention from critics and historians of varying points of view, satirical as well as sentimental (see Arthur Bryant, *The National Character* [London, 1934], pp. 37–53; H. J. Massingham, *The English Countryman: A Study of the English Tradition* [London, 1942], chap. 5, "The Squire").
    Aspects of the building mania of the eighteenth century are further explored by Allen, *Tides in English Taste*, chap. 2; and by John Summerson, "The Classical Country House in the Eighteenth Century," *Journal of the Royal Society of Arts* 107 (1959): 544–45. For a suggestive analysis of the improvement of an actual estate, Stourhead, and its symbolic as well as social implications, see Kenneth Woodbridge, "Henry Hoare's Paradise," *Art Bulletin* 17 (March 1965): 83–116. "While gardens and picture collections are made to enhance the prestige of the owners," Woodbridge comments, "art is a symbol-making activity, giving outward form to inward states. . . . At one level the iconography of Stourhead is drawn from the classical sources accepted at the time, particularly from the *Aeneid;* at another, it represents Henry's own life and aspirations" (p. 108).
    See also *Architecture in English Literature*, pp. 6–8.
13. Watt, *Rise of the Novel*, p. 26.
14. Richardson, *The History of Sir Charles Grandison: In a Series of Letters Published from the Originals by the Editor of Pamela and Clarissa*, 7 vols., (Oxford, 1936), vol. 6, letter 5, p. 25.
15. Malins, *English Landscaping and Literature*, p. 110.
16. Bland, "Endangering the Reader's Neck," pp. 124–26. Fielding, *The History of Tom Jones* (New York, 1943), pp. 8–9. In describing the landscape surrounding Allworthy's house, Fielding apparently had in mind as his model Prior Park as designed by its owner, Ralph Allen—himself the prototype of Allworthy.
17. See Malins, *English Landscaping and Literature*, pp. 43–44.
18. *Humphry Clinker* (Baltimore, 1967), p. 150. Horace is quoted several times in the novel and provides the epigraph to the original title page, as Angus Ross notes in his introduction to this edition, p. 17.
19. Ibid., p. 325.
20. For detailed consideration, see Smith, *Architecture in English Literature*, pp. 68–75.
21. Leslie A. Fiedler speculates interestingly on the serious psychological and social implications of the Gothic romance in *Love and Death in the American Novel* (New York, 1960), pp. 96–124. Kenneth Clark, in his

classic study *The Gothic Revival* (London, 1928), examines the Gothic romance as an aspect of the neo-Gothic movement of the eighteenth and nineteenth centuries.
22. Introduction to his edition of *The Castle of Otranto* (London, 1925), p. xix.
23. Smith, *Architecture in English Literature*, p. 110.
24. *The Mysteries of Udolpho*, 2 vols. (London, 1931), 1 : 230.
25. See Martha Banta, "The House of the Seven Ushers and How They Grew: A Look at Jamesian Gothicism," *Yale Review* 57, no. 1 (Autumn 1967) : 56–65.
26. Smith, *Architecture in English Literature*, p. 142.
27. For analysis of *Castle Rackrent*, see P. H. Newby, *Maria Edgeworth* (Denver, 1950), pp. 39–45; and Thomas Flanagan, *The Irish Novelists, 1800–1850* (New York, 1959), pp. 77–78. See also Dorothy Brewster, *East-West Passage: A Study in Literary Relationships* (London, 1954), p. 55; and Cyril Connolly, ed., *Great English Short Novels* (New York, 1933), p. x.
28. General preface, *Waverley*, ed. Andrew Lang, (Boston, 1892), p. xxi. For a comparison of *Waverley* and *Castle Rackrent*, see Donald Davie, *The Heyday of Sir Walter Scott* (New York, 1961), pp. 65–66. For discussion of Scott as a serious student of cultural differences, see David Daiches, "Scott's Achievement as a Novelist," *Literary Essays* (London, 1956).
29. Davie, *The Heyday of Sir Walter Scott*, pp. 30–33.
30. "Fiction and Sir Walter Scott," *Notes and Reviews*, with a Preface by Pierre de Chaignon La Rose (Cambridge, 1921), p. 110.
31. See Lord David Cecil, "A Note on Jane Austen's Scenery," *The Fine Art of Reading* (New York, 1957); and Bland, "Endangering the Reader's Neck," pp. 128–31. For recent discussion of Jane Austen and the Gothic tradition, see Frank W. Bradbrook, *Jane Austen and Her Predecessors* (Cambridge, 1966), pp. 102–08.
32. *Pride and Prejudice* (London, 1950), p. 210. Discussion of Elizabeth's reaction in relation to the contemporary preoccupation with landscape may be found in Martin Price, "The Picturesque Moment," *From Sensibility to Romanticism: Essays Presented to Frederick A. Pottle*, ed. Frederick W. Hilles and Harold Bloom (New York, 1965), pp. 267–68.
33. *Emma* (London, 1906), p. 315.
34. Trilling, "Mansfield Park," *The Opposing Self* (New York, 1955), p. 227; Fleishman, *A Reading of Mansfield Park: An Essay in Critical Synthesis* (Minneapolis, 1967), p. 66.
35. Introduction, *Mansfield Park* (Baltimore, 1966), p. 16.
36. Ibid., pp. 24–26.
37. Fleishman, *A Reading of Mansfield Park*, pp. 74–75; Tanner, introduction, p. 35; Trilling, "Mansfield Park," p. 227. Like Yeats, Jane Austen apparently modeled her ideal house on a real one, though no single candidate seems agreed upon. F. Alan Walbank proposes Harleston Hall, Northamptonshire, which came under the auctioneer's hammer in 1940 (*The English Scene* [London, 1941], p. 8). On the other hand, R. W. Chapman identifies Mansfield Park with Cottesbrooke, also in Northamptonshire (*Jane Austen's Letters* [Oxford, 1952], notes, addenda, p. 149).

After Jane Austen, Victorian women novelists—such as Charlotte M. Yonge and Mrs. Gaskell—displayed a special zest for domestic buildings, though not necessarily giving them symbolic meaning. For a discussion of Mrs. Gaskell's settings, see Marjory A. Bold, *Women Writers of the Nineteenth Century* (New York, 1963), pp. 105–06. Margaret Mare and Alicia C. Percival in *Victorian Best Seller: The World of Charlotte M. Yonge* (London, 1948), chap. 8, consider this novelist's predilection for describing stately mansions.

38. *The Novels of Thomas Love Peacock*, ed. David Garnett, 2 vols. (London, 1963), 1 : 355.

39. O. W. Campbell, *Peacock* (London, 1953), p. 69. It might be added that the alliterative title of R. S. Surtee's *Hillingdon Hall* (1845) reminds us that the country house could be the subject of more boisterous humor than Peacock's.

40. Lesser figures like Harrison Ainsworth, Edward George Bulwer-Lytton, and Henry Kingsley might at least be mentioned (see Edith Birkhead, *The Tale of Terror* [London, 1921], pp. 185–96).

See William York Tindall, *The Literary Symbol* (New York, 1955), p. 72. For an early, rather sketchy study of the house and the poets of the nineteenth century, see H. Heathcote Stotham, *Architecture Among the Poets* (London, 1898).

41. In *The Gothic Flame* (London, 1957), Devendra P. Varma points out the close resemblance between Miss Havisham's room and the chamber of the dead marchioness in *The Mysteries of Udolpho* (p. 200). The general appearance of the house was of course modeled on Restoration House in Rochester. Discussion of its symbolism may be found in Tindall, *The Literary Symbol*, p. 72, and in J. Hillis Miller, *Charles Dickens: The World of His Novels* (Cambridge, Mass., 1958), p. 267.

42. Hardy, *Jane Eyre* (*Charlotte Brontë*), (Oxford, 1964), pp. 16–29. In *The Brontës Came Here* (Halifax, Yorkshire, n.d.), Phyllis Whitehead discusses the actual houses and locations the Brontës probably had in mind as models for their fictional settings.

43. For detailed analysis of the house in *Bleak House*, see Miller, *Charles Dickens*, pp. 219–20. Oddly enough, the original of Chesney Wold is Rockingham Castle in Northamptonshire, where Dickens enjoyed theatricals. Bowen, introduction to *Uncle Silas* (London, 1947), pp. 10, 19.

44. Edward Wagenknecht, *Cavalcade of the English Novel* (New York, 1943), p. 235.

45. Henry James, *Literary Reviews and Essays*, ed. Albert Mordell (New York, 1957), p. 307; Disraeli, *Sybil; or, The Two Nations* (London, 1954), pp. 71–72, *Coningsby; or, The New Generation* (London, 1911), p. 122. Holloway, *The Victorian Sage* (London, 1953), pp. 93, 106. Despite the obvious idealization, Disraeli's houses are usually based on actual places. Palatial Coningsby Castle is modeled after Chatsworth or Welbeck, and Lady Diana Cooper maintains that Beaumanoir is a reproduction of Belvoir Castle (*The Rainbow Comes and Goes* [Boston, 1958], p. 29).

46. *Vanity Fair*, ed. Geoffrey and Kathleen Tillotson (Boston, 1963), p. 76; Williamson, "A Note on the Function of Castlewood in *Henry Esmond*," *Nineteenth-Century Fiction* 18, no. 1 (June 1963) : 72–75. On Thackeray's symbolism in general, see Dorothy Van Ghent, *The English Novel: Form and Function* (New York, 1953), pp. 145–52.

47. Cecil, *Early Victorian Novelists* (New York, 1935), pp. 264–65 (but see

also Bland, "Endangering the Reader's Neck," pp. 134–35); Sadleir, *Trollope: A Commentary* (London, 1927), pp. 191, 193; *Henry James: Autobiography*, ed. F. W. Dupee (New York, 1956), p. 251; and James, *The Art of Fiction and Other Essays*, ed. Morris Roberts (New York, 1948), p. 61. Matcham, the house which appears in both *The Wings of the Dove* and *The Golden Bowl*, appears to echo Matching Priory, which is in several of Trollope's novels.

48. Eliot, *Scenes of Clerical Life* (Boston and New York, 1907), 1 : 138–39.
49. James, *The Wings of the Dove*, New York Ed., 19 : 208.
50. Bland, "Endangering the Reader's Neck," pp. 135–36. In *The Novels of George Eliot* (New York, 1959), Jerome Thale has noted how Dorothea's boudoir at Lowick reflects the decline of the marriage (pp. 158–60).
51. For a discussion of the socio-economic condition of the historic country house, see F. M. L. Thompson, *English Landed Society in the Nineteenth Century* (Toronto, 1963), chaps. 9 and 10.
52. For an account of Hardy's boyhood acquaintance with Kingston Maurward manor near Dorchester and his remarkable devotion to its mistress, Julia Augusta Marin, see Evelyn Hardy, *Thomas Hardy: A Critical Biography* (London, 1954), chap. 2. Details of houses connected with Hardy's novels may be found in *Country Houses of Dorset* (London, n.d.).
53. Brown, *Rhythm in the Novel* (Toronto, 1950), p. 13.

APPENDIX B

1. Oscar Cargill, *The Novels of Henry James* (New York, 1961), pp. 15–16.
2. *Hawthorne* (Ithaca, N.Y., 1956), p. 94.
3. Robert W. Stallman, *The Houses That James Built and Other Studies* (East Lansing, Mich., 1961), pp. 7–8. Stallman, however, does not consider James's preoccupation with the English country house as such.
   Some of the motifs that attend the house symbol in James might also be traced to Hawthorne's influence. The garden imagery, for instance, may have its source in the Pyncheon garden, whose Edenic attributes Hawthorne elaborately describes in chap. 10 of *The House of the Seven Gables*. Again, the device of the portrait in *The Sense of the Past* may have been suggested by the portrait of Colonel Pyncheon, as has been noted by T. S. Eliot ("Henry James, II," *The Shock of Recognition*, ed. Edmund Wilson [New York, 1943], pp. 863–65); and Marius Bewley (*The Complex Fate* [London, 1952], p. 29). On the other hand, it must be remembered that mysterious portraits play their part in the Gothic fiction with which James was also highly familiar.
   Harry Levin, moreover, has remarked on the similarity between James's regard for England and what he calls Hawthorne's "homing instinct," revealed in titles like *Our Old Home* (see *The Power of Blackness*, p. 96).
4. *French Poets and Novelists* (London, 1919), pp. 92, 95.
5. "Honoré de Balzac," *The Art of Fiction* (New York, 1948), p. 34. In the essay that he wrote as a young man, James was even more severe in attacking Balzac's "ineffable snobbishness." Noting that Balzac "began very early in his career to write about countesses and duchesses," James observes that even after he became famous "the manner in which he usually portrays the denizens of the Faubourg St. Germain obliges us to

believe that the place they occupy in his books is larger than they occupied in his experience" *(French Poets and Novelists,* pp. 112–13, p. 73).

6. "Honoré de Balzac," pp. 34, 35.

7. *The Ghostly Tales of Henry James* (New Brunswick, N.J., 1948), p. 104. In " 'The Turn of the Screw': Jamesian Gothic," *Essays in Criticism* 12 (January 1962) : 34–39, Manfred Mackenzie argues that James probably had the Gothic novelists in mind while writing his most famous horror story. Mackenzie, however, does not refer to the many other allusions to Gothic romances to be found in James, though these would strengthen his argument.

8. *The Notebooks of Henry James,* ed. F. O. Matthiessen and Kenneth B. Murdock (New York, 1955), p. 37.

❧ Index ❧

❧ Acknowledgments ❧

Grateful acknowledgment is made to the following for permission to quote from publications in copyright:

Collins Publishers for *English Country Houses* by V. Sackville-West.

Harcourt Brace Jovanovich, Inc., and Jonathan Cape, Ltd., for *Dodsworth* by Sinclair Lewis.

Houghton Mifflin Co., Hamish Hamilton Ltd., A. P. Watt & Son, and Vincent Sheean for *Personal History* by Vincent Sheean.

Holt, Rinehart and Winston, Inc., and Routledge & Kegan Paul, Ltd., for *Escape from Freedom* by Erich Fromm.

Oxford University Press for *The Notebooks of Henry James,* ed. F. O. Matthiessen and Kenneth B. Murdock.

Oxford University Press for *The Notebooks of Henry James,* ed. F. O. Matthiessen and Kenneth B. Murdock.

Charles Scribner's Sons for *The Novels and Tales of Henry James.*

A. P. Watt & Son and the Estate of H. G. Wells for *Experiment in Autobiography* by H. G. Wells.

Harcourt Brace Jovanovich, Inc., and Edward Arnold, Ltd., for *Marianne Thornton* by E. M. Forster.

Alfred A. Knopf, Inc., The Bodley Head, Ltd., David Higham Associates, Ltd., and Janice Biala for *Parade's End* by Ford

Madox Ford and *The Bodley Head Ford Madox Ford* Volume III.

Alfred A. Knopf, Inc., Random House, Inc., and Faber & Faber, Ltd., for *The Dog Beneath the Skin, or Where is Francis?* by W. H. Auden and Christopher Isherwood.

The Society of Authors, on behalf of the Bernard Shaw Estate, for *Heartbreak House* by Bernard Shaw.

Harper & Row, Inc., Chatto & Windus, Ltd., and Mrs. Laura Huxley for *Crome Yellow* by Aldous Huxley.

Ernst Benn, Ltd., for *Knole and the Sackvilles* by V. Sackville-West.

Grove Press, Inc., William Heinemann, Ltd., Laurence Pollinger, Ltd., and the Estate of the late Frieda Lawrence for the Grove Press Edition of *Lady Chatterley's Lover* by D. H. Lawrence. Text from the third manuscript version, first published by Guiseppe Orioli, Florence, 1928.

Harcourt Brace Jovanovich, Inc., and Faber & Faber, Ltd., for *The Complete Poems and Plays: 1909–1962* by T. S. Eliot.

The Viking Press, Inc., and the Hogarth Press, Ltd., for *Loving* by Henry Green.

Alfred A. Knopf, Inc., Random House, Inc., and Curtis Brown, Ltd., for *Bowen's Court* by Elizabeth Bowen.

Barrie & Jenkins, Ltd., and The Cresset Press for Elizabeth Bowen's introduction to *Uncle Silas* by Sheridan Le Fanu.

Alfred A. Knopf, Inc., and Jonathan Cape, Ltd., for *The Heat of the Day* by Elizabeth Bowen.

Harcourt Brace Jovanovich, Inc., The Hogarth Press, Ltd., and the Author's Literary Estate, for *Orlando, To the Lighthouse, and A Writer's Diary* by Virginia Woolf.

Harper & Row, Inc., for *Art and Reality* by Joyce Cary.

Harper & Row, Inc., and Michael Joseph, Ltd., for *To Be a Pilgrim* by Joyce Cary.

Little, Brown and Co., Chapman & Hall, Ltd., and A. D. Peters & Co. for *Brideshead Revisited* by Evelyn Waugh.